ETHICS AND
ECONOMICS

ETHICS AND ECONOMICS

Edited by
Ellen Frankel Paul
Jeffrey Paul
Fred D Miller Jr

87-627

BASIL BLACKWELL
for the
Social Philosophy and Policy Center
Bowling Green State University

© Social Philosophy and Policy 1985
First Published 1985
Basil Blackwell Publisher Limited
108 Cowley Road, Oxford OX4 1JF, England

British Library Cataloguing in Publication Data

Ethics and economics.
1. Business ethics.
I. Paul, Ellen Frankel   II. Miller, Fred D.
III. Paul, Jeffrey
174'.4   HF5387

ISBN 0-631-14359-9

Library of Congress Cataloging in Publication Data

Ethics and economics.
Includes index.
Contents: Rule utilitarianism, equality, and justice/John C. Harsanyi
—Morality, reason and management science/David Copp—What's
morally special about free exchange?/Alan Gibbard—[etc.]
1. Economics—Moral and ethical aspects—Addresses, essays,
lectures.
I. Paul, Ellen Frankel.   II. Miller, Fred Dycus, 1944–
III. Paul, Jeffrey.
HB72.E78   1985   174'.9339   85-11238
ISBN 0-631-14359-9

Printed in Great Britain
by Whitstable Litho, Kent

CONTENTS

INTRODUCTION

The moral status of economic systems is one of the central issues of contemporary social and political philosophy. Many recent discussions focus on the moral standing of market economies, which are characterized by private ownership and extensive economic freedom. Others, following the lead of Rawls and Nozick, address the much more fundamental question of how we should choose principles of justice in terms of which to assess economic and other social institutions. And there is a wealth of literature on the ethical questions raised by the application of social decision procedures to economic matters. What these discussions have in common is the recognition that economic questions are not merely questions of practicality and efficiency, but also questions of morality and justice.

The contributors to this volume represent a variety of disciplines and perspectives, and the questions they address cover the spectrum from the most fundamental questions of moral theory to practical questions of individual and social decision-making. But all these authors share the recognition of the interplay between moral and economic questions. All of them are concerned to enhance our understanding of social institutions and, thereby, improve the working of these institutions.

David Gauthier and John Harsanyi are both concerned with the fundamental question of which principles of justice should be used to assess social institutions and arrangements. Gauthier argues that justice is a matter of agreement among rational individuals. Unlike rational individual choice, however, which is choice according to principles which maximize utility, bargaining about principles of justice does not result in an agreement to *maximize* anything. Rather, it results in an agreement to distribute the benefits of cooperative endeavors in a certain way. Harsanyi, taking an opposite tack, argues that rule utilitarianism is the correct approach to the assessment of economic and other social arrangements, and that the pursuit of values like equality and justice must not be allowed to undermine social utility.

Amartya Sen and Allan Gibbard are more directly concerned with the moral assessment of market economies. Sen rejects "procedural" defenses of the market, which argue that the market is justified as an exercise of individuals' prior rights. Rather, he argues, the moral standing of the market is derivative and contingent upon the outcomes of market processes; and "outcomes" must be construed broadly enough to include such factors as the protection of rights and the enhancement of freedom. Gibbard also rejects procedural defenses, but he is no more persuaded by the pragmatic argument that the market produces optimal incentives and, hence the most desirable outcome. Even if the conditions of perfect competition could be realized, he argues, there is "no practicable way of arranging initial endowments so as to achieve equitable distribution as exchanges proceed."

In addition to attempts to justify the market, there is an established tradition in Western philosophy of using the market paradigm to explain and justify political and legal institutions. Jules Coleman's paper considers the extent to which this is a viable approach. His discussion focuses on market contractarianism – a market theory of political association – and the unanimity rule – a rule of collective choice. Coleman distinguishes two versions of market contractarianism and provides extensive criticisms of the unanimity rule.

The remaining papers in this volume are primarily concerned with methodological issues. Alexander Rosenberg focuses on a central problem of neoclassical economics: that it provides no explanation of the central concept of tastes (or preferences) and, thus, is really not a very good explanation of individual economic behavior. Rosenberg suggests a way of replacing the concept of tastes with that of biological needs which can, in principle, be measured. This allows the economist to explain tastes by reference to needs and to make objective assessments of individual welfare. Rosenberg concludes with a discussion of how to avoid the paternalistic implications of his views.

David Copp offers searching criticisms of cost-benefit analysis. The prevailing view is that cost-benefit analysis contributes to the rationality of social decisions because it allows us to measure economic efficiency. However, Copp argues, it is not clear that cost-benefit analysis can measure economic efficiency because it is not clear that we can always, or even usually distinguish economic from non-economic costs. Further, even limited reliance on cost-benefit analysis carries the risk that we will be tempted to quantify in inappropriate contexts, in order to make all factors involved in a decision readily comparable to economic costs and benefits.

Finally, E. J. Mishan and Dan Usher address the problem of how to determine the value of a life. Mishan argues that any attempt to determine the value of a life without reference to the expressed or revealed preferences of individuals is superfluous, since it must be vindicated by the very preferences it professes to ignore; and any attempt to derive a unique value of life from these preferences is destined to fail, since preferences vary with the level of existing risk, kinds of risk, and other factors. Thus, we should abandon the attempt to find a value of life. Usher, on the other hand, argues that we must attempt to derive a value of life from individual preferences; if we do not, social decisions will be thoroughly arbitrary.

The papers in this volume range from the highly theoretical to the eminently practical. What they share is a concern to illuminate the interplay between ethical questions and economic institutions in a way that will contribute to our understanding of what a just society is and how to achieve it.

THE MORAL STANDING OF THE MARKET*

Amartya Sen

How valuable is the market mechanism for practical morality? What is its moral standing? We can scarcely doubt that as individuals we do value tremendously the opportunity of using markets. Indeed, without access to markets most of us would perish, since we don't typically produce the things that we need to survive. If we could somehow survive without using markets at all, our quality of life would be rather abysmal. It is natural to feel that an institution that is so crucial to our well-being *must be* valuable. And since moral evaluation can hardly be indifferent to our interests and their fulfillment, it might appear that there is nothing much to discuss here. The market's moral standing "has to be" high.

However, the value to an individual of a particular institution when society has been organized around that institution must be distinguished from how the society – and even that person – might have fared had the society been organized differently. We, as individuals, are thoroughly dependent on the market (as things stand), but that does not tell us much about the value of the market *as an institution*. We have to consider alternative ways of doing the things that the market does. The assessment of an institution cannot be based on examining the predicament of an individual who is suddenly denied access to it, without having the opportunity of being in another social arrangement with other types of institutions.

A second difficulty in treating the question as straightforward arises from problems in formulating the nature of the choice that is being considered. When somebody questions the value of the market, he or she is typically not considering the alternative of having no market transactions *at all*. In fact, that is hard even to visualize. Markets, in the widest sense, enter into an enormous range of activities. Some social activities are formal market transactions; others are quite informal; and some have only a few market-type features. Those who rail against the market mechanism are not about to

*I am most grateful to Allan Gibbard for his discussion of the paper following my presentation at Bowling Green on 21 September 1984. I have also benefited from the general discussion, including comments by Jules Coleman, Donald Regan, Alexander Rosenberg, and Hal Varian, and from later correspondence with Varian.

recommend the cessation of all such transactions. To see it as an "all or nothing" question is to miss the point of the criticism altogether. It is a question of "how much," "how unrestrained," "how supplemented." Even the most ferocious critic of the market mechanism is unlikely to be looking for a world in which every person must produce every bit of the goods and services that he or she can consume. The question must be posed differently.

A third problem comes from a different direction. Insofar as the market mechanism is valued as an instrument, its moral value must ultimately derive from somewhere else. We cannot begin to assess the moral standing of the market mechanism without first asking, "To what intrinsically valuable things is the market mechanism instrumental?" We have to place the role of markets in a fuller moral context.

I shall take up the question of instrumentality in the next section, and then go on to the problem of integration.

The Consequent Good or the Antecedent Freedom?

Most defenses of the market are instrumental in terms of the goodness of the *results* achieved. It works "efficiently"; it serves our "interests"; it is "mutually beneficial"; it delivers "the goods"; it contributes to "utility"; it serves as the "invisible hand" by which man is led to promote an end which was no part of his intention.[1] On this view, the market is good because its results are. For example, Friedman and Friedman argue: "on the whole, market competition, when it is permitted to work, protects the consumer better than do alternative government mechanisms that have been increasingly superimposed on the market."[2] We need, of course, a criterion for judging the interests of the consumers and the relevance of these interests to the overall moral assessment of the market. We also need some methodology for interpreting the exact content of the Friedmans' claim before it can be

---

[1] The last phrase comes from Adam Smith, *The Wealth of Nations* (1776). Aside from indicating wherein the virtue of the market mechanism lies, it points to the fact that no individual participant in the process aims at *all* the results the market achieves. Friedrich von Hayek has seen in this a great new insight – indeed a great theory of "the result of human action but not of human design" – initiated allegedly by Adam Smith, "revived" by Carl Menger, and now enshrined by Hayek; see his *Studies in Philosophy, Politics, and Economics* (Chicago: University of Chicago Press, 1967), pp. 96–105. One has to be careful about what is being asserted here. It would be wrong to say that no one aims at *any* of the results achieved. In this model, each person is assumed to pursue, as far as is feasible, his own interest, and this pursuit is *fulfilled* by the market transaction. "The butcher, the brewer, or the baker" did not aim at "our dinner," but *we* presumably *did*. The fact that not *all* the results, nor the *pattern* of the results, was anyone's "design" seems to be an unremarkable fact. Surely, Adam Smith's main contribution, in this area of analysis, was to show how the results of different people's "designs" are *coordinated and achieved* by the market. I have discussed this question, among other issues, in "The Profit Motive," *Lloyds Bank Review*, vol. 147 (1983).

[2] Milton and Rose Friedman, *Free to Choose* (London: Secker and Warburg, 1980), p. 222.

properly assessed. But there can be little doubt that this approach to the value of the market mechanism – whatever its exact content and force – rests on assessing *results*.

Perhaps less obvious – but obvious enough – so is the claim that the market makes people "free to choose," a freedom that might be seen to be valuable in itself (whether or not it also helps in other ways, such as the protection of the interests of the consumers). The goal of "freedom to choose" provides an alternative (though not unrelated) basis for the assessment of markets by its results. "That is the basic difference between the market and a political agency. You are free to choose. There is no policeman to take the money out of your pocket to pay for something you do not want or to make you do something you do not want to do."[3] Whether the freedom to choose is *itself* a fundamental value – not only instrumentally so at some "higher level" of analysis – is a difficult question that need not be addressed in the present context.[4] The importance of the market, on this "free to choose" view, derives from the *more basic* value of that freedom (no matter how the value of that freedom is itself obtained).

But there is also a different possibility that must be considered. It could be the case that what is at issue is not the value of the freedom to choose. People may be seen as having fundamental "rights," and the exercise of those rights may be seen as not requiring any justification at all. If the market is seen as being part and parcel of the exercise of such rights, then markets may be defended on the basis of antecedent rights, rather than in terms of the results, including freedom of choice, that they may achieve. To assert that "individuals have rights, and there are things no person or group may do to them (without violating their rights)"[5] would *imply* the freedom to make market transactions (given the way the rights referred to are characterized). The question of the consequences, in this procedure, arises later, *after* the right to transact (and thus to engage in market relations, in the broad sense) has already been given a stable moral status.

In this formulation, rights specify rules – of ownership, transfer, etc. – that have to be followed for making a person's actual "holdings" legitimate. The results of these rules are accepted precisely because they have resulted from following the right rules, not because the results judged as *outcomes* are in themselves good. The results (including serving the interests of consumers, or even enjoying the "freedom to choose") may or may not, in fact, be judged to be good *as results*. But whatever the conclusion of that outcome analysis

[3] *ibid.*, p. 223.
[4] See R. M. Hare, *Moral Thinking: Its Levels, Methods and Point* (Oxford: Clarendon Press, 1981), on "levels" of moral thinking, and on the distinction between the "intuitive" and the "critical." See also John Gray, *Mill on Liberty: A Defence* (London: Routledge, 1983).
[5] Robert Nozick, *Anarchy, State and Utopia* (Oxford: Blackwell, 1974), p. 1.

might be, the justification of the market, in this aproach, is not based on the merits of the results. Indeed, it is apparent that there are consistency problems in an attempt to combine this approach with another that justifies actions (including, of course, transactions) in terms of preferring one "pattern" of outcomes over another, since that would "over-determine" the system.[6]

If this rights-based "procedural" view is accepted, then the traditional assessment of the merits and demerits of the market, in terms of the goodness of outcomes, would be quite misplaced. The moral necessity of having markets would follow from the status of rights and not from the efficiency or optimality of market outcomes. This approach, incidentally, involves the rejection of the way economists – the professional group most immediately concerned with the assessment of the role of markets – have typically examined the case for and against the market. In the economist's picture of "social welfare," rights are seen as purely institutional (typically legal) artifacts, without any importance of their own: rights are judged – in the typical welfare economic framework – in terms of how they fulfill or thwart people's interests.

The failure to consider the "procedural" approach at all is certainly an omission that deserves some comment. Robert Nozick's analysis represents one example of nonconsequentialist moral reasoning, and this type of reasoning must be seriously considered by welfare economists. Even if such reasoning is ultimately rejected, there is no question that that approach deserves the most serious consideration.

It is also worth noting in this context that the force of a rights-based procedural justification of market operations is independent of our under-standing of empirical regularities in the real world, in a way that any consequentialist justification for market operations cannot be. For example, one could have a lively debate as to whether Friedman and Friedman are right about what they say on the relative merits of the market mechanism in safeguarding the interest of consumers, or whether, in fact, it is the case that "the freedom to choose" in any substantive sense is better guaranteed by the market mechanism than by some feasible alternative. If it is shown that the empirical relationships on which the consequentialist justifications depend are erroneous, then the case for the market mechanism, derived from such reasoning, would collapse.

The same applies to a moral assessment of the market based on the

---

[6] Robert Nozick does point to (what he calls) "invisible-hand explanations" of the emergence of social institutions (such as markets), quoting Adam Smith (*ibid.*, p. 18). But, consistently with his own approach, he does not proceed to assess such institutions in terms of the goodness of interest-fulfilling outcomes.

"freedom" resulting from it. If that freedom is shown to be "illusory,"[7] then the case for the market mechanism would be dis-established. That assessment would have to be thoroughly dependent on the truth of the causal hypotheses linking markets and the resulting freedom. Questions can be raised on the empirical acceptability of the presumed causal connection.

In contrast, one interesting feature of the *a priori* rights-based justification of market operations is that it is not contingent on the empirical regularities that hold in the real world. The results of market transactions may be good, but even if they are bad or unassessable, they are still legitimate because they are sanctioned by antecedent rights. This can be seen as giving the nonconsequentialist approach a "robustness" that the consequentialist approach lacks, especially since empirical regularities are hard to establish, and predictive theories in this field can be extremely flimsy.

On the other hand, this "robustness" and the immunity from empirical critiques are also plausible sources of skepticism about that ethical structure. Why must we accept the priority of these rights?[8] Do the rights of ownership and exchange have "foundational" status? Must we really accept the notion that some arrangements required by the recognition of these rights are morally acceptable irrespective of their consequences – however bad they might be? What if the consequences are totally disastrous?

The last is not only a matter of purely theoretical speculation. As I have tried to argue elsewhere,[9] many large famines – in which millions of people have perished from hunger and hunger-related diseases – have taken place (even in the recent past) without any overall decline in food availability at all, with no "natural cause" making the famines inescapable. People have been deprived of food precisely because of sudden and violent shifts in "entitlements," resulting from the exercise of rights that people "legitimately" have within the given legal system. Loss of employment and wage income have often led to starvation. Changes of relative prices have

---

[7] See, for example, the different analyses of this issue by Z. Husami, "Marx on Distributive Justice," *Philosophy and Public Affairs*, vol. 7 (1978); H. Steiner, "Individual Liberty," *Proceedings of the Aristotelian Society*, vol. 74 (1974); G. A. Cohen, "Capitalism, Freedom and the Proletariat," A. Ryan, ed., *The Idea of Freedom: Essays in Honour of Isaiah Berlin* (Oxford: Clarendon Press, 1979); G. A. Cohen, "Illusions about Private Property and Freedom," J. Mepham and D. Rubens, eds., *Issues in Marxist Philosophy* (Hassocks: Harvester Press, 1981); O. O'Neill, "The Most Extensive Liberty," *Proceedings of the Aristotelian Society*, vol. 79 (1979–80); and others. See also Gerald Dworkin, *et al.*, *Markets and Morals* (Washington: Hemisphere Publishing, 1977).

[8] Allan Gibbard, "Natural Property Rights," *Nous*, vol. 10 (1976). Gibbard examines the possible claim of "property rights" to be "grounded in principles of natural liberty," with or without John Locke's [John Locke, *The Second Treatise of Government* (1764)] qualification regarding the libertarian position, and shows why the claim is hard to justify.

[9] Amartya Sen, *Poverty and Famines: An Essay on Entitlement and Deprivation* (Oxford: Clarendon Press, and New York: Oxford University Press, 1981).

sometimes driven the losers to the wall. The legal systems in question differ, of course, from an *idealized* legal structure of the kind required by a theory of rights of the type we are examining, but, nevertheless, in many respects they have a good deal of similarity. In fact, it is easy to show that, with a system of rights justified independently of consequences, it is possible to have disasters of this kind occurring without anyone violating anyone else's rights at all. The contingency of ownership, as well as influences that determine transfers and terms of trade, can easily lead a particular occupation group into absolute deprivation, destitution, and decimation, without anything illegitimate and perverse having happened from a rights' perspective.

It is not irrelevant to ask the question: If such starvation and famine were to occur, must the results of the market operation be taken as "acceptable," simply because they have followed from people legitimately exercising the rights they have? It is not easy to understand why rules of ownership, transfer, etc., should have such absolute priority over the life and death of millions of people.

In response to this it can, of course, be claimed that only in these extreme cases will it be right to override the requirements imposed by rights and their legitimate exercise. There could be a caveat that nullifies rights in these cases, but not in others.[10]

Robert Nozick himself keeps the question open as to whether "catastrophic moral horrors" should provide a ground for violating rights. There *is* a dilemma here. If disastrous consequences can be used as a ground for nullifying deep-seated rights, surely that completely undermines the consequence-independent way of looking at rights. If disastrous consequences would be adequate to nullify any rights (even the most important ones), perhaps bad-but-not-so-disastrous consequences would be adequate to nullify other, less central, rights? Some of the rights related to the ownership and use of property may well be seen to be less "deep-seated" than some other rights, e.g., the personal-liberty rights with which civil libertarians have been, understandably, most concerned. Once rejection, based on consequential evaluation, is admitted into the picture of moral reckoning, it is difficult to find an obvious stopping place for a theory of rights that is based on a purely procedural approach.

[10] Contrast the model of "alienable rights" in A. Gibbard, "A Pareto-Consistent Libertarian Claim," *Journal of Economic Theory*, vol. 7 (1974), in which rights have extreme sensitivity to the nature of the outcome. It is arguable that such a system of outcome sensitivity may not do full justice to the procedural nature of rights, but on the other hand it is very hard to see why rights should continue to be not alienable at all even when the results of the exercise of rights are plainly terrible. Some connections between outcomes and rights are discussed in my "Rights and Agency," *Philosophy and Public Affairs*, vol. 11 (1982). See also D. H. Regan, "Against Evaluator Relativity: A Response to Sen," *Philosophy and Public Affairs*, vol. 12 (1983); and Amartya Sen, "Liberty and Social Choice," *Journal of Philosophy*, vol. 80 (1983).

It is hard to argue that the value of the market can be divorced from the value of its results and achievements. This is not to say that the assessment of market operations, or the evaluation of the market mechanism, must be based only on *utility* consequences (defined in terms of satisfaction, desire-fulfillment, etc.). For example, it is quite possible to take into account what the market mechanism in general, and specific market operations in particular, would do to such things as the freedom of the individuals in society. If being "free to choose" is regarded as an important part of a person's well-being (*or* regarded as morally important despite its not being a part of personal well-being), it would be perfectly sensible to include this in the assessment of the consequences of market operations. This would obviously be inadequate for producing a procedural moral system of the kind that Robert Nozick and others have tried to develop. But by taking freedom into account in our calculation of consequences, the force of their criticism of narrow consequential systems can be partly accommodated.

I have, in fact, tried to argue elsewhere that taking note of the fulfillment or violation of rights, and of the realization or nonrealization of freedom, in the assessment of social arrangements, does more justice to the *importance* of rights and freedoms than a purely constraint-based (e.g., Nozickian) system of rights and freedom can do.[11] This is not, as is often assumed, only a matter of the contrast between "negative" and "positive" freedom. Even if one ignores altogether "positive" freedom, and confines one's attention to assessing "negative" freedom, there is still a strong case for including the badness of violation of negative freedom in evaluating consequent states. Given imperfect compliance, the violation of negative freedom of A by B can sensibly figure in C's calculation regarding what to do, and a consequence-sensitive system can deal with such links. It is inadequate to try to deal with negative freedom through constraints only, since they have no relevance to C's calculations if it is B who violates A's negative freedom, even if C could have helped to stop this violation.

It could be argued that the consequential way of taking note of rights may not be able to pay adequate attention to the "deontological" aspects of agent-relative action assessment. This might be thought to be particularly so for the special role of "negative" freedom. To this point some responses may be made, which I shall note here without elaboration or development. First, this is really a separate matter requiring *additional* structure,[12] and the correct starting point for "deontological" issues may not be rights at all, but some notion of duty linked with the position-relativity (in

[11] Amartya Sen, "Rights and Agency".
[12] See my "Evaluator Relativity and Consequential Evaluation," *Philosophy and Public Affairs*, vol. 12 (1983), and "Well-being, Agency and Freedom: The Dewey Lectures 1984," *Journal of Philosophy*, vol. 82 (1985).

particular, "doer relativity") of moral evaluation.[13] Second, such additional structure for personal morals may be quite consistent with a result-oriented assessment of institutions such as markets and property.

No matter how that additional deontological question is dealt with, the *valuation* of freedom – even of "negative" freedom – would demand a more consequence-sensitive approach, not reliant only on imposing constraints. Those who have argued that the traditional consequentialist approaches – most notably the utilitarian systems – take inadequate note of the importance of freedom, have not been, in my view, mistaken in this claim. But the failure arises not so much from the concentration on consequences, but from the way consequences are assessed. If utilitarianism is split into three distinct parts,[14] viz., "welfarism" (judging states of affairs only by utility information), "sum-ranking" (dealing with utility information by simply adding them), and "consequentialism" (judging actions, rules, etc., ultimately by the goodness of the states of affairs resulting from them), then the primary failing, it can be argued, arises from "welfarism."

This is, of course, a more general question, and one which we need not really take up in this paper. If it is accepted that the moral importance of the market mechanism and market operations has to be seen primarily in terms of its results, then the need to go more deeply into consequential systems has to be recognized. The value of the market instrument is, then, consequential, derivative, and contingent. To assess that value we have to understand the more fundamental social values of well-being, freedom, and justice.[15] We have to examine also the causal links between the institutional arrangements and the realization of the more fundamental values.

---

[13] One way of seeing the problem of personal morality in this type of context is in terms of a system of action evaluation that is consequence-sensitive, but not fully "consequentialist." Another way of dealing with it is to make the evaluation of states of affairs *position-relative* to the person doing the evaluation (including his or her own agency). There is, in fact, a case for such position-relativity on grounds of ethical cogency; or at least so I have tried to argue in "Rights and Agency"; see also the exchange between Donald Regan, "Against Evaluator Relativity," and A. K. Sen, "Evaluator Relativity and Consequential Evaluation," *Philosophy and Public Affairs*, vol. 12 (1983).

[14] Discussed in Amartya Sen, "Utilitarianism and Welfarism," *Journal of Philosophy*, vol. 76 (1979).

[15] On questions as to how these moral values may be interpreted, assessed and integrated, there are – not surprisingly – enormous differences; see for example K. J. Arrow, *Social Choice and Individual Values* (New York: Wiley, 1951); J. C. Harsanyi, "Cardinal Welfare, Individualistic Ethics, and Interpersonal Comparisons of Utility," *Journal of Political Economy*, vol. 63 (1955); and *Essays on Ethics, Social Behaviour and Scientific Explanation* (Dordrecht: Reidel, 1976); I. M. D. Little, *A Critique of Welfare Economics* (Oxford: Clarendon Press, 2nd edition, 1957); J. M. Buchanan and G. Tullock, *The Calculus of Consent* (Ann Arbor, MI: University of Michigan Press, 1962); J. Rawls, *A Theory of Justice* (Cambridge, MA: Harvard University Press, 1971); and "Kantian Constructivism in Moral Theory: The Dewey Lectures 1980," *Journal of Philosophy*, vol. 77 (1980); R. Dworkin, *Taking Rights Seriously* (London: Duckworth, 1977); and "What is Equality," *Philosophy and Public Affairs*, vol. 10 (1981). On

Optimality and Inequality

The assessment of the market mechanism in welfare economics has tended to rely – at least in recent decades – on the so-called "basic theorem of welfare economics."[16] Indeed, in the theory of welfare economics, the main rationale of the market mechanism has been typically viewed in the light of the dual relationship captured by this theorem.[17]

The first part of this "basic theorem," asserting that every competitive equilibrium is a Pareto optimum, has been called the "direct theorem." The other part, claiming that every Pareto optimum is a competitive equilibrium, may be called the "converse theorem." Both theorems are established by making a set of restrictive assumptions. The assumptions are not exactly the same in the two cases, but they have several requirements in common (e.g., the absence of externalities[18]).

---

related matters, see also H. Varian, "Distributive Justice, Welfare Economics and The Theory of Fairness," *Philosophy and Public Affairs*, vol. 4 (1975); G. Dworkin, et al, *Markets and Morals*; G. Calabresi and P. Bobbitt, *Tragic Choices* (New York: Norton, 1978); D. Usher, *The Economic Prerequisites to Democracy* (New York: Columbia University Press, 1981); J. Roemer, *A General Theory of Exploitation and Class* (Cambridge, MA: Harvard University Press, 1982); and "Equality of Talent," Working Paper 239, Economics Department, University of California, Davis, (1984); B. C. Frey, *Democratic Economic Policy* (Oxford: Martin Robertson, 1983); A. M. McLeod, "Justice and the Market," *Canadian Journal of Philosophy*, vol. 13 (1983); P. K. Pattanaik and M. Salles, *Social Choice and Welfare* (Amsterdam: North-Holland, 1983). I have tried to discuss some of these issues in Amartya Sen, *Collective Choice and Social Welfare* (San Francisco: Holden-Day, 1970; republished, Amsterdam: North-Holland, 1979); "Equality of What?" in S. McMurrin, ed., *Tanner Lectures on Human Values*, vol. 1 (Cambridge: Cambridge University Press, 1980, reprinted in my *Choice, Welfare and Measurement* (Oxford: Blackwell; and Cambridge, MA: M.I.T. Press, 1982); "Rights and Agency," *Philosophy and Public Affairs*; "Well-being, Agency and Freedom: The Dewey Lectures 1984."

[16] K. J. Arrow, "An Extension of the Basic Theorems of Classical Welfare Economics," in J. Neyman, ed., *Proceedings of the Second Berkeley Symposium on Mathematical Statistics and Probability* (Berkeley, CA: University of California Press, 1951); G. Debreu, *Theory of Value* (New York: Wiley, 1959); K. J. Arrow and F. H. Hahn, *General Competitive Analysis* (San Francisco: Holden-Day, 1971; republished, Amsterdam: North-Holland, 1979).

[17] As Dorfman, Samuelson and Solow put it: "More recently it has become common to sum up all these in one brief and easily understood theorem which comprises everything of significance and provides the backbone of welfare economics. This fundamental theorem states 'every competitive equilbrium is a Pareto optimum; and every Pareto optimum is a competitive equilibrium.'" R. Dorfman, P. Samuelson, and R. Solow, *Linear Programming and Economic Analysis* (New York: McGraw-Hill, 1958), pp. 409–410.

[18] This assumption is not in fact fully needed for each of the results; see S. Winter, "A Simple Remark on the Second Optimality Theorem of Welfare Economics," *Journal of Economic Theory*, vol. 1 (1969); and G. C. Archibald and D. Donaldson, "Non-paternalism and the Basic Theorems of Welfare Economics," *Canadian Journal of Economics*, vol. 9 (1976). These further results indicate the presence of an asymmetry, in the required assumptions regarding "externalities," between the direct theorem and the converse theorem. Some other properties (e.g., convexity) have very disparate relevance, indeed, to the two theorems (the direct theorem does not require any convexity assumption, whereas the convex theorem certainly requires it in some form or other).

The ethical force of the direct theorem in establishing the case for the market mechanism may be seen to be quite limited. A Pareto optimum does, of course, have the valuable property that not all the parties can be made better-off (in terms of utility) in any alternative feasible state. But it is easily seen that a situation can be Pareto optimal but nevertheless highly objectionable – indeed, possibly disastrous. If the utility of the deprived cannot be raised without cutting into the utility of the rich, the situation can be Pareto optimal but truly awful.

There are two standard responses to this criticism of the relevance of the direct theorem. One is to argue that the criticism is based on making explicit or implicit use of "egalitarian" values, and many people would dispute whether such values have force. I have tried to address that issue elsewhere,[19] and this is perhaps not the occasion to go again into that old question. I shall have a little more to say on this in the next section, but for the moment I simply assert that indifference to the inequality of well-being requires some justification. The fact that equality is widely valued does not, of course, establish its validity. But it does demand a response, and a presumption of this kind calls for some serious argument as to why, in this case, inequality is acceptable. If the direct theorem is to be treated as one of great ethical significance, we must be told more about the *general moral irrelevance* of inequality of well-being, *or* of the moral case for the *particular* inequalities that would contingently occur *in each case*.

The other counterargument suggests that we should shift our attention from the "direct theorem" to the "converse theorem." Given "welfarism," i.e., assuming that "social welfare" is a function of utility information only (and this seems to be the common assumption in welfare economics), it is plausible to argue that the best of the feasible social states must be *at least* Pareto optimal. Since, according to the "converse theorem," *every* Pareto-optimal feasible state is a perfectly competitive equlibrium, with respect to some set of prices (and some initial distribution of resources), it follows that it is invariably "possible" to achieve the very best through some market mechanism (provided the market is perfectly competitive). The fact that some particular Pareto-optimal states may be morally revolting does not affect this argument one iota, since we could have chosen another – better – Pareto optimum (not this awful one) by having a different initial distribution of resources, and by relying on the perfectly competitive mechanism to take us to the appropriate social optimum. Not surprisingly, Debreu describes the converse theorem as a "deeper" result, and Koopmans notes that it is the

---

[19] Amartya Sen, *On Economic Inequality* (Oxford: Clarendon Press; and New York: Norton, 1973).

converse theorem, rather than the direct theorem, which is "the central proposition of the 'new welfare economics'."[20]

The converse theorem is undoubtedly a major theorem in the literature of resources allocation. But to use it as a justification for the market mechanism requires further argumentation. The converse theorem points to the possibility that, if we get the initial distribution of resources right, we can reach the very best state of affairs through the competitive market mechanism *without requiring any political interference with the market mechanism*. That can certainly be seen as a conditional rejection of the necessity of a political mechanism.

On the other hand, *how* do we get the appropriate initial distribution of resources? The need for the redistribution of ownership is, of course, one of the central political issues that divides the "right" from the "left." Classical socialist arguments have been concerned primarily with the ownership of "means of production," and only secondarily with such questions as "externalities" and other "vices" with which the market mechanism cannot allegedly cope. If the real case for the market mechanism – through the highroad of the "converse theorem" – is dependent on a major revolution in the distribution of resource ownership, then the case for *laissez-faire* and for using the allegedly "non-political" route of the market mechanism is thoroughly undermined. The "converse theorem" belongs to the "revolutionist's handbook."

There is, in fact, a further difficulty, and this concerns the issue of incentives. Once the initial distribution is appropriate to the optimal outcome, the perfectly competitive outcome, if unique and globally stable,[21] will take us in the direction of the very best state of affairs. However, in order to determine the *appropriate* initial distribution of resources (for optimality in terms of the values usually invoked in traditional welfare economics, including "equity"), one would need a great deal of information about each person's productivity, tastes, etc. It will not be in the interest of those who are likely to lose out in the process of redistribution to reveal these facts. The incentive to reveal information is absent in such a system, under the standard assumption of self-interested behavior.[22]

---

[20] G. Debreu, *Theory of Value*; T. C. Koopmans, *Three Essays on the State of Economic Science* (New York: McGraw-Hill, 1957), p. 27.

[21] Uniqueness and global stability, incidentally, are additional assumptions and no mean demands either. See Arrow and Hahn, *General Competitive Analysis*.

[22] This problem of the incentive to reveal information has to be distinguished from the problem of informational economy, to which the precedures for "decentralized resource allocation" are addressed (see, for example, E. Malinvaud, "Decentralized Procedures for Planning," in E. Malinvaud and M. O. L. Bacharach, eds., *Activity Analysis in the Theory of Growth and Planning* (London: Macmillan, 1967); G. M. Heal, *The Theory of Economic Planning*

It would, thus, appear that while the converse theorem is intellectually much more attractive, it is not easy to translate it into a practical case for the market mechanism.[23] If the *information* regarding individuals is inadequate for determining what the initial distribution of resources should be, *or* if there is an absence of – or reluctance to use – a political mechanism that would *actually* redistribute resource-ownership and endowments appropriately, then the practical relevance of the converse theorem is severely limited. On the other hand, the direct theorem continues to apply without these qualifications (provided the other assumptions, such as the absence of externalities of particular kinds can be legitimately made.)[24] Indeed, for the "non-omniscient," or the "non-revolutionary," government, it is the direct theorem rather than the converse theorem that is of immediate interest in judging the market mechanism.

This, of course, does bring us back to the earlier question as to how good an outcome we might regard a Pareto optimum to be. If one is concerned about income distribution, or about inequalities of utility or well-being, it is

---

(Amsterdam: Horth-Holland, 1973); M. Weitzman, "Prices versus Quantities," *Review of Economic Studies*, vol. 41 (1974); P. Dagsputa, *The Control of Resources* (Oxford: Blackwell, 1982). In such "decentralized" procedures, each agent acts as a member of a "team," and it is typically assumed that they have *shared objectives*, though disparate access to information. The problem of decentralized resource allocation, when the agents have their own respective goals, which may conflict, has not been much studied in the literature, and will certainly not lead to simple and comforting results.

[23] There are various "incentive compatible" mechanisms (see, for examples, T. Groves and J. Ledyard, "Optimal Allocation of Public Goods: A Solution to the 'Free Rider' Problem," *Econometrica*, vol. 45 (1977); J. Green and J.-J. Laffont, "Characterization of Satisfactory Mechanisms for the Revelation of Preferences for Public Goods," *Econometrica*, vol. 45 (1977); P. Dagsputa, P. Hammond, and E. Maskin, "The Implementation of Social Choice Rules: Some General Results in Incentive Compatibility," *Review of Economic Studies*, vol. 46 (1979); which deal effectively with the problem of "the free rider" in terms of the incentive to *do* the right thing, *given* the initial distribution of resources, despite the presence of such problems as "public goods." These "solutions" are not, however, addressed to the problem of how to deal with the incentive to reveal information of a kind that would permit the policy makers to make judgments about the right initial distribution of resources (in line with the distributional objectives of policy making). Nor do they address the problem of revelation of individual *judgments* to be combined in an "aggregate" judgment (e.g., to decide on equity). On the last, see A. Gibbard, "Manipulation of Voting Schemes: A General Result," *Econometrica*, vol. 41 (1973); M. A. Satterthwaite, "Strategy-Proofness and Arrow's Conditions: Existence and Correspondence Theorems for Voting Procedures and Social Welfare Functions," *Journal of Economic Theory*, vol. 10 (1975); P. K. Pattanaik, *Strategy and Group Choice* (Amsterdam: North-Holland, 1978); J.-J. Laffont, ed., *Aggregation and Revelation of Preferences* (Amsterdam: North-Holland, 1979); H. Moulin, *The Strategy of Social Choice* (Amsterdam: North-Holland, 1983); B. Peleg, *Game Theoretic Analysis of Voting in Committees* (Cambridge: Cambridge University Press, 1984).

[24] In fact, insofar as we value the market achievement not in terms of Pareto-optimality (i.e., reaching an "undominated" vector of utilities), but in terms of the corresponding notion of being "free to choose" (i.e., having an "undominated" n-tuple of individual freedoms to pursue *whatever* they decide to seek), the assumption of self-interested behavior can be also significantly relaxed.

very hard to settle just for "any Pareto-optimal state," without looking further.

This particular difficulty brings out an extraordinary aspect of the market mechanism that is often overlooked. It is that the specification of the market mechanism is an essentially *incomplete* specification of a social arrangement. Even with the purest, perfectly competitive market mechanism, we are not in a position to understand precisely what will happen until we know something more about the rest of the social arrangement, in particular the distribution of endowments and resource ownership. It is an extraordinarily ambitious program to judge one part of the social arrangement (the market mechanism) without assuming something specific about the other parts. It is not surprising, therefore, that our view of the market mechanism may well be thoroughly dependent on how the incomplete description of the social arrangement given by the market mechanism is completed by other substantive descriptions. For any moral approach that responds positively to equality of one kind or another (of well-being, or of resources[25]), the assessment of the market mechanism must be integrally related to the rest of the picture.[26]

I ought to mention, in this context, that there are a number of other "results" that are often cited in the literature dealing with the moral case for the market mechanism based on achievement assessment. For example, in dealing with the *effects* of property rights, reference is often made to Ronald Coase's theorem[27] – that the optimality of the outcome is independent of the initial distribution of property rights, provided certain assumptions (such as absence of transactions costs) are made. However, the result depends upon a very weak definition of "optimality," and the difficult issues discussed in the last few paragraphs are essentially not addressed.[28]

The only way of dealing with the problem of inequality in the outcome of market mechanism is to face that issue directly, rather than avoiding it, either

---

[25] See R. Dworkin, "What is Equality." See also J. Roemer, "Equality of Talent"; and H. Varian, "Dworkin on Equality of Resources," mimeographed, University of Michigan, Ann Arbor (1984).

[26] There can, however, be useful *partial* criteria of judging achievements, e.g., whether the mechanism satisfies specific requirements of "horizontal equity" or "symmetry preservation." The market mechanism can be partially defended from these particular perspectives. See, for example, D. Schmeidler and K. Vind, "Fair Net Trade," *Econometrica*, vol. 40 (1972); H. Varian, "Equity, Envy and Efficiency," *Journal of Economic Theory*, vol. 9 (1974).

[27] R. H. Coase, "The Problem of Social Cost," *Journal of Law and Economics*, vol. 3 (1960).

[28] For different interpretations of what Coase's line of reasoning achieves, see J. M. Buchanan, *Freedom in Constitutional Contract* (College Station: Texas A & M University, 1977); and "Rights, Efficiency and Exchange: The Irrelevance of Transactions Cost," mimeographed, Center for Study of Public Choice, George Mason University (1983); G. Calabresi and P. Bobbit, *Tragic Choices*; R. Cooter, "The Cost of Coase," *Journal of Legal Studies*, vol. 11 (1982); E. J. Green, "Equilibrium and Efficiency under Pure Entitlement Systems," in A. H. Meltzer and T. Romer, eds., *Proceedings of the Conference on Political Economy*, vol. 2, Supplement to *Public Choice* (1982).

by silence, or by some peculiar definition of "optimality." It might be the case that inequality of well-being or of resources is of no moral concern, but if so, that position has to be made and defended. It becomes, of course, particularly hard to defend that proposition when inequalities are so great that some people live in extreme misery, or indeed die of starvation or hunger. But even otherwise the question is far too important to be neglected.

The Producers' Rights to the Product

One other line of moral defense of the market mechanism (traced to different "foundational" values) raises the question of who is "producing" what, and argues for the right of the producer to enjoy the fruits. On this view, inequalities in the outcome are of no concern, unless they are out of line with the productive contributions made by the different individuals. This approach does directly address the issue of inequality, suggesting a method of dealing with it which is based on *the right of the producer* rather than on *the right of the needy*. I examine that approach next, by scrutinizing a powerful exposition of it by P. T. Bauer.[29]

Bauer's attack on "the unholy grail of economic equality" has several features, but it includes *inter alia* what I have elsewhere called "the personal production view."[30] This issue is quite central to the moral assessment of the market mechanism. Bauer argues that "economic differences are largely the result of people's varied capacities and motivations." (p. 19) Given this interpretation of economic differences, he sees little that is wrong with such inequality: ". . . it is by no means obvious why it should be unjust that those who produce more should enjoy higher income." (p. 17)

Bauer argues that the high income of "the relatively prosperous or the owners of property" are "normally . . . *produced* by their recipients and the resources they own." (p. 12, emphasis added) Given this "personal production view" of inequality, the moral assertion of the appropriateness of such an inequality can be seen as a variant of an "entitlement" argument. However, the entitlement reasoning here does not take the procedural form it takes in the system of Nozick and others, since the rights that people have, on Bauer's view, are not that of ownership, transfer, etc., but of actually getting what one has "produced." Bauer is concerned with results and not just with procedural rules of contract, etc.

In this respect, the entitlement reasoning of Bauer relates to a labor-entitlement system of the kind that one interpretation of the Marxian theory

---

[29] P. T. Bauer, *Equality, The Third World and Economic Delusion* (Cambridge, MA: Harvard University Press, 1981).

[30] See Amartya Sen, "Just Desert," *New York Review of Books*, vol. 19 (March 4, 1982). See also P. T. Bauer's rejoinder in the same journal, June 10, 1982; also P. T. Bauer, *Reality and Rhetoric: Studies in the Economics of Development* (London: Weidenfeld, 1984).

of "exploitation" leads to. According to that view, labor "produces" all the value of the output (or "nature" and labor do, with no "residual" left), and the entitlement of labor to get the output is related to the fact. Any "shortfall" reflects "exploitation."[31] In Bauer's system, the output is produced not only (nor, in any Lockean sense, "ultimately") by labor, but by the different factors of production (including capital). And the marginal productivity theory is given an interpretation of real contribution, as opposed to having only allocational usefulness in terms of counterfactual calculations.

It is not at all implausible to think that "the personal production view," if correct, can lead to some case for inequality, even though it would still have to compete with claims arising from other considerations, such as that of needs. If, for example, a person has himself produced – unaided by others – some food, and another person wants to snatch that food away from the first, then the case for the first person rather than the second having that food might well be seen to be strong. While this judgment may be countered with competing arguments for a different distribution (the stronger need of the second person, if that is the case), there is undoubtedly some plausibility in arguing that the fact that the first person has produced the good in question *is* a matter of moral relevance. Also, if there are no strong contrary arguments, i.e., if the second person's needs are not noticeably different from those of the first, the case for the first having the food on grounds of having "produced" it would seem to be quite strong, at least in terms of common-sense morality.

"The personal production view" is, however, rather difficult to sustain. If production is an interdependent process, involving the joint use of different resources, it is not generally possible to separate out which resource has produced how much of the total output. There is no obvious way of determining that "this part" of the output is due to resource 1, and "that part" due to resource 2, etc. The method of attribution according to "the marginal product" concentrates on the extra output that one incremental unit of the resource would produce, *given* the amounts of the other resources. This method of accounting can lead to problems of internal consistency, except under some special assumptions (in particular, constant returns to scale). But even if these assumptions are made, the relevance of the accounting to "the personal production view" is deeply problematic.

---

[31] There are, of course, a great many difficulties in this way of seeing the Marxian system, as many contributions by Marxian economists have brought out. There is, in fact, a strong case for seeing the relevance of Marxian exploitation theory from a perspective different from that of production entitlement. On these issues, see M. Morishima, *Marx's Economics* (Cambridge: Cambridge University Press, 1973); I. Steedman, *Marx after Sraffa* (London: NLB, 1977); G. A. Cohen, *Karl Marx's Theory of History* (Oxford: Clarendon Press, 1978); J. Elster, "Exploitation and the Theory of Justice," mimeographed, Historisk Institute, University of Oslo (1980); J. Roemer, *A General Theory of Exploitation and Class*.

In fact, the marginalist calculus is not concerned with finding out who "actually" produced what. Marginal accounting, when consistent, has an important function in decision making regarding the use of resources, suggesting when it would be appropriate to apply an additional unit of resource, and when it would not. To read in that counter-factual marginal story one of "actual production" – who in fact produced what part of the total output – is to take the marginal calculus well beyond its logical limits.

For example, if it turns out that, using the marginalist calculus to evaluate factor contributions, yields the result that 40 percent of the output is due to labor, 40 percent due to machinery, and 20 percent due to management, that just tells us something about the respective relative values of the marginal contributions multiplied by the total amounts of the respective resources. It would not, of course, follow that any of these three factors of production could produce their respective shares unaided by the others. Indeed, the apportioning is not even one that is done by adding together the marginal contributions of all the respective units one after another, but rather goes by weighting the *entire* amount of the resource input by the marginal valuation of the counterfactual additional contribution of that resource *at the point of equilibrium*. Under the competitive distributive process, that is what will determine the relative shares of income, and in this sense, it has predictive value as well as allocational use. But "the personal production view" adds to this real use a spurious interpretation as to who has "produced" what. This comes, as it were, from nowhere, and it is essentially a fiction. It might, of course, be seen as a "convenient fiction," but that fiction is a whole lot more convenient for some than for others.

The problem becomes even more complicated when the comparison extends to incomes generated from the production of *different* goods, since the relative incomes would then depend on the relative prices of these products, introducing an additional element of arbitrariness into "the personal production view." The significance of the relative prices in terms of "productive contributions" would require a further fiction in translating the "marginal rates of transformation" – again, a set of counterfactual magnitudes – into a set of actual production weights.

There is the further problem that "the personal production view" applies only to resources, and to move from there to the contribution of the person *owning* the resources is a considerable jump. The right of the owners of productive resources to receive high income requires some justification of the moral relevance of ownership. It is not justified on the simple ground, to which Bauer refers, of the income-rights of "those *who* are more productive and contribute more to output." (p. 11; emphasis added) Once again, the traditional socialist literature has not been so concerned with disputing the productive contribution of different resources as it has been with disputing the right of the *owners* of productive resources to grab what the resources produce.

If this reasoning is correct, the problem of inequality raised in the context of the other defenses of the market mechanism is not disposed of by moving to "the personal production view." This is not because there is no intuitive appeal whatever to the idea that one ought to have a right to something one has produced "oneself." But (1) in a world of interdependent production, that condition is difficult to apply to resources; and (2) in a world of nonpersonal resources, it is difficult to translate it from resources to persons.

There are, of course, circumstances in which "the personal production view" might be very powerful. If, for example, we are asked to arbitrate between two children fighting over a wooden toy, which has been made unaided and with free wood by one of them, and if we know nothing more about the two children, then it would be not unreasonable to be swayed by the fact of "personal production."[32] Utilitarians (and many others) will claim that this appeal is entirely explainable by some instrumental reasoning. Whether this is so is unclear. What is clear, and cannot be doubted, is that there is a strong moral intuition in that direction. But no matter what this appeal arises from, the possibility of applying it to judging actual market outcomes is so restricted by the fact of interdependence and the contrast between owning and producing, that this approach may be of little use in practical reasoning.

Concluding Remarks

The moral standing of the market mechanism has to be related to results, and it is, thus, derivative and contingent. While it is important to examine the possibility that market operations might be justified on grounds of the exercise of peoples' "prior" rights (irrespective of consequences), the implausibility and the arbitrariness of that approach are difficult to avoid. I have argued for the alternative of assessing market operations in terms of achievements, but also for treating achievements much more widely than "welfarism" permits (including such factors as the importance of "freedom to choose"). This has the advantage of taking note of the moral force of some of the arguments presented by the "procedural" view, while making that force compete with other moral claims in the overall decision.

The second approach examined finds the moral standing of the market mechanism in the values of the outcomes. This is the standard approach in welfare economics, which then proceeds to take the more specialist form of

---

[32] I have discussed this question in "Ethical Issues in Income Distribution: National and International," in S. Grassman and E. Lunberg, eds., *The World Economic Order: Past and Prospects* (London: Macmillan, 1981); reprinted in Amartya Sen, *Resources, Values and Development* (Oxford: Blackwell, and Cambridge, MA: Harvard University Press, 1984).

judging the outcomes exclusively by the utilities generated. In terms of that general approach of "optimality," while a case could be made for saying some nice things about the market mechanism, it is hard to go beyond some highly tentative statements. The crucial issue turns out to be our assessment of inequality. The "direct theorem" ignores it. The "converse theorem" deals with it in a way that is self-defeating, insofar as the noninterventionist "moral" of the market mechanism is concerned.[33] Of course, we might refuse to judge the outcome in terms of utility information only. I have tried to argue elsewhere[34] against the "welfarist" method of evaluation of states of affairs. But the issue of inequality does have to be addressed, whether inequality is seen in terms of utilities, well-being, incomes, resources, or freedoms (including the real "freedom to choose").[35] The practice of avoiding this question through evasion or silence, on the one hand, or through peculiar definitions of "optimality," on the other, seems hard to defend.

The third approach that was examined is one based on "the personal production view." Despite the possible relevance and force of that moral consideration, it appears that this gives us very little help in morally assessing market mechanisms in a world with (1) interdependent production, and (2) owned impersonal resources.

The argument that is much harder to dismiss is one that claims little for the market mechanism except superiority over other *practical* alternatives. Samuel Brittan has argued that "too often the defects of real world market are compared with the hypothetical action of a benevolent and omniscient dictator (as frequently – in the more technical writing – for reasons of mathematical convenience as from any deeply held conviction)."[36] Indeed, it is not unfair to ask a critic of the market mechanism what precise system he would put forward *instead*, how well does it work, and how does it compare?

Once the issue is seen in this way, it is clear that the question of the moral standing of the market mechanism cannot be given the kind of simple answer that some of the approaches examined have tried to give. It might well be the case that many alternatives suggested as substitutes for the market mechanism would do worse than the market mechanism, even in terms of

---

[33] It is not surprising, in view of this, that the early contributions to the efficiency of the market mechanism came from socialist writers like O. Lange, "The Foundations of Welfare Economics," *Econometrica*, vol. 10 (1938); and A. P. Lerner, *The Economics of Control* (London: Macmillan, 1944).

[34] Amartya Sen, *Collective Choice and Social Welfare*; "Utilitarianism and Welfarism"; "Rights and Agency."

[35] On the last, see Amartya Sen, "Equality of What?"; Well-being, Agency and Freedom: The Dewey Lectures 1984."

[36] S. Brittan, *The Role and Limits of Government: Essays in Political Economy* (London: Temple Smith, 1983); p. 37. See also I. M. D. Little, *Economic Development: Theory, Policy and International Relations* (New York: Basic Books, 1982).

the criteria used by the advocates of the change. It is also possible that, in terms of the criteria put forward by defenders of the market mechanism, replacement of the market in many spheres by other procedures would do much better.

The Chinese produced chaos by trying to do away with some features of the market mechanism. At the same time, they did expand the positive freedoms of many. For example, despite a per capita GNP only a fraction (about a seventh) of Brazil's and Mexico's, China has succeeded, through an interventionist regime, in raising life expectancy beyond that of Brazil and Mexico. It is also higher than that of South Korea, a country with a much higher level of income and a much faster rate of growth (based on a market economy with an active government policy). If we look at actual achievements across the world, the picture is a divided one, and there are many conditional conclusions to be drawn based on such empirical comparisons.[37] The difficulties in making the comparisons arise partly from the problem of isolating empirical regularities, but also from the formidable complications in getting an adequate moral criterion in terms of which the instrumentality of the market mechanism and its rivals can be judged.

When all the qualifications have been put in, the market mechanism certainly has some instrumental moral relevance, related to its handling of information and incentives. The result-oriented and contingent nature of that relevance does not make the lessons unimportant. The defenders of the market mechanism have often seen in hesitant acknowledgments like this one a tendency to damn the market with "faint praise." But while faint praise is no doubt one method of damning, unjustified and ferocious praise is certainly another. The vigor of the defense of the market mechanism examined earlier in the paper is not matched by its ability to meet criticisms. It also distracts us from the contingent importance of the use of the market mechanism in many real circumstances, and tends to make us overlook the relevance of these lessons for practical reasoning. There *is* a case for *faint* praise – not any less, nor much more.

Economics, All Souls College, Oxford

---

[37] The question is discussed in Amartya Sen, "Public Action and the Quality of Life in Developing Countries," *Oxford Bulletin of Economics and Statistics*, vol. 43 (1981); and "Development: Which Way Now?", *Economic Journal*, vol. 93 (1973).

WHAT'S MORALLY SPECIAL
ABOUT FREE EXCHANGE?*

ALLAN GIBBARD

Is there anything morally special about free exchange? In asking this, I am asking not only about extreme, so-called "libertarian" views, on which free exchange is sacrosanct, but about more widespread, moderate views, on which there is at least something morally special about free exchange. On these more compromising views, other moral considerations may override the moral importance of free exchange, but even when rights of free exchange are restricted for good reason, something morally important is lost. For some, free exchange may preserve liberty, in some morally significant sense, or realize some such moral value as "to each his own." Alternatively, a system of free exchange may have a special moral status by virtue of the kinds of pragmatic arguments that economists give, arguments that free exchange produces good social results. Whether free exchange has any such virtues as these is the broad question I address in this paper. I offer what I have to say somewhat in the spirit of an overview. Philosophical scrutiny and economic analysis combine, it seems to me, to delineate fairly clearly what is, and what is not, morally special about free exchange.

More specifically, my concern is this. A system of free exchange can be expected to give rise to a market with a system of prices. Other economic orders too, including most extant ones, involve an extensive price system, even though they are not systems of pure free exchange or pure *laissez faire*. Now, it is clear enough what can be morally special about a market with prices. Given a suitable distribution of assets and a suitable system of prices, each person has a choice among a wide range of ways of leading his life. At the same time, as he decides how to lead his life, each person must take into account the resources his choices divert from others, and decide in light of their cost what he really wants most. A price system, then, can harmonize the conflicting demands people make on limited resources, while leaving each person a wide latitude of choice. Now price systems, as I have said, can arise without unfettered free exchange – as is demonstrated by every actual economy in the world. It is often supposed, though, that there is something

*Some of the work on this paper was done while the author was a Fellow at the Center for Advanced Study in the Behavioral Sciences, with support from a Fellowship for Independent Study and Research of the National Endowment for the Humanities, and from the Andrew W. Mellon Foundation. The author is extremely grateful to all these sources of support.

morally special, not only about a price system in general, but about a particular kind of price system: a price system that arises from an economic order of pure free exchange. My chief question, then, is what, if anything, is morally special about a system of pure free exchange, as opposed to other economic orders that yield a system of prices.

By free exchange, then, I mean something more than a price system. I mean something like the full economic order supported by nineteenth century liberals and those who now call themselves libertarians. What peculiarly characterizes such a system? I will attempt no full elucidation, but the crux lies in the free transferability of the rights of private ownership. That is to say, there is something called "ownership" of things, land, and the like. This "ownership" includes extensive rights to the use of whatever is owned, circumscribed in ways that protect the person and the property of others. There is probably nothing general and rigorous to be said about what these rights of use are, but there is something important to be said about the transfer of these rights. We have a system of *free exchange* if, first, whatever these use-rights of ownership may be, they are transferable by gift or contractual exchange, subject only to those restrictions which the parties involved have accepted. In addition, we might require that each adult be counted as "owning" himself, in the sense that he has wide latitude in deciding what to do. It will follow that in a pure system of free exchange, whatever a person is permitted to do, he may obligate himself to do – often as part of an exchange of property rights. Finally, we may stipulate that all property rights are acquired by the transfer of rights of ownership. Thus, the main distinguishing feature of a system of free exchange is that the rights of ownership, whatever they may be, are transferable, subject only to restrictions that arise from contract. In a system of free exchange, then, the rights of ownership go well beyond the rights of ownership as we know them in our own economic order; I shall be referring to ownership in the former sense as *extreme ownership*.

I have contrasted a *pure system of free exchange* with a *market price system*; the former is a specific version of the latter. A person with property rights faces a price system if he faces a set of prices at which he can exchange those property rights for others. A price system, then, may offer a person with transferable property rights a choice among a wide range of activities involving the use and consumption of scarce resources. A person faced with a price system may chart his life voluntarily, in the sense that he may choose it from a wide range of options. Whether the range is wide and the options are attractive will depend on the person's assets and the prices he faces, as well as on his needs and tastes. Price systems can exist without having developed from a system of pure free exchange, as I have defined it, and indeed the familiar price systems are not systems of pure free exchange.

Capitalism with redistributive taxation, for instance, involves a price system, but not a system of pure free exchange. For if exchange is taxed, then although I have the various rights of use that go with full ownership, I cannot exchange those rights without paying a tax. Likewise, most state economies confront individuals with a price system, though in those economies, exchange is tightly controlled.

Now a suitable price system, as I have said, offers a person with sufficient assets a wide range of attractive alternatives for leading his life. It may be highly desirable, then, that everyone face a suitable price system with sufficient assets, and one attraction of free exchange may be that it promises to bring about such a desirable state of affairs. Since, though, we can have a price system without free exchange, the virtues of a price system are not peculiarly virtues of a pure system of free exchange. My question is, is there anything morally special about free exchange itself? Is there anything special about free exchange, as opposed to a price system without pure free exchange?

Free exchange has been advocated on many grounds, but we might divide them into "pragmatic" and "intuitionistic" defenses. "Pragmatic" defenses tell us why we should want free exchange, moral grounds aside, and then derive the moral desirability of the system from that nonmoral point of view. Prime examples are utilitarianism, the efficiency arguments of economists, and, I think, the hypothetical contract view in Rawls's book, *A Theory of Justice*.[1] I include Rawls here because, on his theory, principles of justice are evaluated by their appeal to mutually disinterested agents behind a veil of ignorance. The reasons these agents have for preferring one set of principles to another are not moral ones. According to Rawls, though, our reason for adhering to these principles in the flux of life – our moral reason – is that we would have chosen them from behind the veil of ignorance. We would have chosen them because of their prospective advantages, and these advantages are reckoned in nonmoral terms. Hence, in Rawls's theory, the moral character of the principles of justice rests ultimately on the advantages they offer us, and in that sense, Rawls's defense of whatever property rights are sanctioned by his principles of justice is pragmatic. What I am calling "intuitionistic" defenses of free exchange, in contrast, appeal directly to a moral value that is taken as fundamental. I have in mind, here, principally arguments that fundamentally rest on the moral importance of freedom and respect for property rights.[2]

My thesis will be that to the extent that any good arguments speak specifically for free exchange, rather than for a price system in general, their

---

[1] John Rawls, *A Theory of Justice* (Cambridge, MA: Harvard University Press, 1971).
[2] See especially Robert Nozick, *Anarchy, State, and Utopia* (New York: Basic Books, 1974).

grounds are ultimately pragmatic. These pragmatic grounds, though, do not support free exchange in any pure form, but only in a highly mitigated form. Hence, there is no simple, clearcut formula for economic justice. If we want to know what systems of property rights would satisfy the demands of justice, we must cope with complex, pragmatic issues.

Institutionistic Justifications of Free Exchange

First, let us examine what I call "intuitionistic" views of free exchange. These views take moral principles directly pertaining to property rights, or to liberty, as fundamental moral principles. We tend to think of "ownership" as a primitive, irreducible feature of the world. We were, after all, taught to think of things as "mine" or "hers" or "his" from earliest childhood, and so, perhaps, were our ancestors since time immemorial. We are apt, in careless moments, to think of a person's property as a part of his person, like an arm or a leg. The first step in thinking about property rights is to realize that property is a matter of complex human contrivance, custom, and convention. Ownership of a thing is, after all, a matter of a complex cluster of rights with respect to it. These "rights" we may think of positively, as those recognized by the community involved, or normatively, as those that ought to be recognized and respected, but in either case, my point holds. If we think positively, then we must realize that property is a matter of a complex array of human attitudes. If we think normatively, we must realize that property is a matter of complex ways things ought to be, and our theory of the ways things ought to be is precisely what we are putting in question when we do normative political philosophy. In thinking about property in either way, we must wrench our minds free of the grip of a fetish – the fetish of a primitive "mine" or "yours", "his" or "hers" mentality.

Now, once we free our minds from *ownership* as a primitive notion, the intuitions to support certain property rights as morally fundamental elude us. I have argued this before,[3] and so here I go quickly. The most promising strategy for defending property rights is that of Locke, who tries to derive property in things from property in one's own person. Robert Nozick calls such a theory a "historical entitlement theory."[4] It is, in essence, a theory of the legitimacy of appropriation, and leads to what I have called "extreme ownership." Now the appeal of appropriation, if we resolutely cast aside ownership as a primitive fetish, seems to me to lie either in considerations of liberty or in considerations of welfare. The appeal to liberty, though, cannot be direct, for ownership primarily involves restrictions on liberty – on the liberty of others to make use, without my leave, of the thing I own. What

---

[3] Allan Gibbard, "Natural Property Rights," *Nous*, vol. 10 (1976), pp. 77–86.
[4] Nozick, *Anarchy*.

recommends appropriation is that a system of property can, in some ways, enhance liberty and welfare. It can enhance welfare in that, Malthusian pressures aside, appropriation can make possible a reasonably satisfactory life for all those not hampered by a natural affliction. This appeal to welfare is, of course, pragmatic, and is not an appeal to intuitions that directly concern property or liberty. As for liberty, in an advanced economy a system of property rights can indeed enhance liberty in an important sense of the term. Given a suitable system of exchangeable property rights, each able person will have a choice among a range of reasonably satisfactory ways of life. Liberty in this sense, however, is achievable in a variety of economic orders that yield a price system. It does not require that all property rights be rooted in what I have been calling "extreme ownership."

I mean all this as a summary of familiar ground. Of course it is no adequate treatment of the class of theories I am dismissing. Even if the criticisms I have sketched can be made to stick we are left with important questions. Isn't free exchange in some sense "free" in a way that taxed exchange or restricted exchange is not? Don't the equilibrium prices in a system of free exchange somehow reflect the value of what is exchanged in a way that other price systems do not? Free exchange, in a sense, internalizes the costs and benefits of what one does. I act to your benefit if you judge the benefit great enough to make it worth my while. In a world of free exchange, the benevolent do not lose and the selfish do not gain, for the benefits of my acts accrue to me and the costs of my acts are borne by me. What it is best for me to do from the point of view of the world as a whole is precisely what it is best for me to do from the point of view of my own benefit. Good works are rewarded and bad works are penalized in exact measure of their worth.

The picture here is one of perfect justice and perfect efficiency. Indeed, on this argument, perfect justice boils down, in a sense, to perfect efficiency. Not only are good works rewarded and bad works penalized, but the penalties are nicely adjusted to draw forth the good work only if its benefits to others are worth its costs to me, and to deter my bad works only if the costs to others outweigh the direct benefits to me.

This talk of perfect incentives, though, is a mirage. Note, first, that in this talk of "costs" and "benefits" we seem to be invoking a standard of interpersonal comparison: I bear the cost I impose on you, or reap the benefit I convey to you. But this supposes that your cost can be made mine, or your benefit mine. What can be said for the incentives of free exchange is something like this: I get a dollar's worth of benefit if I give you a dollar's worth of benefit. More precisely, I benefit you at a dollar's cost to me only if you can, with net gain to you, convey to me a benefit I find worth at least a dollar. Now, if we suppose that an extra dollar buys more benefit for one person than for another – in particular, for the poor than for the rich – then costs and benefits are not traded at par. Dollars are traded at par. Suppose John Churchmouse, who is poor, gets from a dollar ten times the benefit that would be gotten from a dollar by Jane Croesus, who is rich. Then she will not convey a benefit to him, in self-interested exchange, unless she can benefit him ten times the amount he can benefit her without net loss. Only a tenth of the cost or benefit she imposes on him is internalized by her, whereas ten times any cost or benefit he conveys to her is internalized by him. Costs and benefits are "internalized" in a lopsided way.

There still remains the question, "If an exchange of property rights can be made to mutual benefit, why forbid it?" The answer is, to induce a pattern of exchanges that is better on the whole. We forbid employment below the minimum wage because we think that more offers of employment will then be made at or above the minimum wage. We forbid untaxed sales because we think that more people will be then willing to make taxed sales. So put, to be sure, these sound like restrictions on liberty. But they are, for the most part, something more complex: they are restrictions on the exchange of property rights, and property rights are rights to restrict the liberty of others to use a thing. They are a part of a pattern of restrictions on liberty, the pattern constituted by a system of property rights. They are not added restrictions on liberty, over and above the restrictions on liberty involved in a system of pure free exchange. They are restrictions on our legal powers to alter the restrictions on liberty that constitute a system of property rights.

I cannot, of course, claim to have disposed of all possible intuitionistic groundings of property rights. Three intuitionistic approaches, though, seem to run aground. In the first place, any argument that appeals directly to intuitions about property is unlikely to survive a full realization of the complex nature of the rights involved when one says a thing is "mine" or "yours." A complex array of rights needs more than a simple intuition to ground it. In the second place, arguments for appropriation extending to extreme ownership that are grounded on the miserable state we would all be in if everything were common property fail to support extreme ownership in particular; they simply support having some system of property rights other than common ownership of everything. Finally, arguments in favor of extreme ownership for the sake of liberty fail in two ways. If liberty is a matter of having a wide range of reasonably attractive alternatives in one's life, regulated systems of exchange may produce more widespread liberty than would a system of pure free exchange. If, on the other hand, liberty is the lack of legal constraints on action, any system of property rights restricts liberty, and there seems to be no way to identify restrictions on exchange as additional restrictions on actions. They are, rather, restrictions on powers to alter restrictions on action.

Pragmatic Justifications of Free Exchange

Return, then, to pragmatic arguments. Much of the work of theoretical welfare economics consists in investigating claims that free exchange produces optimal incentives. This work elaborates and assesses Adam Smith's claim that under a system of free exchange, economic agents act "as if guided by an invisible hand" to produce an outcome that is best in some sense. The story theoretical welfare economics tells has been a mixed one.[5] One version of the claim of the invisible hand is that it achieves Pareto-efficiency: that things work out so that, given the constraints of technological feasibility, no one could have been better off without someone else having been worse off. Applied to a perfectly competitive economy, that is the "First Fundamental Theorem of Welfare Economics."[6] The theorem claims no virtue for the distribution of benefits in a perfectly competitive market. It may be, for all the theorem says, that some people will live in the lap of luxury and others will be miserable. The virtue of Pareto-efficiency is simply that no one could have been less miserable without someone else being more miserable or less happy. Pareto-efficiency is consistent with the grossest inequity.[7]

A "Second Fundamental Theorem of Welfare Economics" apparently rights this deficiency. Although some Pareto-efficient distributions are horrendous, presumably the best economic distributions are Pareto-efficient. The Second Fundamental Theorem says that in a perfectly competitive market, any Pareto-efficient distribution whatsoever may be achieved with a suitable distribution of initial endowments. That means, in particular, that the best distribution can be achieved by free exchange. This holds true whatever your conception of "best" is, so long as the "best" feasible distribution, as you conceive it, is Pareto-efficient.[8]

The two Fundamental Theorems of Welfare Economics, then, seem to say this: although not every distribution resulting from free exchange will be morally satisfactory, some distribution achievable with free exchange will be. Even this limited endorsement of free exchange, though, is deceptive. In the first place, the nice invisible hand results come only when certain idealized conditions are met: that everything that matters in life comes from the private consumption of goods; and that information is perfect, commodities

---

[5] See, for example, Adam Smith, *The Wealth of Nations* (Edinburgh, 1976, and New York: The Modern Library, 1937), and Hal R. Varian, *Microeconomic Analysis* (New York: Norton, 1978).

[6] See Varian, *Microeconomic Analysis*, p. 147, and Varian, "Distributive Justice, Welfare Economics, and the Theory of Fairness," *Philosophy and Public Affairs*, vol. 4 (1975), pp. 223–247.

[7] For a review of fallacies involving the Pareto principle, see Lawrence G. Sager, "Pareto Superiority, Consent, and Justice," *Hofstra Law Review*, vol. 8 (1980), pp. 913–938.

[8] See Varian, "Distributive Justice."

infinitely divisible, and economic agents perfectly rational. Much of theoretical welfare economics consists of the study of inevitable "market failure": the failure of free exchange to produce results that are Pareto-efficient – not to mention equitable – when these ideal conditions are not realized. In the second place, reaping the benefits of the Second Fundamental Theorem would require a perfect omniscience on the part of whomever distributed the "initial endowments." Even if the fairy tale conditions of perfect competition could be realized, there would be no practicable way of arranging initial endowments so as to achieve equitable distribution as exchanges proceed. So long as no god has arranged things so that we can have justice on earth without human striving after justice, the best we can hope for is tolerable, but Pareto-inefficient, distributions of property rights – distributions that we would not know how to match or better by a system of pure free exchange.

Given limited foresight, both on the part of the designers of an economic order and on the part of individual economic agents, the problem of economic justice becomes in some ways a problem of insurance.[9] Life is uncertain, and that makes it prudent for a person to be insured against great calamities in his life, such as lacking the ability to earn a decent income. Insurance, though, brings with it problems of moral hazard. Being insured, that is to say, leaves us with less than optimal incentive to take care. The market for insurance is inevitably inefficient, so long as there is no costless way to bind insurees to take optimal care. The "invisible hand" results of economists' general equilibrium theory do not hold in a world where insurance is needed and moral hazard is unavoidable. Thus, the Second Fundamental Theorem of Welfare Economics cannot reasonably be interpreted as telling us that we can achieve our favorite Pareto-efficient distribution through a system of pure free exchange. We cannot achieve that distribution in any economic order, and the theorem gives us no reason to suppose that the best distribution attainable through public policy will be attainable through a pure system of free exchange.

It might be thought that a system of voluntary income insurance would do as well as or better than any compulsory, public scheme – at least if all economic agents were perfectly rational in their insurance decisions. The kind of social insurance we need, though, cannot be supplied by a market of adults acting on their own behalf. It would be in my interest to be insured, to some degree, against being unable to earn a living, long before I reached the age of competence to buy that insurance for myself. To be

---

[9] I draw this from Ronald Dworkin, "What is Equality? Part 2: Equality of Resources," *Philosophy and Public Affairs*, vol. 10 (1981), pp. 283–345, and from recent unpublished work of Hal Varian.

committed, from childhood, to a scheme of income insurance is in effect to be subject to redistributive taxation.[10]

If there is anything to be said for untempered free exchange, it is its salience as a solution to a political bargaining problem. The "old-time religion" of *laissez faire* is just that; its only rational support comes from an extreme skepticism about the ability of any political process to mitigate the inequities of *laissez faire*. Its chief recommendation, in other words, is as an arbitrary fetish: that to settle matters by taboo may beat settling them by struggle.

Recent work in the theory of social choice and the possibility of "incentive-compatible" systems has indicated that no possible economic order will have the best of "invisible hand" properties.[11] Hence, if I am right that intuitionistic arguments reduce, on scrutiny, to fetish and pragmatism, then all that can be reasonably supported, for any political system capable of permitting enlightened, morally sensitive economic policy, is a mitigated system of free exchange, i.e., a price system with taxation to mitigate income inequalities. Nothing economists or philosophers know tells us otherwise.

Philosophy, University of Michigan

---

[10] This is argued in Allan Gibbard, "Health Care and the Prospective Pareto Principle," *Ethics*, vol. 94 (1984), pp. 261–282.

[11] See, for example, Allan Gibbard, "Social Decision, Strategic Behavior, and Best Outcomes," H. Gottinger and W. Leinfellner, eds., *Decision Theory and Social Ethics* (Boston: Reidel, 1978), pp. 153–168; "Social Choice and the Imperfectability of a Legal Order," *Hofstra Law Review*, vol. 10 (1982), pp. 401–413; and Theodore Groves and John Ledyard, "Some Limitations of Demand Revealing Processes," *Public Choice*, vol. 29 (1977), pp. 107–124.

BARGAINING AND JUSTICE

David Gauthier

My concern in this paper is with the illumination that the theory of rational bargaining sheds on the formulation of principles of justice. I shall first set out the bargaining problem, as treated in the theory of games, and the Nash solution, or solution F.[1] I shall then argue against the axiom, labeled "independence of irrelevant alternatives," which distinguishes solution F, and also against the Zeuthen model of the bargaining process which F formalizes.[2]

I shall then characterize an alternative solution, G, and relate it to the Kalai-Smorodinsky axiomatization.[3] Unfortunately, as Alvin Roth has shown, solution G and the Kalai-Smorodinsky axioms part company when they move beyond two-person bargaining games; I shall mention Roth's result and its implications for both solution G and the axiomatization.[4] This will lead me to propose a modification of G, solution G', which has been at the center of my own inquiries into bargaining, although for some time I failed to realize that G' was not, or at least not always, G.[5] I shall develop a Zeuthen model of the bargaining process which corresponds to G', and show its appealing features.

G' in hand, I shall note a startling resemblance between it and Rawls's difference principle; this will enable me to make the transition between bargaining and justice.[6] A bargaining model of morality captures, as a decision-theoretic model does not, Rawls's essential, but too often ignored,

---

[1] See J. F. Nash, "The Bargaining Problem," *Econometrica*, vol. 18 (1950), pp. 155–162. See also Alvin E. Roth, *Axiomatic Models of Bargaining* (Berlin: Springer Verlag, 1979), pp. 4–19.

[2] See Frederik Zeuthen, *Problems of Monopoly and Economic Warfare* (London: Routledge, 1930), pp. 104–121. For the relation between Nash and Zeuthen, see John F. Harsanyi, "Approaches to the Bargaining Problem Before and After the Theory of Games," *Econometrica*, vol. 24 (1956), pp. 144–156.

[3] See Ehud Kalai and Meir Smorodinsky, "Other Solutions to Nash's Bargaining Problem," *Econometrica*, vol. 43 (1975), pp. 513–518.

[4] See Roth, *Axiomatic Models*, pp. 98–107.

[5] Solution G' appears (although not under that label) initially in "Rational Cooperation," *Noûs*, vol. 8 (1974), pp. 53–65. See also "The Social Contract: Individual Decision or Collective Bargain?," in C. A. Hooker, J. J. Leach, and E. F. McClennen, eds., *Foundations and Applications of Decision Theory* (Dordrecht: Reidel, 1978), vol. 2, pp. 47–67.

[6] For the difference principle, see John Rawls, *A Theory of Justice* (Cambridge, Mass: Harvard, 1971), especially pp. 75–83.

requirement that moral theory "take seriously the distinction between persons." And it permits a decisive rebuttal, both of the claim that "average-utilitarianism" correctly captures moral or social rationality, and of the claim that maximin principles provide an irrational basis for *moral* choice.[7] The result will be, not to vindicate Rawls's aberrant Kantianism, but rather to defend the contractrarian theory that might have been developed from the insights in his early papers, most especially "Justice as Fairness."[8] Indeed, the result will be to defend precisely the moral theory that I have been developing.[9]

I turn now to the bargaining problem. Consider a finite set of actors, n in number, each of whom defines a Von Neumann-Morgenstern utility-function as a measure of his or her preferences over a continuous but bounded range of possible outcomes (continuity may be assured by treating any lottery over outcomes as an outcome).[10] Each outcome may then be represented as a point in n-dimensional utility-space, and the set of outcomes constitutes a compact, convex region in that space. Suppose that any point in this region may be realized by agreement among the actors; we may then call it the *bargaining region*, S. Suppose also that, should the actors fail to agree, the outcome will be a designated point in S, d. Then the bargaining problem, classically conceived, is the problem of determining a point of agreement, x, as a function of the bargaining region S and of the disagreement point d: $f(S,d) = x$. We suppose that the disagreement point is not Pareto-optimal in S, so that there is a point y in S such that $y > d$.

Here, a few notational points are in order. For any point x in utility-space, we write $x = (x_1, x_2, \ldots, x_n)$, where x_i is the utility of x to the i-th individual. We write $x > y$ if and only if for each i, $x_i > y_i$. And we write S^+ for the set of points x in S such that $x > d$.

The Nash solution, or solution F, to the bargaining problem may be simply characterized as follows:

$$F(S,d) = x, \text{ such that } \prod_{i=1}^{n} (x_i - d_i) > \prod_{i=1}^{n} (y_i - d_i) \text{ for all } y \ (\neq x) \text{ in } S^+.$$

$(x_i - d_i)$ is a measure of the gain to the i-th player of the outcome x over the disagreement outcome d. Thus, the Nash solution maximizes the geometric

---

[7] The quotation is from Rawls, *A Theory of Justice*, p. 27. The views to be rebutted are advocated in particular by John C. Harsanyi; see especially "Can the Maximin Principle Serve as a Basis for Morality? A Critique of John Rawls's Theory," in *Essays on Ethics, Social Behavior, and Scientific Explanation* (Dordrecht: Reidel, 1976), pp. 37–63.

[8] "Justice as Fairness" appeared in the *Philosophical Review*, vol. 67 (1958), pp. 164–194. Rawls's Kantianism is emphasized in *A Theory of Justice*, pp. 251–257, and in "Kantian Constructivism in Moral Theory," *Journal of Philosophy*, vol. 77 (1980), pp. 515–572.

[9] The full account of this theory will appear in *Morals by Agreement*, Oxford, in press.

[10] A Von Neumann-Morgenstern utility-function is one having the expected utility property: see J. C. Harsanyi, *Rational Behavior and Bagaining Equilibrium in Games and Social Situations* (Cambridge: Cambridge University Press, 1977), p. 34.

average of the gains realized by the actors in relation to what they would have achieved without agreement.

John F. Nash proved that solution F is uniquely determined by four axioms. Three of these I propose to accept as uncontroversial. They are:

Pareto-optimality: if f(s,d) = x, then $-\exists$ y: y∈S & y>x.

Symmetry: if (S,d) is symmetric and if f(S,d) = x, then for all i, j, $x_i = x_j$.

Independence of Equivalent Utility Representations: let (S',d') be obtained from (S,d) by positive linear transformations of the actors' utility-functions:

if f(S,d) = x, then f(S',d') = x', where x' is obtained from x by the same transformations.

The appeal of Pareto-optimality is evident. Without it, some person will fail to obtain a utility that he might have obtained at no cost to the others. Symmetry seems an evident requirement; if nothing in the information enables us to distinguish the actors, then the solution equally should not distinguish them. And independence of equivalent utility representations reflects the fact that Von Neumann-Morgenstern utility-functions are defined only up to a positive linear transformation. The bargaining outcome should not be affected by the purely arbitrary choices of zero-point and unit in the individual utility-functions that may be used indifferently to measure the same preferences.

The fourth axiom is rather different. It is:

Independence of Irrelevant Alternatives: let dε⊂TcS: if f(S,d) = x and if xεT, then f(T,d) = x.

This condition, to be distinguished from the Arrovian condition of the same name, is an application of Sen's rationality property *alpha* to the bargaining problem.[11] Property *alpha* states that a best item in any set must be a best item in any subset of which it is a member. The rationale for its application to the bargaining problem would seem to be this. Consider the solution to a bargain over a given range of outcomes and with a fixed disagreement point. Suppose that the range is restricted, without affecting the disagreement point, and that the original solution falls within the restricted range. Then, surely, it should be the solution to the restricted bargain. In the original bargain, it was selected over all of the alternative outcomes now available; what reason could there now be for selecting one of those alternatives? The axiom states that removing alternatives should not affect the bargaining

---

[11] See Amartya K. Sen, *Collective Choice and Social Welfare* (San Francisco: Holden-Day, 1970), p. 17. For the Arrovian "independence of irrelevant alternatives" condition, see Kenneth J. Arrow, *Social Choice and Individual Values*, 2nd edition (New York: Wiley, 1963), pp. 26–28.

solution, unless either the original solution is removed, or the disagreement point is affected.

We stated the axiom in terms of contracting the bargaining region; we may reformulate it in terms of expanding the region. Let $T \subset S$: if $f(T,d) = x$, then $f(S,d) = y$ where either $y = x$, or $y \in S$. Suppose that the range of available outcomes is expanded, without affecting the disagreement point. Then, surely, the solution to the original bargain should still be selected over any alternatives previously available; what reason could there be for selecting one of those alternatives? The axiom states that adding alternatives should not affect the bargaining solution, unless either one of the added alternatives is selected, or the disagreement point is affected.

Sen's *alpha* property is a condition on the presence of a maximal element in a set. An element that is maximal in relation to given alternatives must remain so in relation to any subset of those alternatives. If we suppose that the solution to the bargaining problem should involve the selection of a maximal element from the available alternatives, then we shall expect Sen's *alpha* property to be satisfied by the solution. Any maximizing problem involves the selection of a maximal element, and so it must have a solution satisfying *alpha*.

But maximization is not a direct concern in bargaining. Each bargainer has a maximizing concern – a concern with maximizing his own payoff – but there is no ground for the supposition that these unite into a single maximizing concern to be resolved in bargaining. The bargaining problem is primarily distributive, a problem of determining the size of the slices into which a pie is to be divided. It is not purely a distributive problem, because the size of the pie may be affected by the way in which it is sliced. But the distributive aspect is clearly focal; each bargainer cares about the size of the pie only insofar as it affects the size of his or her slice.

The supposition that what the bargainers aim at is the maximization of some quantity, such as the geometric average of the gains, rests on a fundamental misconception about distributive problems. Underlying standard bargaining theory, and also the economic version of utilitarian moral theory, is the attempt to convert a question of distribution into one of production – to represent a concern with the division of some quantity as a concern with maximization. Maximization, as a feature of individual behavior, is, understandably, deeply rooted in economic thought. And the search for maximizing solutions to problems is mathematically appealing; maximization is generally well-behaved. But the attempt to provide a maximizing solution to the bargaining problem resembles the attempt of the drunk to find his watch under the lamp post rather than in the shadows where he dropped it: "There's more light here." I shall return to this inappropriate insistence on maximization again before our inquiry is concluded.

The weakness of the Nash solution may be appreciated from another perspective if we consider the Zeuthen model of the bargaining process to which it corresponds. The model is most easily constructed for two-person bargaining, and I shall restrict my attention to that case. Faced with a possibly variable pie to be divided, two bargainers – let them be management and labor – advance proposals, which we may suppose take the form of a set of payoffs, one to each party. If their proposals are incompatible, agreement will be reached only through concessions. Zeuthen provides a measure of concession, and a rule for determining, given that measure, who should concede.

Let management's proposed outcome be $m = (m_1,m_2)$, where m_1 is management's payoff, and m_2 is labor's. Let labor's proposed outcome be $l = (l_1,l_2)$. The disagreement point – the expected outcome if no bargain is reached – is $d = (d_1,d_2)$. Then the Zeuthen formula for measuring the concession that would be involved were management to accept labor's proposal is $(m_1-l_1)/(m_1-d_1)$. (m_1-l_1) represents what management would forgo in accepting labor's proposal; (m_1-d_1) represents management's proposed gain in relation to disagreement; the Zeuthen formula measures the concession as the proportion of this total gain that would be forgone. Similarly, labor's concession is $(l_2-m_2)/(l_2-d_2)$. Now, the larger the concession, the less willing one is to make it. Therefore, Zeuthen argues that the party whose concession, as measured by the ratios of the Zeuthen formula, is smaller, must make a concession – that is, must put forward a revised proposal. And the revised proposal must be such that the other party will be required to make the next concession; otherwise the initial party would simply have to make a further concession or accept the other's proposal. Thus let $(m_1-l_1)/(m_1-d_1)$ be smaller than $(l_2-m_2)/(l_2-d_2)$. Management must make a concession; it puts forward a new proposal, say $m' = (m'_1,m'_2)$ such that $(l_2-m'_2)/(l_2-d_2)$ is smaller than $(m'_1-l_1)/(m'_1-d_1)$. Labor must now offer a concession; the process continues until one party is unable to make a concession forcing the other to a further concession, and can only accept the other's proposal. At that point agreement is reached.

By simple algebraic manipulation, it is easily shown that if management's current proposal is m^* and labor's is l^0, management must make a concession if $(m^*_1-d_1)(m^*_2-d_2)$ is smaller than $(l^0_1-d_1)(l^0_2-d_2)$, and labor must make a concession otherwise. Agreement clearly results on that proposal $x = (x_1,x_2)$ such that for any y ($\neq x$) in S^+, $(x_1-d_1)(x_2-d_2) > (y_1-d_1)(y_2-d_2)$. And this is solution F.

Let us reflect on the bargaining process just sketched. I have no objection to the use of the Zeuthen formula as a measure of concession, or to the Zeuthen rule for determining who must concede, given meaningful proposals and a meaningful disagreement point. But in the process as sketched, the proposals play no role. The bargainers converge on the same outcome, whatever their proposals at any stage may be, as long as each always proposes an outcome at least as favorable to himself as the outcome provided by solution F. The series of proposals and concessions seems to model a process of bargaining, but, given that the proposals play no role in determining the outcome, the concessions from meaningless proposals are equally meaningless, and so the modeling is entirely spurious.

Although in the model we talk of concessions, when the outcome is reached we are unable to determine whether one party has conceded more than the other. It is not possible to add together the several concessions that each party makes, since each concession is measured only relative to the proposal at the stage in the bargaining process when it occurs. Even if there were but one stage, and so one concession by each party, the measure of their concessions would depend on the particular proposals they had happened to advance. These proposals play a dummy role, however, and do not affect the outcome. By a suitable choice of proposal, one can make one's concession appear as large or as small as one pleases. And so concession is given no real significance in the Zeuthen model corresponding to solution F.

I turn now from solution F to solution G. To characterize solution G, we introduce the ideal point. For a bargaining situation (S,d) we write the ideal point as $\bar{x}(S) = (\bar{x}_1, \bar{x}_2, \ldots, \bar{x}_n)$, where $\bar{x}_i = \max \{x_i / x \varepsilon S^+\}$. The ideal point would represent that outcome, normally inaccessible and so not part of the bargaining region, at which each actor i would receive the greatest payoff that he could receive from any outcome in the bargaining region, given that every other actor j must receive at least his disagreement payoff d_j. Obviously, if uninterestingly, we should require that if $\bar{x}(S)\varepsilon S$, then $f(S,d) = \bar{x}(S)$.

The introduction of the ideal point enables us to capture directly the relevant maximizing considerations. Each individual bargainer seeks to do as well for himself as possible; each, therefore, seeks his greatest utility, given that a bargain is possible at all. And so each seeks the utility he would receive at the ideal point. In rejecting the relevance of the ideal point, solution F excludes the individual maximizing concerns of the bargainers in favor of an ungrounded, joint maximizing concern. Solution G makes no such error.

We now characterize solution G: $G(S,d) = x$, such that x is the maximal point (in S) for which, for all i, j, $(x_i - d_i)/(\bar{x}_i - d_i) = (x_j - d_j)/(\bar{x}_j - d_j)$. $(x_i - d_i)$ represents an actor's gain from the outcome x in relation to disagreement;

$(\bar{x}_i - d_i)$ represents an actor's gain from the ideal point in relation to disagreement, and so his gain from the most he could receive from any outcome in S^+, in relation to disagreement. $(x_i - d_i)/(\bar{x}_i - d_i)$ thus represents the proportion of possible gain that is afforded to actor i by outcome x. The solution G equalizes proportions of possible gain, and equalizes them at the maximum level.

G may seem a very plausible solution to the bargaining problem. Each person wants as big a slice of the pie for himself as possible. Solution G divides the pie into slices, each of which represents the same proportion of its recipient's maximal share – the share one could get leaving others with as much pie as in the absence of agreement. And no pie is left over – the slices are as large as possible, given that each is to be the same proportion of its recipient's maximum as every other slice.

Ehud Kalai and Meir Smorodinsky have provided a very neat axiomatization of solution G for two-person bargains. The first three axioms are the same as those for solution F: Pareto-optimality, symmetry, and independence of equivalent utility representations. But instead of the independence of irrelevant alternatives, which gives solution F its maximizing character, solution G satisfies a monotonicity condition. I shall follow Alvin Roth in stating the weakest such condition satisfied by G, because it relates the solution directly to the ideal point, and because it is intuitively clearer than the actual Kalai-Smorodinsky condition; this is:

Restricted Monotonicity: let $T \subset S$: if (T,d) and (S,d) are such that $\bar{x}(T) = \bar{x}(S)$, then f $(S,D) \geqslant f(T,d)$.

The very plausible idea expressed by this condition is that, if a bargaining situation is enlarged without changing either the disagreement point or the ideal point, the solution to the enlarged bargain should afford each actor a payoff at least equal to what he would receive from the solution to the original bargain.

Appealing as solution G and the Kalai-Smorodinsky axiomatization may be, they coincide only for two-person bargains. Solution G is well defined for all bargains but, as we shall shortly note, it loses its appeal for certain bargains involving three or more persons. And the Kalai-Smorodinsky axiomatization, alas, gives rise to an impossibility theorem for n-person bargains. Not all four of the axioms can be simultaneously satisfied for all bargains in which three or more persons are involved.

The argument here is due to Roth, whose example I adapt for illustration. Consider a three-person bargain, T, with a bargaining region the convex hull formed by the points $(0,0,0)$, $(1,0,1)$, and $(0,1,1)$, and d = $(0,0,0)$. It is evident that the Pareto-optimal points fall on the line joining $(1,0,1)$ to

(0,1,1), so that any solution satisfying Pareto-optimality must afford the third person a utility = 1. The ideal point, $\bar{x}(T) = (1,1,1)$.

Now, consider a game S with a bargaining region formed by the points (0,0,0), (1,0,1), (0,1,1), and (1,1,0), and d = (0,0,0). The ideal point, $\bar{x}(S)$ = (1,1,1). Note that S contains T. S is a symmetric game; thus, the only solution satisfying the symmetry axiom must be $f(S,d) = (2/3,2/3,2/3)$. But since S contains T and has the same disagreement and ideal points, by the restricted monotonicity axiom $f(S,d) \geq f(T,d)$, and so $f_3(S,d) = 1$. Thus Pareto-optimality, symmetry, and restricted monotonicity cannot all be satisfied.

Consider the solution G for these bargaining games. For S, unsurprisingly, $G(S,d) = (2/3,2/3,2/3)$. This is the maximal point x such that $(x_1-d_1)/(\bar{x}_1-d_1) = (x_2-d_2)/(\bar{x}_2-d_2) = (x_3-d_3)/(\bar{x}_3-d_3)$. But for game T, perhaps surprisingly, $G(T,d) = (0,0,0) = d$. The disagreement point is the only point in T such that the actors receive equal proportions of their possible gains. For game T, the solution G is not Pareto-optimal.

We should not be prepared to sacrifice Pareto-optimality, at least not in a normative theory of bargaining. Solution G must therefore be rejected – although we may want an acceptable solution to be identical with G for two-person bargains. And the monotonicity axiom must also be rejected because, in conjunction with the three axioms we accept as uncontroversial, it yields an impossibility theorem. What is to be done?

I propose the following modification of solution G; let us call it solution G':

$G'(s,d) = x$, such that $\min_i (x_i-d_i)/(\bar{x}_i-d_i) > \min_j (y_j-d_j)/(\bar{x}_j-d_j)$ for all y ($\neq x$) in S^+.

Recall that $(x_i-d_i)/(\bar{x}_i-d_i)$ represents the proportion of i's maximum gain that he receives from outcome x. Thus $\min_i (x_i-d_i)/(\bar{x}_i-d_i)$ represents the smallest, or minimum, proportion of possible gain yielded by outcome x to any person. G' therefore requires that the minimum proportion of possible gain yielded by the bargaining outcome be greater than the minimum proportion of possible gain yielded by any alternative outcome in the bargaining region. The worst-off person, in terms of the proportion of gain from bargaining that he receives, must be as well-off as possible.

The solution G' satisfies our three uncontroversial conditions – Pareto-optimality, symmetry, and independence of equivalent utility representations. It does not satisfy Sen's *alpha* property as applied to the bargaining problem; it is not a maximizing solution. And it is not monotonic, even in the restricted sense satisfied by G. We may easily verify, however, that if solution G is Pareto-optimal, then $G(S,d) = G'(S,d)$. For let $G(S,d) = x$. If x is Pareto-optimal, then for all y ($\neq x$) in S, there is some person j for whom y_j is less than x_j. But then $(y_j-d_j)/(\bar{x}_j-d_j)$ must be less than $(x_j-d_j)/(\bar{x}_j-d_j)$. Since solution G yields equal proportions of possible gain to all, for all persons $i,(x_j-d_j)/(\bar{x}_j-d_j) = (x_i-d_i)/(\bar{x}_i-d_i)$. And so $\min_i (x_i-d_i)/(\bar{x}_i-d_i)$ is greater than $\min_i (y_j-d_j)/(\bar{x}_j-d_j)$. But then $G(S',d) = x$.

At this point I should produce the axiom that, added to Pareto-optimality, symmetry, and independence of equivalent utility representations, yields solution G'. But instead, I offer a Zeuthen model of the bargaining process corresponding to solution G'.

Each bargainer makes a proposal, and each proposes that he receive the greatest utility compatible with every other person receiving at least the disagreement payoff. In other words, each person proposes his ideal payoff. Now, let x be any outcome in S^+; then the concession required by person i if he accepts x, as measured by the Zeuthen formula, is clearly $(\bar{x}_i-x_i)/(\bar{x}_i-d_i)$ – the proportion of his proposed gain over the disagreement payoff that he forgoes. As before, the larger one's concession, the less willing one must be to make it. Consider, therefore, the largest, or maximum, concession required for agreement on an outcome; if the outcome is x, then this will be $\max_i (\bar{x}_i-x_i)/(\bar{x}_i-d_i)$. The person who must make this largest concession will be least willing to agree on outcome x. Now, compare the largest concessions required for each of the possible outcomes. We may suppose that these represent the maximum degree of resistance to agreement on each outcome. The Zeuthen argument is, clearly, that the outcome exciting the least maximum degree of resistance must be accepted; the person required to make the maximum concession needed to yield this outcome is more willing to concede than any person required to make the maximum concession needed to yield any other outcome. Thus, the outcome with the least, or minimum, maximum concession is the bargaining solution, or, in other words, the outcome x such that $\max_i (\bar{x}_i-x_i)/(\bar{x}_i-d_i) < \max_j (\bar{x}_j-y_j)/(\bar{x}_j-d_j)$ for any outcome y $(\neq x)$ in S^+.

But $(\bar{x}_i-x_i)/(\bar{x}_i-d_i) = 1 - (x_i-d_i)/(\bar{x}_i-d_i)$. Thus, maximizing the former is equivalent to minimizing the latter. And minimizing the maximum value of the former for outcomes in S^+ is equivalent to maximizing the minimum value of the latter for these outcomes. Therefore, the requirement that the maximum concession be minimized is equivalent to the requirement that the minimum proportion of possible gain be maximized. And so the solution yielded by our Zeuthen model is solution G'.

Indeed, we may derive solution G' from the following postulates about rational behavior in bargaining:

1. Each person must propose the greatest utility for himself compatible with no person expecting less utility than from disagreement.

2. Given proposals satisfying 1, each person must suppose that there is a

set of concessions leading to an outcome in the bargaining region such that every rational person is willing to make the concession required of him in the set, provided every other person is so willing.

3. Each person must be willing to make a concession (provided others are similarly willing) if its size (as measured by the Zeuthen formula) is not greater than the size of the largest concession that he supposes that some rational person is willing to make (again, provided that others are similarly willing).

4. No person is willing to make a concession if he is not required to do so by conditions 2 and 3.

Every set of concessions leading to an outcome in the bargaining region requires a concession at least as large as the minimum maximum concession. From condition 2, each person must suppose that every rational person is willing to make the concession required of him by a set containing a concession at least as large as the minimum maximum concession. This means that some rational person is willing to make a concession at least as large as the minimum maximum concession. By condition 3, each person must be willing to make a concession at least as large as the minimum maximum concession. Since this suffices to yield agreement on an outcome in the bargaining region, conditions 2 and 3 cannot require any person to be willing to make a concession larger than the minimum maximum concession, and so, by condition 4, no person is so willing. Thus, rational bargainers reach agreement on, and only on, an outcome requiring a concession no larger than the minimum maximum concession, or, in other words, rational bargainers reach solution G'.

If we reflect on the Zeuthen model corresponding to solution G', we note that the magnitude of each person's proposal enters into the measurement of concession and so proves directly relevant to the solution. Each individual has good reason to propose as much utility for himself as is compatible with no one losing utility by agreement. The relevance of the ideal point to the bargaining solution thus corresponds to the demand in the model that each person propose his greatest feasible utility. Since the proposal each person makes is meaningful, the concession each then makes is also meaningful. And since each person makes but one, we may readily determine the total magnitude of his concession. Indeed, the bargaining solution depends directly on these magnitudes; we compare them and select that outcome requiring the minimum maximum total concession.

It might be thought that the Zeuthen model corresponding to solution F is more realistic than that corresponding to solution G', because it represents bargaining as a multi-stage process, rather than as a single-stage process. But the stages of that model are, as we have seen, without significance. The outcome to be reached is fixed without regard either to the proposals made or to the particular sequence, single-stage or multi-stage, of concessions made from those proposals. If we suppose that the Zeuthen rule for determining concessions is to be applied to determine the overall or total concessions to be made by the several parties to a bargain, then we find that it yields a meaningful one-stage representation of the bargaining process supporting solution G'.

In solution G' and in the associated Zeuthen model, we compare the proportionate gains, or equivalently the concessions, made by all of the parties to a bargain. We should note, first, that these comparisons are strictly independent of equivalent utility representations; the arbitrary choices of zero-point and unit in the individual utility-functions have no effect on the magnitudes compared. We should also note that these comparisons are not interpersonal utility comparisons. We do not suppose that persons making equal concessions, as measured by the Zeuthen formula, give up equal amounts of utility, whatever that would mean. We do not suppose that persons obtaining different proportions of possible gain obtain similarly different amounts of utility. If our disagreement payoffs are $0, and your ideal payoff is $500 and mine $50, then we receive equal proportions of possible gain if you get $300 and I get $30; we do not suppose that the utility value of money is ten times for me what it is for you.

In our argument, we give no meaning to interpersonal comparisons of utility. Each person's utility is a measure of outcomes based on that person's preferences. There is no common measure involved. The notion that utilities are interpersonally comparable rests on sheer confusion; it involves the illegitimate supposition that utility is a measure of something like the extent of overall preference-satisfaction obtained by a person. Perhaps we could introduce such a measure by treating objects of preference as possible worlds, requiring each person to order all possible worlds, and then normalizing each person's resulting utility-function to a 0–1 scale. But carrying out this Herculean task would shed not the slightest light on the bargaining problem. Bargainers have no reason to be concerned with comparative overall preference-satisfaction.

Solution G' introduces maximin or minimax considerations into bargaining. We suppose that rational bargainers will agree on an outcome that maximizes the minimum proportion of possible gain or minimizes the maximum concession. We should at once notice the connection between solution G' and John Rawls's difference principle. Suppose that we apply G' to the distribution of social values. The difference principle, it will be remembered, states that the minimum representative share of some subset of social values is to be maximized. As Rawls notes, his general conception of justice, that "All social values . . . are to be distributed equally unless an unequal distribution of any, or all, of these values is to everyone's advantage," is "simply the difference principle applied to all primary goods."[12] Now, as formulated by Rawls, the difference principle does not distinguish between the share of social values, or primary goods, or whatever, that would be obtained without social cooperation and the share obtained through cooperation. By introducing the disagreement point, solution G' enables us to take account of this difference; we suppose that each person seeks to maximize his gain over the outcome of no cooperation, and so is concerned with his share of socially or cooperatively produced values. Identifying the disagreement point with the outcome of no cooperation, solution G' yields a distribution of the cooperative *product*.

Furthermore, Rawls requires an interpersonal comparison of values, or primary goods, to determine the minimum share under different social arrangements, selecting that arrangement in which the least share is maximized. By invoking the notion of proportionate shares, solution G' enables us to avoid this problem of interpersonal comparison, and, furthermore, to avoid the exploitation of the more-advantaged that Nozick and others have criticized in Rawls's argument. But here my concern is not to berate Rawls for supposing that social cooperation should involve compensation. Rather, let us note that the solution G', as applied to agreement on the distribution of social values, works in a way similar to Rawls's difference principle, of which it may be considered a generalization. The difference principle would result from G' in the special case in which: first, what was to be distributed could be made the object of interpersonal comparison; second, in terms of that comparison, persons would suffer equally at the disagreement outcome; and third, also in terms of that comparison, persons would benefit equally from the ideal point.

Rawls supposes, or supposed, that the difference principle, requiring the maximization of the minimum share of some subset of social values, is itself chosen by a decision process conducted in accordance with a maximin principle of choice. John Harsanyi has correctly and decisively shown the irrationality of such a principle for the individual decision making to which Rawls appeals.[13] As a critique of Rawls, Harsanyi's argument turns out to be futile because, as Rawls's later writings make evident, the decision process is not part of the core of his moral theory, but only part of its dispensable heuristic.[14] How we get the difference principle is, for Rawls, less important than that we get it – since this principle relates to his Kantian conception of moral persons. But we are concerned with bargaining and justice, not with

---

[12] Rawls, *A Theory of Justice*, pp. 62, 83.
[13] See note 7 for reference.
[14] Note the absence of the decision process from the argument of "Kantian Constructivism in Moral Theory."

Kantian moral persons. And we are now in a position to see that Harsanyi's criticism (decisive as it is against the supposition that moral principles, or principles of justice, may be arrived at through a process of individual decision making based on maximin reasoning) would be entirely beside the point had Rawls developed the original contractarian insight of his theory and taken seriously the idea of bargaining, as the procedure by which principles of justice are selected. For in bargaining we do not have an individual decision maker, or even a group of individual decision makers, concerned with maximizing some single quantity. As I have argued, the attempt to invoke Sen's *alpha* property in the guise of Nash's axiom of the independence of irrelevant alternatives is simply an attempt to fit bargaining into a maximizing strait-jacket. Although rational individual decision making is correctly represented by a maximizing model, bargaining is not, and in bargaining the use of maximin considerations comes into its own. For in bargaining the distinction between persons is, and is to be, taken seriously, and the maximization of a single quantity, however conceived, fails to do this. In requiring that slices of the pie be determined by a maximin principle, in which each person is assured that the smallest proportionate gain is as large as possible, each is assured that his concerns are not being sacrificed to those of any other person. No maximizing procedure can do this.

Let me emphasize that my argument is not a criticism of maximization where it belongs. Economics, and rational choice, are properly concerned with maximization; as a first approximation, one might endorse Jon Elster's view that "man may indeed be seen as a *globally maximizing machine*."[15] But individual maximizers, interacting, do not a single maximizer make. My argument is a criticism of the imperialism of maximization that is represented, in our concern with bargaining and justice, by Nash's solution F, and by John Harsanyi's utilitarian moral theory.[16] Both of these confound distribution with production and mutual agreement with individual decision. They are paradigmatic cases of barking brilliantly up the wrong tree.

As preliminary to what follows, I want to distinguish clearly between the procedure in accordance with which principles of justice or, more generally, moral principles, are selected, and the content of the principles. We may bring the distinction into focus by a contrast between Harsanyi and Rawls. Harsanyi supposes that the "function . . . that [an] individual . . . will use in evaluating various social situations from a moral point of view will be called his *social welfare function*" as contrasted with the utility-function that he uses

---

[15] Jon Elster, *Ulysses and the Sirens* (Cambridge: Cambridge University Press, 1979), p. 10.

[16] Perhaps the best statement of Harsanyi's theory is in "Morality and the Theory of Rational Behaviour," in Amartya Sen and Bernard Williams, eds., *Utilitarianism and Beyond* (Cambridge: Cambridge University Press, 1982), pp. 39–62 (reprinted from *Social Research*, vol. 4 (1977)).

in evaluating situations from his personal point of view.[17] The social welfare function is, Harsanyi argues, the function an individual would use were he evaluating situations from a personal point of view, but from behind a veil of ignorance in which he assigned equal probability to occupying each of the positions in society with the preferences and capacities of the person in that position. In effect, we may say that, for Harsanyi, a moral principle corresponds to the principle for rational individual choice under complete ignorance of one's position among those affected by the choice. The principle, he claims, is the principle of maximizing average expected utility (where obviously interpersonal comparability of utility must be assumed), and it is determined by considering choice in complete ignorance of one's position.

Rawls does not identify the principles of justice with the principles one would use in choosing from behind a veil of ignorance. Rather, the principles of justice are the objects of such choice. Thus, for Rawls, the principles an individual would use for his most basic evaluations of social situations – the principles of justice – are not identical with the principles he would use for making individual decisions behind a veil of ignorance. They are, instead, the principles he would choose for social evaluation from behind that veil. For Harsanyi, moral principles are those that would characterize individual choice behind a veil of ignorance; for Rawls, moral principles are those that would be chosen from behind such a veil.

We should expect that the principles one would choose from behind a veil of ignorance would be related in a significant and deep way to the principles one would employ in choosing. Thus, we could recast Harsayni's argument into a Rawlsian form, and claim that, reasoning in accordance with the principle of expected utility-maximization, one would choose principles for maximizing average utility if one were choosing in ignorance of one's identity. We could also recast Rawls's argument into Harsanyian form and claim that, reasoning on a maximin principle from behind a veil of ignorance, one would evaluate social situations from the perspective of the position receiving the maximin share – thus arriving at the difference principle. The more specific features of Rawls's two principles of justice depend, as Rawls makes clear, on further limiting assumptions.

Although we can move back and forth between the two approaches exemplified by Harsanyi and Rawls, we should keep procedure separate from content, and in our present enquiry we must focus on procedure. It is, of course, not to be taken for granted that a procedural derivation of moral principles, or of principles of justice, is appropriate. But it is, I think, natural to suppose this if one begins with the idea that individuals are concerned

---

[17] Harsanyi, *Rational Behavior and Bargaining Equilibrium* . . ., p. 50.

with realizing a conception of their own, individual good – a conception that need not be a selfish one, but one that does not necessarily harmonize fully with the conceptions of others – and with the idea that society is, as in Rawls's useful phrase, a "cooperative venture for mutual advantage," where mutual advantage is to be related to the concern of each individual to realize his own good.[18] The claim is that, through social cooperation, each of us is better able to realize, or able to realize to a greater extent, a conception of his own good, than would be possible in the absence of such cooperation. However, it is clearly necessary, if there is to be social cooperation, that certain principles be accepted as determining the institutions and practices of the society within which cooperation is to be effected. Given that each individual is concerned to advance his own good, and that society is conceived as promoting mutual advancement, it is natural to suppose that the acceptability of social principles must be related to agreement among individuals. Acceptable principles are those individuals would agree to under suitably constrained circumstances.

We shall return to the implications of this reference to constraint. First, let us trace the implications of the idea that the principles should be the object of agreement. This must immediately suggest the relevance of rational bargaining. The outcome of a bargain may reflect the circumstances in which the parties find themselves, but the idea of a bargain is independent of circumstances. We suppose that the principles of justice constitute the solution to an appropriately specified bargaining problem, and so, given our acceptance of solution G', we suppose that the principles of justice may be represented as maximizing the minimum proportionate gain expected by the parties to the bargain. Principles of justice are principles for maximizing minimum proportionate gain.

If, indeed, G' is the rational solution to the bargaining problem, then an outcome-maximizing minimum proportionate gain must be rationally acceptable from the standpoint of every individual. Each person, recognizing the equal rationality of all, considers it rational to tailor his own proposal and concession so that minimum proportionate gain is realized. Thus, an agreement based on solution G' is fully impartial, not in abstracting from the interests of the individuals concerned, but in giving recognition to each of their interests in a way rationally acceptable from the standpoint of each. In bargaining, we attain impartiality among real persons by taking their distinctness seriously.

To be sure, we need not suppose that all real-life bargaining exhibits the impartiality of solution G'. For in real-life bargaining, the differential bargaining skills of the bargainers will lead to solutions that often differ

---

[18] Rawls, *A Theory of Justice*, p. 4.

markedly from G'. Furthermore, G' is impartial given the circumstances of bargaining. If you are holding a gun to my head, the agreement we may reach may be rational and impartial in relation to that initial situation, but questions about its impartiality are apt to arise. Remember that we have yet to talk about suitably constrained circumstances.

Rawls makes a fatal misstep in his argument to the principles of justice when he supposes that, persons being placed behind a veil of ignorance in order to secure an appropriate agreement, they are left with "no basis for bargaining," so that their agreement may be represented as one individual's choice. Thus, Rawls says that, "If anyone after due reflection prefers a conception of justice to another, then they all do, and a unanimous agreement can be reached."[19]

Even behind a veil of ignorance, however thick, each person must be aware that he is concerned with realizing a conception of his own good. Without this, the parties have no basis for agreement; they would have no interest in reaching agreement or in anything else. But given this, each must be concerned with reaching an agreement that maximally advances his own interests, and each must recognize the equal and parallel concern of every other person. The only way in which an individual can rationally protect his unknown conception of the good that he would advance is by bargaining to an agreement that – because it is rationally acceptable from the standpoint of every bargainer – is rationally acceptable from the standpoint of his own conception of the good, whatever it may be. (The only condition required here is that each person's conception of the good be such that it can be advanced by a cooperative venture for mutual advantage. This, it will be remembered, is given in the way our problem is posed.) In this bargaining, the distinction between persons is preserved. Thus, the procedure by which the principles of justice are determined respects, as Rawls's own procedure does not, our individuality. Rawls sacrifices the distinction between persons behind the veil of ignorance when he replaces bargaining by individual choice. Then, to protect his theory from the apparently utilitarian consequences of this sacrifice, he supposes that the choice of principles is made in accordance with what, as Harsanyi has correctly argued, is a highly irrational rule. Had Rawls carried through the idea of a bargain, he could have preserved the distinctness of persons and derived a maximin principle with solution G'.

It might be thought that there are two quite different procedures for arriving at principles of justice from behind a veil of ignorance – one, which I have developed, based on bargaining, and another, found in different versions in Rawls and Harsanyi, based on individual decision. But, in my

[19] Rawls, *A Theory of Justice*, p. 139.

view, the only possible procedure is based on bargaining. Individual choice of principles of justice behind the veil is impossible, because one would lack a sufficient basis for making such a choice – a system of aims, or a coherent set of preferences, or a conception of one's own good. One chooses rationally by maximizing utility, which is a measure of outcomes based on preference; one can then normally set about to maximize utility only if one has a known set of preferences over which one may define a utility-function. And the veil of ignorance denies one knowledge of one's preferences.

Harsanyi seeks to escape this impasse by supposing that, behind the veil, one assumes an equal chance of being each person, with that person's preferences, and then one chooses by maximizing average utility – the average level of preference-satisfaction. But the equiprobable mix of each person's set of preferences is not itself a coherent set of preferences; it does not afford a conception of any person's own good. Even if one can define a measure of outcomes, average utility, based on the equiprobable mix of each person's set of preferences, is not itself utility, and maximizing it is irrelevant to rational choice.

Were there a principle, the choice of which would maximize, not average utility, but one's expected utility, whatever one's preferences were, then even behind the veil of ignorance one would have sufficient basis for rationally choosing it. One would need to know only that one had a set of preferences, and not what those preferences were. But no principle or set of principles of justice is best from every standpoint, or best advances one's own good whatever that good might be.

Turning Rawls around, then, I claim that, behind the veil of ignorance, persons seeking social principles or principles of justice have no basis for anything but bargaining. Seemingly paradoxically (but only seemingly so), they cannot choose but they can agree. They cannot choose, because choice is rational only from a determinate standpoint, a known set of preferences, however indeterminate the prospects over which one chooses. But they can agree, because agreement is rational from every standpoint, and so from whatever standpoint each unknowingly occupies. Only the idea of agreement makes possible the unanimity required for rationally arriving at principles of justice behind a veil of ignorance.

We have identified the procedure by which principles of justice are to be selected. As the outcomes of a rational bargain, we know that they must satisfy the maximin requirements of solution G′. We must now consider the light shed on principles of justice by the rider that they be the outcome of a bargain in suitably constrained circumstances. Here, the basic point is that the circumstances must be such as to assure the *ex ante* character of the agreement. The circumstances must, then, abstract from all actual advantages enjoyed and disadvantages suffered under existing social arrangements; these are not bargaining counters appropriate to an agreement deciding on or evaluating social arrangements. Thus, the disagreement point for a bargain yielding principles of justice must be a state of nature – a condition characterized by the absence of social cooperation – and not a particular, historically given state of society.

I shall not attempt here to show that a Lockean, and not a Hobbesian, state of nature affords the appropriate disagreement point.[20] What I shall note is that the abstraction required to yield suitably constrained circumstances leads to an identification between the procedures leading to agreement and the content of the principles that are the objects of agreement. Since no basis for establishing a more determinate content is available, we can say only that the principles of justice that satisfy the requirements of solution G' must be principles that evaluate and determine social institutions and practices in terms of solution G' – in terms, that is, of the extent to which the institutions and practices assure maximin proportionate gain, taking the absence of social cooperation as the disagreement point from which gain is measured.

If we equate these principles with the idea of a social welfare function, then we may conclude that a social welfare function should not be a maximizing function. Our argument shows that it is quite mistaken to relate each person's moral choices to a function defined over a set of preferences, moral or impartial rather than personal, but satisfying the usual axioms for rational behavior under risk. Harsanyi, who has been foremost in maintaining this view, insists that morality should exhibit the same form of rationality as individual decision making.[21] But I note once more that this is to introduce maximizing requirements in the wrong place. The individual seeks to maximize his own utility – seeks to realize to the fullest possible extent a conception of his own good. Morality is not concerned with maximizing some quantity analogous to individual good; rather, morality is concerned with the way in which the benefits society makes possible are distributed among individuals each pursuing his own good. Morality relates this distribution to agreement among those individuals. And so, the rationality of moral choice is assured, not by modeling it on the rationality of individual, personal choice under risk, but rather by modeling it on the rationality of a bargain. Each should choose morally in such a way that the socially agreed upon standard of maximizing minimum proportionate gain is realized. The maximin character of solution G' carries over to determine the nature of

[20] I endeavor to show this in *Morals by Agreement*.

[21] "I propose to consider *ethics*, also, as a branch of the general theory of rational behavior, since ethical theory can be based on axioms which represent specializations of some of the axioms used in decision theory . . ." Harsanyi, "Advances in Understanding Rational Behavior", in *Essays on Ethics . . .*, p. 97.

moral choice by the individual who seeks to act in accordance with the principles of justice. This represents the application of solution G' to social practices and institutions.

Morality – or at least that part of it constituted by justice – is a matter of agreement. And, although agreement is arrived at by individual maximizers, it is not an agreement to maximize anything. Each is concerned with his share of social goods, which contributes to the realization of his own concept of the good life. There is no greater whole of which these good lives are a part. As Robert Nozick says, "There are only individual people, different individual people, with their own individual lives."[22] When these people agree, they agree on a mode of cooperation that better enables each of them to assure that his life is a good one by his own standards. The rational way to do this leaves the person who receives the least extensive share of social benefit, measured in relation to what he might have received, with the knowledge that any alternative social arrangements would have afforded someone a yet smaller share.

If my argument has been successful, I have shown how a theory of bargaining is linked to a theory of justice. In developing both, I have taken "seriously the distinction between persons."[23] Agreeing that productive concerns and individual decisions are to be linked to a conception of maximizing rationality, I have nonetheless shown that distributive concerns and moral decisions are to be linked to a conception of maximining rationality – a conception, however, that is itself linked to maximization by the argument that individually rational bargainers would reach agreement on maximizing minimum proportional gain. Thus, I have shown the congruence of three fundamental ideas: the individual, as a rational being, concerned with realizing a conception of his own good; society, as a cooperative venture that contributes to the realization of these several goods; and morality, as a set of principles agreed to by rational individuals and requiring that society contribute to individual realization in a way that maximizes the minimum proportionate gain. Such are the fruits of solution G'.

Philosophy, University of Pittsburgh

---

[22] Robert Nozick, *Anarchy, State, and Utopia* (New York: Basic Books, 1974), p. 33.
[23] Rawls, *A Theory of Justice*, p. 27.

PROSPECTS FOR THE ELIMINATION OF TASTES FROM ECONOMICS AND ETHICS

ALEXANDER ROSENBERG

De gustibus non est disputandum. This maxim reflects a fundamental problem both for the study of markets and for the concern with morals. The problem is the intractability of tastes coupled with their indispensability for both positive and normative economics. Tastes are indispensable in positive microeconomic theory because, under the label 'preferences,' they, together with expectations, determine choice and behavior. Tastes are equally indispensable to welfare economics' conception of morally permissible arrangements, because these arrangements must reflect compromises between competing and conflicting preferences.

But tastes are intractable in ways well-known to economists. When described in terms of utilities, they are neither intrapersonally comparable in respect of cardinality nor interpersonally comparable ordinally. They are close-knit and interdependent. Nor is there in economics or elsewhere anything remotely like a theory of how tastes are determined, and more important, how they differ between agents and how they change over time. Neoclassical microeconomic theory circumvents these problems by treating tastes as "exogenous." They are determined by noneconomic forces and are "given" for the purposes of explaining and predicting behavior. They are subject only to ordinal intrapersonal comparisons – and they sometimes are treated as mere notational variants on actual choice-behavior, systematized in the theory of revealed preference. Their structure, and changes in it, are never the effects of changes in prices and quantities of commodities available. Tastes are, rather, among the noneconomic causes of price and quantity produced. This is in many ways a reasonable approach to take towards preferences, for there are good grounds to suppose that tastes and preferences are formed by noneconomic forces. On the other hand, this approach seriously compromises the explanatory and predictive power of economic theory, as we shall see.

For welfare economics, the consequences of the intractability of tastes seem at first blush more serious and certainly more obvious. The limitations on normative conclusions about welfare that are enshrined in the criterion of Pareto-optimality testify to the effects of enforced agnosticism about tastes. Because tastes are exogenous there is no scope within welfare economics for even so elementary a distinction as that between wants and needs (beyond an altogether inadequate account in terms of differences in elasticity). Moreover, considerations of Pareto-optimality cannot distinguish between societies characterized by widespread slavery or starvation and affluent, democratic ones, just so long as, in each case, no one can be advantaged without disadvantaging someone else. The reason is, of course, that within these societies one agent's preferences cannot be compared, weighed, adjudicated, or traded-off against another's. For tastes are incomparable. There is no disputing them. More generally, if the socially-preferred alternative is not to be entirely independent of individual preferences, its selection will be no more determinate than that of the individual preferences it reflects.

In this paper I want to discuss an alternative, a "new theory of consumer behavior" outlined by Gary Becker,[1] which aims at solutions to these two problems – the exogeneity of tastes and the weakness of welfare conclusions that follow from the intractability of tastes. I shall then provide a stronger interpretation of this theory than Becker explicity endorses, justify it, and examine its ramifications for these two problems. I do so not just because Becker's theory aims to solve the first problem and seems easily adapted to solving the second, but because it is the most important, influential, and empirically powerful reformulation of the theory of economic behavior offered since ordinal utility replaced marginalism.

Becker's work[2] has spawned a movement called "Human Capital Theory" which comes close to being a revolution in economics. It has greatly influenced the economic treatment of public policy. In addition, it has vastly broadened the applicability of economic theory to a large number of apparently noneconomic choices. Among those areas to which the new theory has been applied with impressive empirical support are marriage, family size, divorce, travel, education, migration, health, and "cross sectional and life-style patterns of consumption expenditure and time allocation." Indeed, Becker holds that his "approach provides a valuable unified framework for understanding *all* human behavior."[3] I think this claim is correct. The theory has far greater explanatory power than traditional microeconomics. But in this paper I shall ignore its powers of deductive systematization of independently generated data and focus on the theory's foundations.

---

[1] Gary Becker, *The Economic Approach to Human Behavior* (Chicago: University of Chicago Press, 1976). All page references to Becker in the text are to this work.
[2] Together with that of K. J. Lancaster, "A New Approach to Consumer Theory," *Journal of Political Economy*, vol. 72 (1966), pp. 132–157.
[3] *ibid.*, p. 14. For many of these applications, see Becker, *Human Behavior*, and his more recent *Treatise on the Family* (Cambridge, MA: Harvard University Press, 1981).

In brief, Becker's theory solves the problem of tastes by attributing to all economic agents exactly the same set of "stable preferences." Accordingly, these preferences can be ignored in the explanation of differences in choice, since they never change and therefore don't produce other changes. I shall argue that these "stable preferences" need to be interpreted as human needs, if they are to do the work Becker wants them to do. So interpreted, "stable preferences" really do solve the problems generated by the exogeneity of tastes for positive theory, and they do so in a way that unshackles welfare economics from the restrictions of Pareto-optimality. But as a theory about the needs of human agents and how they respond to them, Becker's claims may help sanction normative conclusions that conflict with well-entrenched convictions about permissible state intervention in individuals' choices. The only way I can see of avoiding this problem is to tie Becker's theory to a doctrine of natural rights, a doctrine with which the neoclassical tradition in welfare economics has not been comfortable.

Economic Theory and the Problem of Tastes

Economics is an intentional science. It holds that economic behavior is determined by tastes and beliefs, that is, by the desire to maximize preferences, subject to the constraint of expectations about available alternatives. Differences between the choices made by individual agents who face the same alternatives are due either to differences in preferences, to differences in expectations, or to both. Similarly, changes in the choices of an individual agent over time are due to changes in one or both of these causal determinants of his behavior.

The trouble is that there are no resources within economics for separating the influence of these two components on changes and differences in actual choices. (Hereafter I will speak of differences, meaning thereby both *intra*personal changes in preferences and *inter*personal differences in them.) Yet such separation is required to preserve microeconomic theory against the joint charges of triviality or falsity. Actual economic agents often enough seem to violate the principles of rational choice, for example, by making purchases at different times that violate the weak axiom of revealed preference. Does this show that the theory is false? No. One apparently reasonable thing to say when an economic agent's behavior appears to be irrational because it violates the preference-ranking previously assigned to him is that his tastes have changed. But if tastes are exogenous and nonfungible, there is no prospect of an economic – or indeed any other systematical – account of such changes, and so there is no prospect of assessing this strategy for explaining away apparent irrationality. The price of theory-preservation here seems to be triviality.

Becker expresses this problem in the following terms:

For economists to rest a large part of their theory of choice on differences in tastes is disturbing since they admittedly have no useful theory of the formation of tastes, nor can they rely on a well-developed theory of tastes from any other social science, since none exists. . . . The weakness in the received theory of choice, then, is the extent to which it relies on differences in tastes to "explain" behavior when it can neither explain how tastes are formed nor predict their effects. (p. 133)

This problem runs very deep in economic theory. Most of the interesting theorems of microeconomics involve holding preferences or expectations or both constant, while varying prices and/or income. Expectations are held constant by the assumption of perfect information. When this assumption is relaxed, expectations turn out to be a function of the agent's tastes and probability assignments. Preferences are held constant by assuming that the individual remains on the same indifference curve, or in the same family of them.

As Becker notes, there is at present no theory elsewhere in social or behavioral science that treats tastes as endogenous, to which the economist can help himself, or which can at least comfort him with the assurance that an account of changes in taste is at least theoretically available. Economists may, however, respond to a charge like Becker's with the claim that such a theory is in principle possible. Meanwhile, the economist can certainly appeal to tastes as a legitimate explanatory variable in his theory. Solving some problems about human behavior need not require solving all problems, especially when these other problems are the business of psychologists and not economists. The trouble with this line is that psychology seems incapable in principle of providing a theory of tastes that does not already presuppose the sort of economic rationality which economists need a theory of tastes to defend.

Much recent work in the philosophy of psychology suggests that beliefs and desires cannot be separated. This thesis, often called "the holism of the mental," asserts that the identity of a preference, or a belief, is a function of the other beliefs and desires the agent has. (It is ironical that the impetus for this thesis is to be found in the same work of Frank Ramsey's[4] to which so much of the economic theory of choice under uncertainty is beholden.) If beliefs and desires are so tightly connected, then we can never hope to distinguish tastes from expectations in such a way as to legitimate a separate appeal to them to explain away apparently actual choices that falsify the theory of consumer behavior.

[4] Frank Ramsey, *Foundations of Mathematics* (London: Routledge and Kegan Paul, 1931), Chapter 3, "Truth and Probability."

We may illustrate the problem that holism creates for economic theory by considering the well-known Slutsky equation, which expresses the separate effects of a change in prices and income on the expenditure of a consumer. For example, a sharp price-drop in one commodity can affect the consumer in two ways: he can now buy more of the cheaper good, and he need spend less to purchase the same amount of it. Indeed, he may find himself so much better off by the price-drop that he can afford to buy a different good he preferred all along, but could not afford. If this good substitutes for the cheaper good, the consumer may buy less of a good whose price has fallen, instead of more. Which of these outcomes will be the case is systematized in the Slutsky equation:

$$\frac{\delta q_i}{\delta p_i} = \left(\frac{\delta q_i}{\delta p_i}\right)_{\text{utility}\,=\,\text{constant}} - q_i \left(\frac{\delta q_i}{\delta y}\right)_{\text{price}\,=\,\text{constant}}$$

The first term describes the rate of change in consumption of commodity, i, q_i for a change in its price, p_i. The equation attributes this effect to two causes. The first is described in the equation's second term as the substitution effect, the rate of change in consumption for a change in price, *holding utility levels, i.e., tastes, constant.* The second is the so-called income effect described in the third term, which reflects how the change in *i*'s price affects the agent's income, y, and through it his consumption of good *i*. If the second term exceeds the third, the consumer buys more of *i* as the price drops; if the third term is larger than the second, he buys less.

But, how are we to assure that the utility level is being held constant through such price changes? This appears to be a question for the psychometrics of taste and preference. The only way the psychologist can measure preferences is by assuming that his subject is rational in assessing the costs and payoffs of varying alternatives presented to him. In other words, the psychologist must adopt the assumption of utility maximization from the economist. In fact, he may be faced with experimental data that can themselves only be explained by the Slutsky equation, thus bringing the inquiry back to where it started.

Thus, suppose the psychologist varies prices and his subject's income in order to see whether choices vary systematically in a way that reflects constancy of preference. If some of the goods whose prices are varied are inferior, then preferences will *appear* to be nonasymmetrical as prices change, and the agent's choices will sometimes seem irrational: he will prefer good *i* to *j*, and *j* to *i*. Either that, or his tastes really have changed. Of course, the Slutsky equation can be invoked in these cases to explain away the apparent irrationality, as due to the income effect of an inferior good, without appeal to exogenous changes in taste. But this equation is the very one we are attempting to assess while holding utilities constant. If the philosophical analysis of the identification of psychological states is right, there is no alternative to this sort of circularity.

Any actual choice can be accommodated to the conventional theory of comsumer behavior because of the indeterminacy of the preferences that give rise to it. Even holding expectations constant through the assumption of perfect information will not take up enough slack, for there is no way to pin down tastes within the theory. Moreover, there seems to be no other theory in which economically exogenous tastes are endogenous. There is no prospect of a psychological theory of preferences that will enable us to identify changes in them independently of the identification of beliefs, either. This is the source of the apparent empirical emptiness of the conventional theory of consumer behavior. Therefore, matters are worse than Becker supposes. It is not just that there is no psychological theory of tastes independent of the assumptions of economic theory: there cannot be one.[5]

One traditional reaction to these problems about the theory of individual economic behavior is to deny that economics really has anything to say about it. Claims about individual agents are treated merely as convenient fictions helpful in systematizing the real subjects of economic concern – markets, industries, and whole economies. Some economists have followed Sir John Hicks's strategy for dealing with the Scylla and Charybdis of falsity or tautology that seems to face the theory. As Hicks wrote, "if our study of the individual consumer is only a step towards the study of a group of consumers, these falsifications can be trusted to disappear when the individual demands are aggregated."[6] Becker has adopted a similar view himself:

Although economists have typically been interested in the reactions of large markets to changes in different variables, economic theory has been developed for the individual firm and household with market responses obtained simply by blowing up, so to speak, the response of a typical unit. Confusion results because comment and analysis were directed away from the market and toward the individual, or *away from the economist's main interest.* (p. 154, emphasis added)

---

[5] The bearing of "holism" about the mental on these issues is spelled out in Donald Davidson, "Philosophy as Psychology," in *Essays on Actions and Events* (Oxford: Oxford University Press, 1981), pp. 229–238. To see the role which such assumptions have come explicity to have in experimental psychology, see Howard Rachlin, "Maximization Theory in Behavioral Psychology," *Behavioral and Brain Sciences*, vol. 4 (1981), pp. 371–418.

[6] Sir John Hicks, *Value and Capital* (Oxford: Oxford University Press, 1939), p. 11.

This attitude towards the conventional theory of consumer behavior is a coherent one. But it incurs considerable costs, costs so great that few economists are willing to pay them, including those like Becker who seem to endorse this strategy.

One cost is that the theory of consumer behavior, treated now as a *facon de parler* for downward sloping demand curves but without any real significance for actual individual behavior, loses its considerable powers to systematize that behavior. Thus, for example, despite its problems, the Slutsky equation really does seem to be an important part of the correct explanation of why the consumption of bread declines when its relative price falls greatly, and why this phenomenon is not incompatible with the more frequently observed phenomenon of increased consumption in the wake of a price decline.

A more serious loss is that this interpretation of microeconomic theory deprives it of any relevance to the whole domain of welfare economics. For in this domain, the chief questions concern the effects of social policies on the utilities of actual individuals, rather than abstractions convenient for the economical expression of regularities about markets and industries. There would be no point to various compensation criteria for changing distributions of commodities, nor any sense in debates about the losses or gains involved in the existence and distribution of a consumer's surplus, unless there were real agents to be advantaged or disadvantaged by these distributions. The very possibility of normative applications of microeconomic theory turns on its actual applicability to real economic agents. And this application is seriously compromised by the lack of a theory of tastes.

Becker's Theory of Identical, Stable Preferences

Becker's new theory circumvents this problem of tastes entirely, by the simple expedient of assuming that every agent has exactly the same set of lifelong tastes for the same set of quite specific goods as every other agent.

Becker's theory involves an imaginative rearrangement[7] of concepts familiar from conventional microeconomics. In particular, it involves adapting the theory of production (where questions of taste do not arise) to the choices of individual agents. Instead of assuming that the agent's utility is directly derived from the consumption of market goods, Becker asumes that it is only indirectly dependent on them. Utility is derived directly from commodities the agent produces for his own consumption by combining market goods together with his own time, in accordance with the techniques of production available to him. The consumer's demand for market goods is identical to that of a firm's demand for inputs or factors of production.

---

[7] I describe it as a rearrangement because, as Becker admits, the conventional exposition of the theory of consumer behavior is derivable from his, although it will contain items in the utility function quite foreign to the conventional theory. See *Human Behavior*, p. 146.

Relatively simple mathematics illustrates these relations. Utility is a function of household commodities only:

$$U = u(Z_1, Z_2, \ldots, Z_n) \tag{1}$$

where U is utility, and Z_i is the quantity of household commodity Z_i. This commodity is produced for direct consumption from goods bought on the market combined with quantities of the agent's time. The amount of Z_i produced is a function of the market goods purchased, the time available, and the technique of production:

$$Z_i = z_i (x_i, t_i, E) \tag{2}$$

Becker calls E the "environmental variable." It describes the productive process or technology which the agent employs to produce Z_i from x_i and t_i. As in the conventional theory, the utility function (1) is maximized subject to the constraint of (2), plus a constraint on income, and a constraint on the household's available time. Total income, I, is all spent on market goods without any savings. It is the sum of the amounts of market goods purchased times their prices:

$$I = \sum_{i=1}^{n} p_i x_i \tag{3}$$

where p_i and x_i are the prices and quantities purchased of market good i. The total time, T, an agent disposes is the sum of the time he spends in the labor market to earn income, t_w, and t_i, the time he devotes to household production of Z_i:

$$T = t_w + \sum_{i=1}^{n} t_i \tag{4}$$

Maximizing the utility function, (1), subject to the constraints of (2), (3), and (4) enables us to derive conditions on optimization of consumer choice familiar from the theory of the firm. Thus, when utility is maximized, the ratio of the marginal products of any two factors of production, i.e., market goods, must be equal to the ratio of their market prices. Similarly, the ratio of the marginal utilities of two household commodities must be equal to the ratio of their marginal costs – their shadow prices for the consumer, determined by the cost of the market goods, the time required to produce them and the respective techniques of production.

Little has been said about E, the "environmental variable" of equation (2). The techniques of production it reflects will be crucial to the shadow prices of household goods (and the productivity of market goods and time in producing them). An inefficient method of production will prevent the highest attainable level of utility – for a given set of market goods and a given amount of available time – from being reached. In fact, E will have to take up the work which tastes are no longer able to do in this theory. Interpersonal and intrapersonal differences in the consumption of market goods will have to be accounted for by differences and changes in E.

Now, the chief virtue that Becker claims for this reformulation of consumer behavior theory is "its reduced emphasis on the role of 'tastes' in interpreting behavior." He recognizes that "this shift in emphasis towards changes in prices and income and away from changes in taste may appear to be simply one of semantics – of hiding an inability to explain tastes behind the camouflage of a production function." (p. 144) Becker's explicit response to this charge – that our knowledge of the quantifiable properties of production functions employed by agents can help us reduce the need for appeals to changes in taste – is inadequate.

First, the problem is not that the old theory's scope for changes in exogenous tastes is too large; it is that we can never tell how large or small it is. We still cannot tell how large it is, even on Becker's new theory. Second, substituting household commodities for market goods in the utility function by itself does nothing to reduce the scope of tastes at all. In principle, consumers' tastes for household commodities can change as easily as their tastes for market goods. Third, defenders of the conventional theory can reduce the role of tastes as effectively as Becker can, simply by weakening the assumption of perfect information and raising the costs of acquiring information. Indeed, various formulations of the conventional theory have done this very thing. This tactic, of course, does not increase the empirical content of the theory, because there is no available measure of an agent's information or how he exploits it, for the same reason that tastes are intractable.

If the new theory is to have a real methodological advantage over the old theory, it cannot be this one. Rather, Becker is committed to a thesis that he seems only to entertain and not explicitly to endorse:

> Consider a logical extension of the view that behavioral differences previously attributed to differences in taste are in fact due to differences in productive efficiency. One might argue that indeed all households have precisely the *same* utility function and that all observed behavioral differences result from differences in relative prices and access to real resources. In the standard theory all consumers behave similarly in the sense that they all maximize the same thing – utility or satisfaction. It is only a further extension then to argue that they all derive that utility from the same "basic pleasures" or preference function, and differ only in their ability to produce these "pleasures." From this point of view, the Latin expression *de gustibus*

non est disputandum suggests not so much that it is impossible to resolve
disputes arising from differences in tastes but rather that in fact no
such disputes arise. (p. 145)

Although Becker does not want to endorse this thesis fully, it seems
evident that he is committed to it, and thereby committed to further
conclusions about the structure of the preference function expressed in
equation (1). Without it, there is no real solution to the problem of tastes for
microeconomic theory. For we can no more easily separate intrapersonal and
interpersonal differences in E, the means of production an agent chooses
to employ, from such changes and differences in the set of household
commodities he chooses to produce. Indeed, without this strong assumption
of identity of utility functions, Becker's formalization is even more prey than
the conventional theory to the exogenous taste problem. To the degree an
agent chooses productive techniques, his choice will be determined by his
tastes for these techniques as well as his factual beliefs about them. Unless
all tastes are the same, so that they cancel out in an explanation of why
different productive techniques are exploited, we have simply increased the
problem of tastes by employing Becker's theory, not decreased it.

Tastes or Needs?

Indeed, Becker requires more than merely a "logical extension" of the
view that *some* behavioral differences attributed to taste differences are really
due to differences in productive technique. It is a difference in kind from the
old theory that he requires. To say that everyone always has the same utility
function is to say that each agent's utility will be maximized by the same
bundle of a limited number of variegated and fungible but independent commodities (given the same income, time, and production-function constraints,
of course). Nothing less than such a utility function will do the job that the
old theory fails to do. But, I shall argue, such a utility function will be a
schedule of needs, not preferences.

To see that the number of household products must be fairly large and
measurable, imagine that there is only one household commodity, say good
health (both physical and psychological), that all agents produce in order to
maximize their utility. It is worth noting that Plato might well be said to have
held this view. The trouble with this supposition is that a given amount of
the commodity in question supervenes on many different combinations of
market goods. It can be produced by many alternative techniques about
which relatively little is known, and each of which is difficult to measure.
Therefore, it bears all the problems of incomparability and nonfungibility
that utility does. A single, global, directly consumed household good that in

effect does nothing but intervene between utility and market goods will be no improvement on the old theory, especially when the "productive techniques" for generating this good from market commodities are so "subjective." To say that smokers and nonsmokers have exactly the same tastes, and maximize utility by maximizing their health, involves either treating health as a mere notational variant on utility, or it raises questions about the efficiency of productive techniques as unanswerable as are questions about the comparisons of utilities.

Suppose we increase the number of basic commodities to three, as Hobbes seems to have advocated. We suppose that utility is maximized by producing as much "safety," "gain," and "reputation" as possible.[8] Here again we have commodities which are scarcely easier to measure than utility. But waive this problem. If there are trade-offs between these or any other household commodities that keep the agent at the same level of utility, the indeterminacy we had hoped to escape reappears. In such a case, inter-personal and intrapersonal differences in the production of household commodities may appear and may be optimal for their respective agents. But distinguishing such cases from irrational choices, or choices dictated by different techniques of production, is the problem of exogenous tastes all over again. We cannot tell whether an agent is indifferent between two different combinations of household commodities attainable by him or whether his tastes for these commodities have changed. If household commodities are subject to trade-offs, then we have merely complicated the methodological problem of tastes, not simplified it.

To implement the new theory beyond the limits of the conventional one, we shall have to identify a fairly large, variegated, but manageable number of universally desired household commodities. Their amounts must be measurable and independent of one another in their effects on utility. Their productive techniques must also be discoverable, as well as quantitatively comparable for efficiency. What are the prospects for discovering such commodities? The first thing to notice is the similarity of household commodities that meet these conditions with what we may independently identify as basic human needs. If we can parlay this similarity into something approaching an identity, then one of the most well-known objections to the economists' view of human behavior will have been circumvented. Micro-economic theory resolutely refuses to distinguish between mere wants or desires, and needs. It does so, of course, because of the incomparability of tastes – of wants and needs. If some or all household commodities are those which meet human needs, then economic theory can take needs seriously, with potentially great advantage for welfare economics.

---

[8] Thomas Hobbes, *Leviathan*, chapter 13.

Why describe the demand for household commodities as needs? First, because it is obvious that individuals have a variety of different needs, that these needs cannot be traded-off, and that in many cases we know, at least in principle, how and in what units to measure them. We know also that few market goods are directly needed in their original state and that most are purchased in order to be combined with others to meet needs – such as nutrition, warmth, shelter, amusement, and psychological well-being. Market goods are combined in a variety of different ways – by different techniques of production – in order to meet these needs.

Another reason for substituting needs for Becker's uniform preferences is that this assumption makes the most sense of the obvious fact that, although each person has different tastes, he explains and justifies his tastes by showing how they fulfill his needs, given constraints. Tastes turn out to be beliefs about how to meet needs. For example, the cultural anthropologist interpreting the desires and values of an alien culture will attempt to show how its values – so different from our own – emerge from that culture's attempts to meet needs common to all cultures. In the past, anthropologists often accounted for these differences by citing fallacious beliefs held by natives, e.g., showing how inefficient their techniques of production were for meeting their needs. Nowadays, anthropologists steer clear of such ethno-centrism. Instead, they attempt to show how ecologically adaptive native productive techniques are, and how they often meet needs the agents themselves do not even recognize – optimizing family size, for example.

Finally, if we do not treat the utility function as one reflecting needs, the advantage of Becker's new theory is again jeopardized. The begin with, if we interpret household commodities in a literal sense, according to which a household commodity is what each family cooks for dinner, chooses for its evening's entertainment, chooses for its mode of bathing, etc., the assumption of uniform and unchanging preferences is simply false. We shall then have to have recourse to all those dodges which the old theory needs to render its unrealistic claims consistent with the facts. If we treat the household commodities as merely fulfilling preferences, interpreted now as psychological wants, we are no more able to identify the common household preference function shared by all individuals than the old theory is able to independently identify the idiosyncratic preference functions of individual agents. This will admittedly be less of a problem for Becker's theory. By assuming that all individuals have the same preference function all the time, the new theory will never need to specify these preferences independently, since they never enter into an explanation of behavioral differences or changes. But this, in effect, simply shifts the entire problem of preferences onto psychology, where it is no more tractable then when it seemed to be part of economics. The shift Becker proposes would not be "simply one of semantics," but it would be one of merely divisional redistricting or gerrymandering in the behavioral sciences. It would not solve a problem so much as ship it to another department.

The treatment of preferences as needs is not the course Becker himself adopts, but it is one his new theory encourages. We already know a fair amount about the common and permanent needs of economic agents. They are specified in the life sciences' findings about minimal levels of sustenance, limits on life sustaining climate and weather, and the other variables on which *Homo sapiens*' persistence and evolutionary fitness depends. We know a great deal about these factors, and we can expect to come to know much more about them. Needs so understood are as tractable as any variable of natural science, and they really do bid fair to solve the problem of tastes. Or rather to dissolve it.

This biological treatment of preferences is one Becker certainly considers. In a long footnote to the claim that there can be no disputes about tastes (previously quoted), he writes:

> To venture one further step, if genetical natural selection and rational behavior reinforce each other in producing speedier and more efficient responses to changes in the environment, perhaps the common preference function has evolved over time by natural selection and rational choice as that preference function best adopted [sic] to human society. That is, in the short run the preference function is fixed and households attempt to maximize the objective function subject to their resource and technology constraints. But in the very long run, perhaps those preferences survive which are most suited to satisfaction given broad technological constraints on human society (e.g., physical size, mental ability, et. cetera). (p. 145)

Becker's claim is not that choices are genetically determined, but that preferences are. Since preferences are not sufficient for choices, there is no tincture of "biological determinism" in this "speculation."

Presumably, a full specification of the biological needs that the individual *Homo sapiens* is functionally organized to meet will explain all or most of his behavior, including his deliberate choices. At present no such list is available, and even when it becomes available it probably will not divide up human behavior into parts that conform neatly to the economist's object of inquiry. Even holding productive techniques constant, it will leave some intra- and interpersonal differences in behavior unexplained. These facts limit the degree to which we can expect improvements in the systematic power of a theory like Becker's, even as more is learned about human needs and how they are fulfilled. In effect, the error term in any specification of shared preferences is not likely to be eliminated, and some rational choices must remain unaccountable. Nevertheless, what the study of human needs can provide should certainly improve the schematic theory Becker offers us. Thus, Becker's theory solves, or rather dissolves, the problem of tastes. It does so by holding them constant, so that they drop out as variables we need to cite in order to explain intra- and interpersonal differences. But holding them constant will only solve the problem if they turn out to be needs and not mere wants.

Implications of Becker's Theory for Welfare Economics

When we turn to welfare economics, the treatment of Becker's stable preferences as needs seems to have even greater advantages, ones that are not reduced or qualified by our temporary ignorance about all the needs an individual has. Or so it seems. For Becker, the application of the new theory to welfare economics is obvious:

> If observed differences in behavior are assumed to result from differences in tastes, and if the satisfaction of each person's tastes is used as a guide to normative statements, then differences in behavior cannot be judged normatively. If, however, the observed behavior is assumed to result from different efficiencies with the same set of tastes, these can be judged by the level of full real income which they produce, i.e., by their level of productivity. For example, if education is said to alter tastes, one cannot speak of the effects of education on the level of utility: what is preferable to the college graduate may not be so to the grade school dropout and the two cannot, even in principle, reach agreement on which set of tastes is "better." But these judgments can be made if education affects the efficiencies of household production functions. Whatever yields greater commodity output is preferable and can be considered as such by both parties. (pp. 145–46)

Of course, this conclusion will not follow unless the strong claims about the identity of preference functions, and the characteristics of their components, are right. Otherwise, there is still scope for exogenous differences to intrude and make the interpersonal comparison indeterminate. Moreover, the effect of education on productive efficiencies must be completely separate from its effect on preferences. Indeed, on Becker's theory, it can have no effect on preferences at all – still another reason to call them basic needs.

In effect, Becker's theory offers us a way of deciding between Bentham's claim that push-penny is as good as poetry and Mill's reply that it is better to be Socrates dissatisfied than a pig satisfied. Bentham is wrong unless the marginal productivity with respect to household goods of push-penny equals that of poetry, and this question is, for Becker, one of fact. Similarly, the marginal productivity of Socratic dissatisfaction must be greater than that of porcine satisfaction for Mill to be vindicated. These points are not intended as ridicule, but rather to show how completely the new theory converts questions of taste into questions of productive efficiency. That these questions seem beyond our technical means to answer does not detract from the fact that, in contrast to questions about taste, they are at least in principle susceptible to answers.

We may thus circumvent one of the most serious theoretical obstacles economics erects against the formulation of a social welfare function. The proof that such a function exists – which ranks the society's alternatives as a function of individual preferences – is one of the chief ornaments of contemporary welfare economics. Arrow's proof that no such function exists, which is compatible with five reasonable assumptions, is both a theoretical *tour de force* and a further spur to those for whom Pareto-optimality is not enough. This class will include most moral philosophers, which partly explains the attraction of nonutilitarian ethical theories based on rights instead of preferences. But if the ultimate determinants of individual choices are needs, if needs are the same between persons, and if levels of satisfaction of needs are cardinally comparable between individuals, then at least one necessary condition of Arrow's impossibility proof is circumvented. For this proof constrains social choices to those that do not presuppose interpersonal comparisons, let alone cardinally measurable differences.

Arrow's impossibility proof hinges on the ethical conviction that individual preferences should determine social choices.[9] They do so, presumably, because preferences are determined by individual needs, and each individual is the best judge of his own needs. Otherwise, why erect individual preferences as the linchpin of a morally permissible social choice function? The Becker theory enables us to honor this ethical conviction about the importance of preferences while enabling us to compare preferences in respect to the needs they answer. Accordingly, a social choice function need not treat them as exogenous in the way required for Arrow's impossibility proof to go through.

The new theory also has implications for the problem of setting the level of supply for a public good. One potential theoretical solution to the problem of market failure in the supply of a public good is to leave its determination to a central planner. He would receive signals about individual preferences and set the level of production and distribution on the basis of these signals. This solution is vitiated by the possibility of strategic preference signals, i.e., false

---

[9] This is an ethical prescription which, as Samuelson puts it, "stems from the individualist philosophy of modern Western Civilization, . . . that individual preferences are to count." Paul A. Samuelson, *Foundations of Economic Analysis* (Cambridge, MA: Harvard University Press, 1947), p. 223.

statements by individuals about their real preferences calculated to enable them to free-ride in the provision and consumption of the public good. But where the planner can consult a theory of the identical needs of each individual, needs that determine his preferences, he may be able to set an optimal level of supply for a public good without appeal to signals about preferences.

There are, of course, more practical implications of the new theory for questions of equity and distribution. The theory permits, in principle, inter-personal comparisons between the levels at which individual needs are satisfied. Since the household commodities, like nutrition, shelter, warmth, amusement, etc., that individuals produce are independent of one another in their effects on the utility function, egalitarianism about welfare will lead us to equalize the level of attainment of each of these needs at a minimum survival level before permitting further distributions. This is something the old theory, with its refusal to differentiate between needs and wants, cannot do. Even where it incompletely specifies the preference function, the new theory will have some bearing on social welfare, just because each of the household commodities it does specify will by itself be relevant to the individual preference functions and, therefore, to the social welfare function too. Thus, with respect to some household commodities like nutrition, we can transcend the limits of Pareto-optimality because we can make specific interpersonal comparisons of the attainment of biologically specified needs, instead of psychologically indeterminate satisfactions. Other goals and ends of individuals we may wish to leave unadjudicated beyond the requirement that satisfying them pass the Pareto test. The reason is that we know as yet too little about the common utility function and the efficiency of alternative means of producing the household commodities that satisfy it.

However, power is dangerous, even explanatory power. The combination of the new theory of consumer behavior with a moral commitment to meet-ing minimal needs or attaining maximal satisfaction is likely to transform utilitarian prescriptions into a very strong paternalism. The old theory provided the utilitarian with immunity against paternalism just because of its explanatory weakness. The old theory limits the implementation of a principle of maximizing satisfactions to distributions that are Pareto-optimal. The new theory allows this same moral principle far greater scope – too much scope, it may seem.

Suppose we are given a market of commodities in which all differences in behavior among economic agents are due exclusively to differences in technologies of production, and these technologies of production determine schedules of the purchase of market goods. Then, to the extent the efficiencies of these techniques are a matter of definite knowledge, we shall have to say that some agents make mistakes in their market purchases. And we shall have to trace these mistakes to false beliefs (implicit or explicit) about the best technology for producing household goods, given the prices and availability of market goods and time. There will be a definite fact about the matter in such cases. Thus, whereas the traditional theory has scope for differences in behavior that do not reflect irrationality or ignorance, Becker's theory does not: beyond differences in biology, it countenances the possibility only of ignorance or irrationality.

But ignorance and irrationality are widely viewed as intolerable, especially when they are harmful to the agent who is ignorant or irrational or both. To the extent an egalitarian principle of distribution demands equal shares of the market commodities that enable an agent to meet his needs for household commodities, it must also underwrite the provision of technical information about productive techniques for meeting those needs. Anyone who refuses to implement them is *a fortiori* irrational. Properly filled out by an identification of household commodities and technologies of production for them, the new theory is nothing less than a recipe for making people as well-off as possible. Given a set of prices for market commodities and labor, there is only one bundle of household commodities that maximizes utility for all healthy, normal agents, and that bundle is determinable without appeal to the subjective tastes or fallacious beliefs of the individual economic agents.

But this is just the theory that a moral paternalist needs. Hitherto restrained by skepticism about what is best for each individual, he can now argue that distribution of market goods, and production in accordance with the most efficient technologies, is clearly optimal for each individual and should be enforced. The false beliefs and "false desires" of agents should be ignored and overridden in favor of welfare presciptions that hinge on the theory, just as the false beliefs and unhealthy desires of the ill should be overriden by the prescriptions of the physician. This is a paternalism, well beyond the enforcement of mandatory motorcycle helmets, to which many, including Becker, will be opposed.

Becker is not any sort of paternalist, nor does paternalism follow from his theory alone. Moreover, he can reject the paternalist's exploitation of his theory on the ground that, short of a full version of the new theory with all the parameters and variables specified, its implementation may do more harm than good. It might enforce the wrong production techniques, allocate the wrong proportion of household commodities, or perhaps even specify the wrong household commodities altogether. But this is not an adequate response to the claim that Becker's theory would turn a utilitarian commitment to maximizing individual preferences into a prescription for paternalism broader than anything we might care to accept.

What is more, fully filled out, this new theory not only provides grist for a paternalism foreign to most people's moral sense, but transforms it into a foundation for central planning utterly distasteful to market advocates like Becker himself. Consider: on the neoclassical theory, the prices of market commodities, wage rates, and the rate of interest are all a function of the aggregation of individual preferences. The justification of the competitive market is that it decentralizes decisions with optimal efficiency by tying prices and output to demand, to preference. Suppose that we can establish the preferences for some or all household commodities by appeal to exogenous factors derived from other sciences dealing with human needs, and suppose further that we can establish the most efficient productive techniques through technical inquiries of equally noneconomic sorts. Then, given information about the available factors of production and techniques of production for market goods, we can establish centrally both shadow prices for household commodities and money prices for market goods without a market mechanism. And we can be sure that this plan will optimize individual welfare – or at least those components of it about which we have reliable knowledge – entirely independently of the mechanisms of a free market. The result would be "production for need," in the Marxist slogan, "instead of for profit."

This conclusion is ironical, for Gary Becker is one of Milton Friedman's most prominent and influential students. Moreover, the new theory is a self-conscious attempt to strengthen the empirical content and systematic power of the neoclassical theory that Friedman and other economists appeal to in arguments for the market approach to social welfare.

The conclusion is more than ironical, however, for it highlights one of the strengths of the traditional theory which Becker's aims to supplant. It is a feature of the old theory which makes a virtue out of what is often seen to be its vice for questions of human welfare. The limitation of neoclassical welfare economics to criteria no stronger than Pareto's is an obstacle to our ability to distinguish slave societies from free ones. But it is also an obstacle to our abilities to legislate morality and to enforce tastes from which many or some will dissent. Toleration as a moral virtue rests in part on skepticism about the possibility of knowing what is in the interests of others. Deprived of the grounds for this skepticism, toleration can be made to look like complicity in evil. A passage from Herbert Marcuse nicely illustrates the moral dangers of moral certainty: "When tolerance mainly serves the protection and preservation of a repressive society, when it serves to neutralize opposition and to render men immune from other *and better* forms of life, then tolerance has been perverted."[10] Moral philosophers and others are well aware of the inimical effects of certainty about what people really

---

[10] "Repressive Tolerance," in R. P.Wolff, B. Moore, H. Marcuse, *Tolerance* (Boston: Beacon Press, 1965), p. 111, emphasis added.

want or need.[11] Through what special faculty of knowledge did Marcuse come to identify a "better form of life?" The problems of metaethics are imposing testimony to the poor prospects of moral knowledge. And toleration is the moral to draw from these prospects. But the new theory of consumer behavior is easily assimilable to a view which fosters intolerance of what its subjects would wrongly describe as differences in subjective preferences, about which they mistakenly believe there is no rational dispute. Taking the new theory seriously as an account of how needs drive choices, requires us to identify some choices as objectively wrong and, therefore, to be tolerated only at a cost borne by the mistaken chooser and perhaps others. To the extent that this conclusion is repugnant to our moral vision of individual agents as autonomous, in at least most of their choices, the strong empirical confirmation of the new theory would be a source of real discomfort.

Needs or Rights?

One approach to human welfare to which neoclassical theorists have been opposed is that based on the ascription of rights. Bentham, the father of welfare economics, is famous for having said that rights are "nonsense on stilts."[12] It is another irony, then, that Becker's theory may both circumvent the threat of encouraging intolerance and undermine the moral teleology of utilitarianism by underwriting a theory of rights. The uniform preference function shared by all agents answers, for example, to the notion of natural rights that Rawls describes in *A Theory of Justice*:

> *Natural rights* depend solely on certain natural attributes the presence of which can be ascertained by natural reason pursuing common sense methods of inquiry. The existence of these attributes and the claims based upon them is established independently from social conventions and legal norms. . . . [T]he concept of natural rights includes the idea that these rights are assigned in the first instance to persons, and that they are given a special weight. Claims easily overridden for other values are not natural rights. Now the rights protected by the first principle [of Rawls' theory of justice] have both of these features in view of the priority rules [of his theory]. Thus, justice as fairness has the characteristic mark of a natural rights theory. Not only does it ground fundamental rights on natural attributes and distinguish their bases from social norms, but it assigns rights to persons by principles

---

[11] This point is made, perhaps to excess, in Karl Popper, *The Open Society and Its Enemies* (London: Routledge and Kegan Paul, 1972).

[12] Jeremy Bentham, "Anarchical Fallacies," *Collected Papers*, reprinted in A. I. Meldin, ed., *Human Rights* (Belmont, CA: Wadsworth, 1970), p. 32.

of equal justice, these principles having a special force against which other values cannot normally prevail.[13]

The needs which household commodities satisfy can be readily viewed as Rawls's natural attributes, ascertainable by reason pursuing common sense methods. They surely exist independently of social conventions and legal norms. After all, they supervene on biological properties of individuals. Their special weight derives from their commonality to all persons, and from the fact that they cannot be traded-off against one another, or against other, say market, commodities, without threatening survival. They represent goals "against which other values cannot normally prevail." These needs are reflected in Rawls's list of natural "primary goods": health and vigor, for instance, which along with social primary goods, are goods all persons prefer more of, and which should be distributed in accordance with two lexically ordered principles of justice. (p. 95) It is worth noting that the lexicality of these principles, and the rights they insure, fit closely together with the new theory's implicit conception of independent household commodities that cannot be traded-off against each other.

Of course, neither Becker's theory nor any other can parlay a theory of needs into an enumeration of rights. "Ought" does not follow from "is." Nevertheless, for anyone disposed to treat questions of welfare in terms of rights, instead of utility or one of its latter day surrogates, Becker's theory is a convenient one. It enables the moral philospher to *unify* a normative theory of rights with a positive theory of choice. Indeed, Becker's theory unifies rights with one possible interpretation of economic theory, a theory widely held both to be the only basis for objective decisions about welfare, and equally widely held to be at best independent of, and at worst incommensurable with, a normative theory of rights.

By treating needs as underlying rights, a moral conception that adopts Becker's theory of consumer behavior can thus avoid intolerance and paternalism. The right to a certain household commodity and to the market goods and technical means to produce it is not a duty to produce or acquire these goods. It entails a duty not to obstruct the acquisition of and production of such goods by others. But it allows the individual agent the freedom to choose and to be "wrong" in his choices. (For all we know such freedoms are among every agent's needs.) At the same time, it squares the moral principle that needs be satisfied with the proof that the market insures allocative efficiency in the satisfaction of these needs. For the new theory of consumer behavior has all the powers of the old one to prove the existence,

---

[13] J. Rawls, *A Theory of Justice* (Cambridge, MA: Harvard University Press, 1971), p. 505f. Page references to Rawls in the text are to this work.

uniqueness and stability of a general equilibrium, and the Pareto-optimality of such an equilibrium.

In this paper I have tried to do three things. First, I have tried to identify the very strong implications of Becker's theory, some of which he does not recognize or does not embrace. Second, I have attempted to make these implications plausible, both by showing that they are shared by others, and that they can be grounded in theories from which economics is at present isolated by its own restrictions. Third, I have explored the ramifications of this theory for some of the normative problems to which welfare economics can and cannot be applied. In this third task I have barely scratched the surface of a potentially fertile field to be cultivated by economists, philosophers, and others.[14]

Philosophy and Social Sciences, Syracuse University

[14] I owe thanks to J. Evinsky, J. Kidder, D. Hausman, R. J. Wolfson, and especially Gary Becker, for useful comments on a previous version of this paper. The current version reflects valuable suggestions by Hal Varian and helpful discussion by Amartya Sen, Allan Gibbard, Jules Coleman, Donald Regan and Jeffrey Paul at the Social Philosophy and Policy Center's conference on Morals and Markets. No agreement with my views, however, should be attributed to these persons, and remaining errors of economics or interpretation are entirely my own.

MARKET CONTRACTARIANISM AND THE UNANIMITY RULE*

Jules L. Coleman

This essay is part of a larger project exploring the extent to which the market paradigm might be usefully employed to explain and in some instances justify nonmarket institutions.[1] The focus of the market paradigm in this essay is the relationship between the idea of a perfectly competitive market and aspects of both the rationality of political association and the theory of collective choice. In particular, this essay seeks to identify what connections, if any, exist between one kind of market account of the rationality of political association and one kind of market-based social choice rule. The market theory of political association I intend to discuss I call "market contractarianism," and the collective choice rule whose relation to it I intend to explore is the unanimity rule. What, if anything, is the relationship between market contractarianism and the unanimity rule?

Market Contractarianism

There are two forms of market contractarianism. In one of its forms, political cooperation is rational to resolve problems arising from Prisoner's Dilemmas, externalities, public goods, asymmetries of information, extreme inequalities in bargaining power, and other sources of *market failure*. In this view, political action is necessary to bridge the gap between the suboptimal equilibrium of interaction that has the payoff structure of the Prisoner's Dilemma and the optimal equilibrium of perfect competition. In the

* Earlier versions of this paper were presented at Bowling Green State University, The University of Toronto Law School, Osgoode Hall Law School, The University of Virginia, Stanford, and Yale Law School, and discussed at a conference on Rationality, Freedom and Responsibility in Tucson, Arizona. I am grateful to participants on each of those occasions for their helpful criticism and commentary. I am especially indebted to Donald Regan, Ned McClennen, James Buchanan, Leslie Green, David Gauthier, Russell Hardin, Mark Isaac, Bruce Chapman, Michael Trebilcock, and Jody Krause, each of whom made substantial contributions to my thinking about the relationships between welfare economics, bargaining theory, and the rationality of political association.

[1] This essay is drawn from work leading to a book length manuscript: *The Market Paradigm*, Oxford University Press, forthcoming. The book is an account of what happens when welfare economics and public choice meet political and legal theory. It is an effort to explore the extent to which welfare economic and rational choice models can account for political institutions, including constitutions, courts, and legislatures, and the extent to which markets themselves presuppose such institutional arrangements.

alternative market contractarian view, political association is necessary, not only to compensate for market failure, but to realize the conditions necessary for *market success* as well. For convenience, I will refer to the version of market contractarianism that grounds the rationality of political association in the failure of perfect competition as the "thin" form of the theory. The version of market contractarianism that sees the need for political association in realizing the conditions of market success as well as in overcoming market failure I call the "thick" form of the theory.

a. *The First and Second Theorems of Welfare Economics*

The best way to illustrate the basic claims of both the thin and thick forms of market contractarianism is first to spell out the idea of perfect competition, including the conditions necessary for its realization, and then to explore ways in which various problems of interaction lead to market failure. I will begin by specifying the conditions of perfect competition, and then I will define three basic concepts: Pareto-optimality, Pareto-superiority, and the core.

D_1: An economy is perfectly competitive if and only if:

C_1: There exists a stable, private allocation of resources. (All resources are privately held and decisions about their use are reserved to those who hold them.)

C_2: Force and fraud in exchange are prohibited.

C_3: There is a sufficient number of buyers and sellers so that no one person's behavior can affect prices.

C_4: All consumption must be private. Each person's consumption enters only his utility function. This condition is alternatively expressed as "nontuism," i.e., each person is uninterested in the interests of others; or as the requirement that individuals have "selfish utility functions"; or as the requirement that no externalities exist.

C_5: Transactions are costless.

C_6: All utility functions are monotonic.

D_2: A state of affairs (S_n) is Pareto-optimal provided there exists no state of affairs (S_i) Pareto-superior to it.

D_3: A state of affairs (S_i) is Pareto-superior to another state (S_n) if and only if no one prefers (S_n) to (S_i) and at least one person prefers (S_i) to (S_n).[2]

---

[2] There is a difference between maximizing the satisfaction of one's preferences, and maximizing one's welfare, well-being, or utility. The Pareto-criteria can be expressed in terms of all four. For ease of exposition, I shall write mostly in terms of preference satisfaction, because nothing in the argument I advance depends on the differences, and because it is common in welfare economics to treat these interchangeably – though in many contexts, doing so is a mistake.

Every distribution of resources in the core is Pareto-optimal, but not every Pareto-optimal allocation is in the core. Suppose we think of exchange as a two person game. Mutual exchange is one of the possible solutions to the game. It is also a Pareto-optimal one. Suppose, however, that the rules of the game do not prohibit theft. Then both individuals could do better by stealing than by exchanging. The exchange solution is Pareto-optimal, then, but not within the core. Generally, an allocation is not within the core even if it is Pareto-optimal whenever one party or a coalition (including the coalition of the whole) can do better independently, on his (or its) own.

D_4: An allocation of resources, S_i, is in the core if and only if it is Pareto-optimal and no person or coalition (including the coalition of the whole) can do better independently.

Thus, in a game that does not prohibit theft, the exchange solution is Pareto-optimal but not within the core. My interest in "The Core" is limited to its application within markets, especially within perfectly competitive ones. Under perfect competition, theft is prohibited, all exchanges must be voluntary. If exchange is voluntary – as it is in perfect competition – the exchange solution to the game is not only optimal, but within the core.

Restricting the discussion of the core to the market introduces the notion of initial endowments. If all exchanges must be voluntary, an individual's initial endowments define how well he can do independently. He will block (veto) any exchange that does not leave him better off than he would be by acting independently. In an exchange economy where force and fraud are prohibited, the core depends on an initial set of endowments, whereas the set of Pareto-optimal allocations does not.

The relationship between optimality and the core can be illustrated by an Edgeworth Box. The set of Pareto-optimal points in a two-person, two-good economy can be represented as points on the contract curve. (See Figure 1).

Points a, b, c, and d are the tangents of A's and B's indifference curves. The line connecting these four points is the contract curve. Points on the contract curve are Pareto-optimal; that is, they are points to which A and B would voluntarily trade, and from which they would not voluntarily depart. The set of attainable Pareto-optimal points can be specified without first specifying an initial distribution of the commodities between A and B. Suppose, however, that the initial allocation of goods is represented by w_1. In that case, although the line through a, b, c, and d represents the contract curve, A would *block* any move from w_1 to, for example, c or d. In going from w_1 to c or d, A would be made worse off than he would be at w_1. Therefore, A would be better off acting independently, i.e., by not cooperating. Given A's and B's indifference curves and the initial distribution w_1, only points between a and b fall within the core.

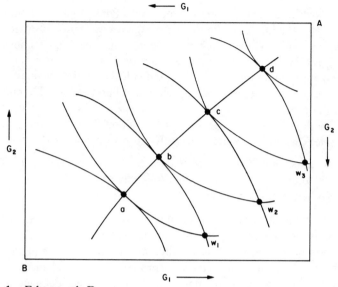

Figure 1   Edgeworth Box

Were resources initially distributed at w_2, only points on the contract curve between b and c would fall within the core. Shifts to other Pareto-optimal allocations, e.g., those between a and b, would be blocked by B; shifts to those between c and d would be blocked by A. Given any initial allocation of resources, only those Pareto-optimal points that make both A and B better off are within the core.

Under conditions of perfect competition, an economy will secure a Pareto-optimal distribution of resoures that is Pareto-superior to the initial allocation. Everyone is better off than each was when trade commenced, and trade ceases when no further mutual gains can be had – when, in other words, the surplus has been exhausted. The first theorem of welfare economics is that the outcome of trade under conditions of perfect competition is in the core.[3]

---

[3] Recent work by "catstrophe," "chaos," or "disequilibrium" theorists has raised doubts about whether even the first theorem of welfare economics obtains. Their view is that the core is empty. The seminal piece is J. Ostroy, "The No-Surplus Condition as a Characteristic of Perfectly Competitive Equilibrium," *Journal of Economic Theory*, vol. 22 (1980), pp. 183–207. The absence of a core in the voting context has been demonstrated by both Norman Schofield and Richard McKelvey. Both prove that simple majority voting rules create cycles under conditions that almost *always* obtain. See N. Schofield, "Instability of Simple Dynamic Games," *Review of Economic Studies*, vol. 45 (1978), pp. 575–594; and R. McKelvey, "General Conditions for Global Intransitivities in Formal Voting Models," *Econometrica*, vol. 47 (1979), pp. 1085–1111. Both papers are extremely technical. The general view, expressed best by Schofield, is that both politics and economics are chaotic – marginalism is out, and anything can happen.

Suppose A and B begin trade from a grossly unequal position. Because the optimal allocation they secure through trade is determined by the initial allocation of resources between them, inequalities that appear in the initial allocation are simply entrenched in the core solution. In general, free trade is mutually beneficial, but only within the domain of possibilities determined by the initial allocation. Left unfettered, perfectly competitive mechanisms are compatible with a great deal of inequality. Can the "distribution" problem be overcome in a way that is compatible with the competitive mechanism? The second theorem of welfare economics claims that it can.

The general problem can be illustrated graphically by representing the contract curve of the Edgeworth Box as a utility possibility or Pareto-frontier. (See Figure 2.)

The points a, b, c, d, e, f, g, and h represent Pareto-optimal allocations of the total resource base. If trade originates at w_1, then A and B will trade voluntarily until they reach a point on the frontier between a and b. If trade begins at w_2, A and B will eventually reach a point on the frontier between b and c. Suppose we have independent reasons for believing that points between c and d are more desirable than are those between a and b, or those between b and c. How can we get to a point on the frontier between c and d?

Points between c and d are Pareto-optimal but, were exchange to begin at either w_1 or w_2, not within the core. That is, points between c and d are

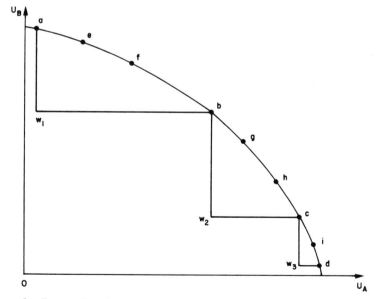

Figure 2   Pareto-frontier

securable from w_1 or w_2 only by violating the condition of individual rationality. We can, however, reach a point between c and d either by lump-sum wealth transfer *ex post* or by rearranging holdings between A and B *ex ante*. The net effect, in either case, is that an area on the frontier is attainable that would constitute a core solution to trade originating at w_3. From w_3 points within c and d satisfy both the individual and collective rationality conditions. The second theorem of welfare economics holds that, for any allocation of resources on the frontier, there exists a set of lump-sum wealth transfers that can move the economy to it.

The conjunction of the first and second theorems of welfare economics imply that a modified (by a zero-sum costless wealth transfer system) competitive mechanism can yield *efficient* and *just* allocations of resources. In claiming this, welfare economists can be understood to be asserting that in competitive markets: (1) rational self-interested behavior secures a social optimum, (2) that this social-optimum can be adjusted to match any desired pattern of distribution by a zero-sum game involving costless lump-sum wealth transfers, and (3) that the optimum secured under conditions of perfect competition is the result of fully voluntary exchange. Together, the first and second theorems provide the standard normative defense of laissez-faire market economies.[4]

b.   *The Two Theorems and the Nonintegration Thesis*
The first theorem of welfare economics specifies the efficiency property of competitive mechanisms; the second specifies the distributive property. What do the two theorems together claim is the relationship between efficiency and distribution?

It is clear that the concepts of efficiency and wealth (or resource) distribution are distinguishable. An allocation of resources may be efficient without being distributively just; or, it may be distributively just without being efficient. On the other hand, because an efficient allocation of resources is, after all, a distribution of resources, every allocation of resources will necessarily have both efficiency and distributive dimensions. It will either be efficient or not; and it will either satisfy certain distributive

---

[4] Within limits. There is a tension between claims (2) and (3). If one advances a Nozickian account, then there exists no way of moving the economy along the frontier that does not create injustice. So an economy can secure both (1) and (2) only by restricting or constraining the competitive mechanism somewhat, i.e., by violating (3). Alternatively, we might consider simply redistributing property rights *ex ante* to satisfy (1), (2), and in a weaker sense (3). This approach follows naturally from what Sen refers to as the Converse Theorem of Welfare Economics, which is roughly: for any point on the frontier, there exists an initial allocation of property rights capable of securing it as a unique outcome of the competitive mechanism. Following the dictates of the Converse Theorem may be no less troublesome to a "noninterventionist" than would be *ex post* redistribution, however. See A. Sen, "The Moral Standing of the Market," *Social Philosophy & Policy* (this issue).

ideals or it will not. In an obvious and unproblematic way, then, considerations of efficiency and distribution are at once conceptually distinct and necessarily connected.

There is, however, a more interesting sense, suggested by the two theorems, in which efficiency and wealth distribution are distinguishable from one another. Suppose we decided to implement policies or institutional mechanisms sufficient to move the economy towards efficiency. Then, if the first theorem is correct, all we need to do is to put in place a perfectly competitive market mechanism. No doubt when the gains from trade have been exhausted the Pareto-optimal allocation that emerges possesses a distributive property. But no need exists to *integrate* any particular distributive ideal into our planning in order to obtain an efficient distribution of resources. In order to secure efficiency, we need not have taken any account of the distributive dimension of the Pareto-optimal allocation that emerges. We need only make competition, albeit perfect competition, possible. By the same token, were we to seek to satisfy a particular principle of wealth distribution – say, a principle of equity – we might follow the guidance given by the second theorem, paying no heed whatsoever to what steps must be taken for our distribution to be efficient. The resulting distribution either will be efficient or not; but promoting distributive principles, by whatever light, does not require that we integrate into the mix those policies or instrumentalities that promote efficiency.

This is the simple but chief inference to be drawn from the first and second theorems about the relationship between efficiency and wealth distribution: namely, that in order to pursue either it is not necessary that we *integrate* considerations of the other sort. When pursuing efficiency, we may be blind to distributive inequalities; and, when rectifying perceived inequities we may be blind to considerations of efficiency. We can first secure the frontier and then move along it *ex post* until we come upon an allocation that is both efficient and just.

In spite of its obvious plausibility, the nonintegration thesis is at best uninformative and very likely misleading or false. It is uninformative for the following reasons. The nonintegration thesis is entailed by the two theorems of welfare economics that are themselves derivable only under conditions of perfect competition. But the welfare-economic theory of rational political association – what I call thin market contractarianism – states that political association is in each person's rational self-interest to overcome market failure. Under conditions of market failure the two theorems do not obtain. Instead, in order to overcome market failure it is necessary to integrate considerations of efficiency *and* wealth distribution. Or so I will argue.

Because the nonintegration thesis implies that, under conditions of perfect competition, concern for the relative distributive shares need not be integrated into the pursuit of efficiency, it may be misleading. The non-integration thesis obtains under conditions of perfect competition. If the argument I alluded to above is sound, however, it does not obtain under conditions of market failure. In the thick market contractarian view, however, perfect competition is itself a bargained solution to what I will call "pre-market market failure." So, market success is itself made possible by solving a market failure problem in which the thesis cannot be sustained. There is a sense, then, in which the failure of the nonintegration thesis is logically prior to its success.[5]

c. *Competition and Rational Political Association*

The point of focusing on the perfectly competitive market and its theorems is that thin market contractarianism holds that political association is rational only if the conditions of perfect competition are not satisfied. Thick market contractarianism holds that political association is rational, not just to overcome market failure, but also to realize the conditions necessary for market success as well.

The remainder of this essay falls into two parts. The first part explores the plausibility and difficulties of both forms of market contractarianism. The general line of argument in both cases will be as follows: markets fail (as do pre-market "markets"). When they do, it is not possible to secure an efficient allocation of resources noncooperatively. The alternative is a cooperative approach to market failure. Cooperation entails both efficiency and distributive components, and they are necessarily linked in a way that undermines the nonintegration thesis. Agreeing to a cooperative or joint strategy requires agreement on the division of the gains obtainable by overcoming market failure – and sometimes a good deal more as well. There are, therefore, two problems in cooperative action: the first is securing *agreement* through rational bargaining; the second is securing *compliance* with bargains that are reached. Problems of both sorts will be discussed, as will their importance, and the relationship between them. The second part of the essay explores the properties of a unanimity rule for collective choice. If commitment to the market paradigm entails a market contractarian approach to the rationality of a political domain, does it also entail commitment to a unanimity rule as a political decision rule within that domain?

Market and Pre-Market Failure: The Case For Rational Political Association

a. *Market Failure*

In this section, we begin by assuming that a market economy is in place.

---

[5] For a more complete discussion, see *Infra*, subsection entitled "Pre-Market Market Failure and the Problem of Rational Agreement."

In a market, rational individual utility maximizers take prices as given to them and seek to advance their own interests *noncooperatively*. If the market economy in place were a perfectly competitive one, it would give rise to a Pareto-optimal allocation of resources. If certain of the conditions of competition are not satisfied, however, consumers and producers in an economy might reach and remain stabilized at inefficient outcomes. When rational, self-interested behavior leads to a suboptimal equilibrium, i.e., a non-optimal equilibrium, market failure occurs.

The standard example of suboptimal equilibrium in the game-theoretic, not the market, setting is the single play Prisoner's Dilemma game characterized by a payoff matrix like the following. (See Figure 3.)

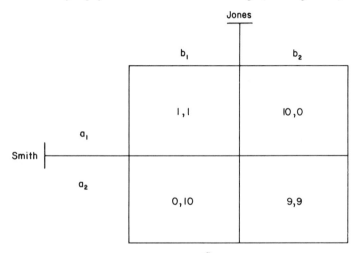

Figure 3   Single Play Prisoner's Dilemma

The joint play a_1, b_1 is the dominant outcome. That is, both players do best, no matter what the other player does, by playing a_1, b_1. Smith can play either a_1 or a_2. With this in mind, Jones must decide whether to play b_1 or b_2. Suppose Smith plays a_1. If Jones plays b_1, he secures 1; had he played b_2 he would have secured 0. Now suppose Smith plays a_2. If Jones plays b_1, he secures 10; had he played b_2, he would have secured 9. No matter which play Smith makes, Jones does best by playing b_1. Similarly, Smith does best by playing a_1. If Jones plays b_1, then, by playing a_1, Smith secures 1 instead of 0; and if Jones plays b_2, by playing a_1 instead of a_2, Smith secures 10 rather than 9. Jones and Smith play a_1, b_1, because in doing so each does the best he can no matter what the other does. Both Jones and Smith would have done better, however, by playing a_2, b_2. Because it is possible to imagine a state of the world, i.e., a_2, b_2, which makes both Jones and Smith better off, that state at which they find themselves, i.e., a_1, b_1, is not Pareto-optimal. The outcome of rational, utility-maximizing behavior in the single play Prisoner's Dilemma is a stable, suboptimal equilibrium. Sometimes individual utility-maximizing behavior is self-defeating.

Every outcome of the Prisoner's Dilemma but a_1, b_1 is Pareto-optimal. Only the move from a_1, b_1 to a_2, b_2, however, constitutes a Pareto-improvement. The relevance of the Pareto relationships among the four outcomes is as follows. Suppose we think of the four outcomes as various alternative starting points for future negotiations or exchanges. The general point of the Prisoner's Dilemma is that we will end up at whichever cell of the game we take as the starting point for negotiations. In the cases of a_1, b_2 and a_2, b_1 and a_2, b_2, that is because each is Pareto-optimal, and it follows from the definition of Pareto-optimality that no further mutually advantageous trades can be made. Suppose, however, that we begin trade at a_1, b_1. While both a_1, b_2 and a_2, b_1 are Pareto-optimal, neither is a Pareto-improvement relative to a_1, b_1. Only a_2, b_2 promises gains for both players. The gains are not obtainable by trade, however: that is, they are not securable by noncoordinated, individual utility-maximizing behavior. For both players there exists a dominant individual utility-maximizing strategy – and it is to play a_1 and b_1 respectively. Both players may agree to play the jointly maximizing or optimizing play, a_2 and b_2 respectively, but the dominant strategy is for each to defect from the agreement he has made.[6]

This discussion illustrates two important features of the suboptimal equilibrium of the Prisoner's Dilemma. The first is that inefficiency results from defection or noncompliance. Where communication is possible, there is no reason for the parties not to agree to the jointly maximizing strategy; the problem is that in the single play, defection from one's agreement is the dominant, utility-maximizing strategy. Secondly, a_2, b_2 represents a net gain for both players from a_1, b_1. It is a mutually advantageous optimum. Moreover, these gains are not obtainable noncooperatively, in the context of the Prisoner's Dilemma. They can be secured instead only by *compliance* with a *cooperative* strategy. We can think of the difference between a_1, b_1 and a_2, b_2 as a "capturable cooperative surplus."

We might draw a further distinction between cooperation and the

---

[6] It is worth distinguishing between two notions of equilibrium: Nashian and dominant. The Prisoner's Dilemma is a dominant equilibrium. That means, in equilibrium no agent will alter his strategy no matter what anyone else does, because his current play constitutes the best he can do no matter what others do. In Nashian equilibrium, an agent might change his play if others do, but he is unwilling to change his play alone. The difference is important. In several approaches to solving the Public Goods Prisoner's Dilemma, it turns out that honestly revealing one's preferences for public goods will *not* be a dominant strategy. Only a weaker, Nashian equilibrium emerges, for example, under a Groves-Ledyard incentive-compatible mechanism.

cooperative surplus. The cooperative surplus is the difference between the suboptimal equilibrium and the efficient equilibrium. In a purely voluntary exchange or market setting, the surplus cannot be captured noncooperatively. That is one way of reading the message of the Prisoner's Dilemma. Cooperation is one way of securing the surplus. If our options for securing the surplus are limited to forms of voluntary interaction, it is the only way. Once we allow coercive measures, or create other sorts of institutional mechanisms – for example, demand-revealing devices – it may be possible to capture the cooperative surplus in ways other than through voluntary cooperation. In short, the cooperative surplus is definable as the gains to be had by overcoming suboptimal equilibria; and cooperation is one way to secure them. In the present context, in which only voluntary measures motivated by rational self-interest are options, it is the only way of doing so.

To sum up: The Prisoner's Dilemma provides the most vivid illustration of the way in which rational, self-interested, noncooperative behavior may lead to stable inefficiencies. In the Prisoner's Dilemma, inefficiency results from noncompliance or defection. It does not result from an inability among the parties to reach an agreement to cooperate. Agreement, albeit insincere agreement, is rational; compliance is not.

Market Failure and The Prisoner's Dilemma: The Problem of Defection. Because the Prisoner's Dilemma arises in contexts in which individuals act non-cooperatively as rational utility maximizers, it is not surprising that economists have analyzed standard cases of market failure in terms of the Prisoner's Dilemma. Markets, after all, are the paradigm of noncooperative utility-maximizing interaction. Under conditions of perfect competition, market behavior is efficient. If the conditions of perfect competition are not satisfied, rational utility maximization may lead to stable suboptimal equilibria, just as in the Prisoner's Dilemma. It is now fashionable to see all such market inefficiencies as resulting from Prisoner's Dilemma inter-actions. I want to illustrate this line of argument by considering two sources of market failure: public goods and externalities.

Let us first consider the problem of pure public goods. A pure public good has two salient properties: one person's consumption of the good does not reduce another person's ability to enjoy it; and once the good is produced there exists no principled or efficient way of excluding anyone from consuming it. National defense is a public good; an apple is a private good. My "consuming" national defense does not prevent others from doing so; whereas, unless one holds a bizarre view about the reincarnation capacities of apples, perhaps fashionable only in California, my eating the apple usually precludes others from doing so. These features of public goods create free-rider problems. To see this, consider the following matrix of the collective goods problem given by Russell Hardin.[7] A collective good is presumed to be produced by a collection of individuals: ten individuals in Hardin's example. Suppose also that each unit of contribution yields two units of the public goods. The payoff for each individual is equal to his benefits less his costs. Each individual must decide whether or not to contribute to the provision of the good. Hardin provides the following matrix to characterize the decision problem facing a potential contributor:

| | | Collective | |
		Contribute	Decline
Individual	Contribute	1,1	−.8, .2
	Decline	1.8, .8	0, 0

Figure 4.

If ten people contribute, twenty units of the commodity are produced at a cost of ten units. There is a net benefit of ten units from the provision of the good: a gain of one unit per person. If everyone contributes, i.e., both Individual and Collective, then the payoff is 1, 1. If one Individual fails to contribute and the nine others do, eighteen units are produced, but because the good is nonexcludable, all ten persons can share in its benefit equally. The benefit per person is 1.8, but the cost of provision for everyone other than Individual is 1. The net gain for Individual is 1.8; for everyone else it is, .8. If Collective contributes, Individual does best by declining.

Consider Individual's potential strategies should Collective fail to contribute. If Collective does not contribute, then by failing to contribute, Individual gains and loses nothing. But if Individual contributes when no one else does, two units of the good are produced to be distributed among ten persons, yielding a benefit of .2 to each. Everyone else free-rides on Individual's contribution, and his payoff is a net loss of .8. If Collective fails to contribute, then so should Individual; but if Collective contributes, Individual should decline to do so. In either case, Individual does best by declining to contribute to the provision of the public good. In effect, this amounts to Individual's agreeing to contribute, thus inducing others to do so as well, then defecting.

---

[7] Russell Hardin, "Collective Action as an Agreeable n-Prisoner's Dilemma," *Behavioral Science*, vol. 16, (1971), p. 473.

The calculus of Individual's choice is the rational calculus of each individual member of the Collective. For each person contemplating whether or not to contribute to the provision of the good, the rational strategy is to decline the contribution and to seek to be a free-rider. But then, the collective good will not be provided. The logic of rational choice in the public goods problem is the same as that in the Prisoner's Dilemma. Cooperation provides a gain for everyone, but the rational strategy is to defect, or in the case of public goods, to decline to contribute to the provision of the good. In a private, competitive market setting, where individual act-strategies are made noncooperatively, public goods tend to be provided at suboptimal levels. The failure to optimize constitutes the classic case of market failure. The difference, then, between the stable but suboptimal equilibrium of market failure and the *ex post* optimal equilibrium of perfect competition constitutes a capturable cooperative surplus.

Market failure also results from externalities. Externalities are byproducts of one person's consumption or production which affect the welfare of others. Externalities may be negative, as in pollution, or positive, as in a lighthouse. To secure an efficient level of externality causing activity, the social costs of the activity must be reflected in the private cost calculation of the externality-causing activity. This is just another way of saying that optimality requires that marginal cost equal marginal benefit. To see this, consider the rancher/farmer example all-too-familiar to followers of the law and economics literature.[8] As the rancher's cows graze on the farmer's land, each additional cow causes marginal damage to the farmer's land. If the social costs of ranching on farming are not reflected in the rancher's decisions about how many cows to raise, he will raise an inefficient number of cows (too many) and the farmer will grow too little corn.

It is tempting to object that we lack an external, objective standard by which we can determine whether too many cattle are being raised and too little corn farmed. What, in other words, is the basis for the claim that the externality leads to inefficiency? The objection can be met by supposing that both the ranching and farming activities are under the direction of one person who owns both adjacent plots of land, and who asks himself, "How much cattle and how much corn ought I to raise?" For this person, there is no avoiding the costs of ranching on farming or farming on ranching; he bears the benefits and costs of both. In the case where externalities are internalized, it is easy to demonstrate that the rancher will raise fewer cows than he would were he not liable for the social costs of ranching on farming. Indeed, because he will cease raising cows at the point at which an additional

---

[8] The seminal piece is R. Coase, "The Problem of Social Cost," *Journal of Law and Economics*, vol. 3 (1960), pp.1–30.

cow results in greater foregone benefits (to him) obtainable by shifting resources to farming, his decision is efficient.

There is no real difficulty in seeing that both the provision of public goods and the existence of externalities lead to suboptimal equilibria or market failure. It is also easy to see how, following Russell Hardin, the public goods problem can be analyzed in terms of the Prisoner's Dilemma. It is more difficult to characterize the problem of externalities in terms of their involving a surplus securable by mutually advantageous cooperative strategies. It can be done, however, and here is how.

The key is to see the externality problem as one in which both the individuals whose conduct generates negative externalities and those who are harmed by them stand to benefit by their elimination; but in the absence of adequate incentives, they are unable to do so. The best illustration of the possibility of mutually advantageous gain through the elimination of externalities is provided by the Coasean approach to externalities. Suppose the following. Had the rancher and the farmer actually been one person – rancher-farmer – he would have raised 50 cows. The 51st cow, and each subsequent one, would have cost him more in foregone corn-crop profits than he would gain by raising additional cows. This means that when there are two distinct persons, a rancher and a farmer, and the rancher raises an inefficient number of cows, say, 51, the farmer loses more than the rancher gains. By negotiating to reduce the number of cows to 50, both parties gain. To make the example concrete, suppose the 51st cow brings the rancher a net gain of $500, but it causes the farmer $600 in crop damage. If an accord is struck between the two that provides the rancher with somewhat more than $500 and costs the farmer somewhat less than $600, both are made better off through cooperation, the net effect of which is to reduce the number of cows to an efficient number – in this case 50. Externalities are not only inefficient, but, like public goods, there are mutually advantageous gains to be had by eliminating them. Externalities exist and persist precisely when these gains are not secured; i.e., when there is a failure to realize the cooperative surplus.

Externalities can create a capturable cooperative surplus. In the Coasean approach, these gains can be captured voluntarily among small numbers of individuals through bargaining. The bargain is, in effect, an exchange: a reduction in output for a negotiated price. But exchange itself has the payoff structure of the Prisoner's Dilemma; and in the *single play*, the dominant strategy is to defect.[9] Externalities, then, are fully analyzable in Prisoner's Dilemma terms. Their existence is inefficient, thus creating a potential cooperative surplus that can be distributed so as to make each person better off. Nevertheless, the agreement to distribute those gains, once secured, is subject to the problem of defection.

It is possible to recast other sources of market failure, including monopoly bargaining power, in the same way. Roughly, the idea is that consumers form coalitions to bargain with the monopolist to sell his product or service at what would be the competitive market, i.e., efficient, price. There are potential gains on both sides by overcoming the source of market failure. The gains to the consumers result from the reduction in prices to the competitive level; the gain to the monopolist comes from the "bribe" consumers pay him to reduce his prices.

Monopoly bargaining power is, therefore, also analyzable in Prisoner's Dilemma terms. Overcoming the inefficiency created by monopolies provides potential gains for everyone. The agreement drawn between monopolists and consumers is in the interest of each, but once again, defection is the dominant strategy in the single play.

In order to understand standard forms of market failure as Prisoner's Dilemmas, it is necessary to show (1) that there are mutually advantageous gains to be had by structuring the problem in order for it to have a cooperative solution, and (2) that any agreement to cooperate, because of

---

[9] Exchange-as-Prisoner's Dilemma

Jones

		exchange apple	keep apple
Smith	**exchange orange**	apple , orange	no apple, orange
	keep orange	apple , no orange	no apple, no orange

Smith does best by withholding the orange from trade no matter what Jones does, and Jones does best, no matter what Smith does, by withholding the apple. It is a fair question why exchange ever proves successful. The answer is twofold: exchange is iterated, and we have a law of contract to enforce agreements by changing the payoff for defection.

the nature of the problem involved, is subject to the problem of defection. In the previous discussion, I attempted to reveal the Prisoner's Dilemma component in the market failure problems of public goods, externalities, and monopolies.

Market Failure and the Prisoner's Dilemma: The Problem of Agreement. Focusing too closely on the Prisoner's Dilemma as the basic structure of market failure may mask several ways in which public goods or externality problems are more complex than the Prisoner's Dilemma. In the Prisoner's Dilemma, inefficiency results from noncompliance. There is, moreover, a specified distribution of the gains from cooperation. Agreement on the distribution of those gains is never at issue, never itself the source of failure. In contrast, in the standard market failure case, there is no efficiency unless the parties can agree on the division of the gains from cooperation. There is no specified division of those stakes, and failures of bargaining are as likely to result in market failure as are problems of defection or noncompliance. Moreover, if we focus entirely on the Prisoner's Dilemma defection dimension of market failure, then we are likely to see the rationality of political association in terms only of *securing*, or coercively enforcing, rational agreements to cooperate. We will, then, underestimate the difficulty of securing such agreements and the role political institutions and mechanisms might play in encouraging agreement – say, by demand revelation mechanisms[10] – as well as the role they play in enforcing agreements once completed.

I want to emphasize that problem of rational cooperation and market failure inadequately addressed by the standard Prisoner's Dilemma analysis of market failure, i.e., the problem of rational bargaining, of agreeing on the division of the gains.

In this section, I want to make good on two modest claims. First, agreeing on the gains from cooperation is a necessary condition of securing the cooperative surplus. Second, the problem of securing agreement is not at all trivial. In the section on pre-market market failures, I will attempt to extend the argument to show that securing agreement in some contexts may be nearly impossible, and, moreover, that even when agreements are reached, they may be self-defeating or seriously unstable on other grounds. For now, I will be content to demonstrate the more modest claims suitable to this context: in particular, that agreement on the gains from providing public

---

[10] This highlights the importance of demand revelation mechanisms. All such mechanisms seek to induce individuals to reveal information, making honesty in each individual's rational self-interest. Bargaining in the absence of such incentives will be swamped by strategic behavior.

goods and eliminating externalities is necessary to achieve efficiency, but difficult to obtain.

First, let me begin by making clear the sense in which market failure integrates considerations of efficiency and distribution in precisely the way these considerations are presumed separable under the conditions of perfect competition. In the case of market failure, there are gains to be had which, *ex hypothesi*, are not capturable by purely voluntary exchange. Securing these gains requires an agreement to act jointly, to cooperate. Efficiency can be secured, then, only if the parties agree to cooperate on a joint strategy. But the rationality of each person's willingness to cooperate depends on his accepting a particular division of the gains. Efficiency, in this context, cannot be secured other than by securing agreement on the division of the cooperative surplus. No agreement on the division of the gains, no gains. No gain, no efficiency. To see this, just recall the rancher/farmer example. Reducing the number of cows to their efficient level, i.e., 50, depends entirely on the rancher and the farmer agreeing on a division of the $100 surplus (the difference between the $500 gain and the $600 loss associated with the 51st cow). Should bargaining fail, inefficiency will remain. Bargaining, moreover (in this context at least), is over the division of the gains and nothing else.

We might put this point as follows. In the circumstances of market failure, individual utility-maximizing behavior can go only so far in securing the Pareto-frontier. When the market model falls short of reaching the frontier, cooperation is necessary. Market failure creates the opportunity for everyone to play a mixed bargaining game. The game is mixed, because it has both redistributive and productive dimensions. Moreover, success in securing the productive goals depends on reaching an accord over the distribution of the productive or cooperative surplus. In the case of overcoming market failure by cooperation, the nonintegration thesis simply does not apply. Consequently, the model of perfect competition has limited force in explaining the nature and scope of rational political association.

The problem we want to focus on is the difficulty of securing agreement. We begin by assuming that a political order or state will enforce whatever agreement individuals reach to overcome the problem of externalities. In deciding how to go about overcoming the inefficiency of externalities, everyone recognizes that externalities can be overcome by bargaining, liability rules, taxes, or subsidies. Consider taxes first: the Pigouvian solution. Tax the offending party at a rate equal to the marginal damage caused by the externality. This will cause the offending party to internalize his costs and, therefore, to bring his level of output down to the efficient level. Then, if the revenue from the tax is transferred to those harmed by the externality, gains that were left uncaptured by virtue of externalities are captured and distributed completely to one side. Efficiency is obtained through taxation, not cooperation.

Efficiency could also be secured by subsidy. In that case, in order to reduce the level of its output, the offending party would be paid a subsidy equal to the marginal gain it secured by imposing the externality. Once again, the efficient or, loosely speaking, the cooperative solution is achieved noncooperatively. And, in the event a tax is imposed on those who were harmed by the externality in order to raise the revenue to subsidize externality-reducing subsidies, the gains would be distributed largely to the advantage of those who cause the harms rather than to those who suffer them.

Both the tax and subsidy schemes overcome the inefficiency of externalities, but they distribute the gains from doing so in vastly different ways. Alternatively, our rational bargainers might contemplate a Coasean approach to externalities. In that case, efficiency would be secured through voluntary exchange, but, in each case, whether efficiency was in fact secured would depend on the success of individual bargaining. That, in turn, would depend on the costs of negotiations, the incentives to reveal information, and the like. Each approach can theoretically overcome the inefficiency of market failure, but which approach would be rational to adopt depends primarily on nonefficiency properties, particularly on the ways in which various schemes distribute the cooperative surplus.

There is another way to illustrate the problem. If individuals choose to solve externality problems in a Coasean way, then, provided transaction costs are acceptably low, whether externalities will be overcome depends in each case on the success of bargaining over the cooperative surplus. On the other hand, if individuals opt for a nonmarket or Pigouvian approach, there is no problem of securing agreement on the division of gains in each case, because the parties do not enter negotiations. On the other hand, there is the problem of securing pertinent information. If the externality-causing activity is to be taxed and the revenues to be transferred to the harmed individuals, members of the latter group have an incentive to overstate the value of the harm they experience. If the level of the negative externality is reduced by subsidizing the offending party, he has an incentive to misrepresent the extent of its benefit.

We are imagining the following: rational bargainers seeking cooperatively to overcome a market failure caused by externalities. They have the following feasible options: taxes, subsidies, bargains, liability rules. Consider the first three. Suppose all are efficient, and thus are capable of capturing the surplus. The solutions differ in how they distribute the gains. Subsidies distribute the gains favorably to those who cause harm; taxes distribute the gains favorably to those who suffer harm. Under Coasean bargaining, the cooperative gains are negotiated among individuals or small groups. These alternatives also differ with regard to other morally relevant characteristics. Both the tax and subsidy approaches capture and distribute the surplus noncooperatively, whereas the Coasean approach distributes the gains according to a principle of voluntary, negotiated settlement. So the problem is complex. Overcoming market failure requires seeking agreement over alternative mechanisms. Without introducing any artificially imposed conditions of uncertainty into the bargaining process, it is hard to imagine that individuals could come to an agreement over alternatives with such different distributional and other properties.

The problem of agreeing on the division of the gains is strictly analogous to the problem of revealing information. It is a problem that is particularly troublesome with respect to public goods. Public goods are positive externalities; their provision by anyone benefits everyone – at least potentially. Consequently, the problem of preference revelation arises. Individuals who stand to gain by the provision of a public good have an incentive to understate the benefit of the good to them whenever the good is to be paid for by some form of benefit tax.

The general issue raised by considering the bargaining problem is that market failure may result in inefficiency; there are potential states of the economy capable of making everyone better off. But obtaining those states may require bargaining, as in the Coase Theorem; or they may require taxation, subsidies, liability rules; or in the case of public goods, they may require a choice among a variety of demand – revelation mechanisms. The rationality of bargaining to any of these mechanisms or institutions depends on a theory of the rational division of the surplus. In the absence of agreement on the division of the cooperative gains, inefficiency remains.

In the thin market contractarian conception of rational political association, to sum up, the state is necessary to overcome market failure. In the case of the Prisoner's Dilemma that just amounts to enforcing compliance. In the case of more complex market failures, political association may entail institutions for encouraging honest revelation of preferences and other inducements to successful negotiations. Failure to reach agreement on the division of the gains from trade is as likely a source of market failure as is failure to comply with agreements once reached. Focusing on the Prisoner's Dilemma aspect of market failure encourages a theory of rational political association that emphasizes the role of the state in enforcing agreements by changing the payoff structures facing each actor. It does little to highlight the problem of agreement formation and, therefore, does little to motivate the rationality of those political institutions designed to reveal information and encourage negotiations.

Whether or not one shares my doubts about rational bargaining, it is

important to see that the entire process of choosing those political
associations of a specific sort that emerge both in securing agreement and in
enforcing compliance is itself analyzable as a mixed bargaining game. By a
mixed game, I mean one that has both *productive* and *redistributive* elements.
Rational political association is a mixed game in that it holds out the
possibility of overcoming market inefficiencies – and is, in that sense,
productive – provided an agreement upon the division of the surplus can be
secured.

I want to close this section by emphasizing how different this view of
rational political association (as both productive and redistributive) is from
the standard view. Political theorists like Lester Thurow who model politics
game-theoretically have claimed that political association is redistributive
only. They argue that decisions pertaining to allocational efficiency are made
elsewhere in a well-ordered society, and that politics is therefore a pure-
redistribution game. If what I have said so far makes sense, this view is
fundamentally mistaken.

b. *Pre-Market Market Failure*

Thin market contractarianism finds in market failure the rationality of
political association. Political institutions are rational, in that view, not only
because they enforce compliance with rational bargains, but because they
encourage rational bargaining as well. Rational bargaining is necessary to
overcome market failure. Overcoming market failure by rational bargaining
requires agreement on the division of the cooperative surplus. The last
section explored some of the difficulties likely to emerge in seeking
agreement on the division of the gains achievable by overcoming market
failure. If agreement is not reached on the distribution of the cooperative
surplus, negotiations or bargaining fails, and market failure remains.

Thick market contractarianism sees the need for rational political
association not just in overcoming a variety of market failures, but in seeking
to realize the conditions of perfect competition as well. Perfect competition
requires the existence of a property rights scheme. The property rights
scheme is itself a bargained solution to what I call a pre-market market
failure problem. The remainder of this section presents the argument for
this claim and explores its implications.

A property rights scheme specifies the domain of an individual's rightful
possessions and enforces certain claims individuals have with respect to
objects in that domain. Borrowing from the law and economics literature,
then, we might think of the property rights scheme as consisting of property
rules, liability rules, and inalienability rules, as well as a criminal law that
serves to enforce the transaction structure specified by the property/liability/

inalienability rule distinctions.[11] We might think of the property rights scheme, therefore, as involving a law of property – which sets out the domain of rightful possessions – and a law of contract (property rules) which gives individuals the right to trade resources as they see fit. A property rights scheme also involves a law of tort (liability rules), which provides individuals with compensation for invasions of those rights, and which, on the standard economic view, specifies the conditions under which others can invade the domain of someone's rightful possessions; and it includes a law of crimes to enforce the above resource transfer mechanism.

Where markets exist, they are subject to market failure. Markets cannot exist, however, in the absence of a system of private property rights. The possible emergence of a system of property rights occurs, then, in a pre-market setting. In the pre-market setting, there are at least two reasons rational, self-interested parties might have for trying to create a property rights scheme: the first is to make possible the gains from trade realizable in a market economy; the other is to reduce the costs of protecting pre-market holdings. We will now explore how considerations of the latter sort might motivate rational political cooperation.

Suppose that individuals have holdings – possessions – but have no rights to these possessions that are themselves secure and enforceable. This is a pre-market state of nature. In this pre-market setting, individuals spend a share of their real resources in defending their holdings from attack and some of the rest of their resources in attacking others. Their decisions about how to live their lives – in effect, what strategies of defense and attack to adopt – can be represented game-theoretically. Each individual has a bundle of property or holdings (H) which he can protect at a certain cost (p), or which he can seek to increase by attacking at a certain cost (a). To simplify the subsequent argument, let's make four additional assumptions: (1) The value of each person's holdings is equal, so that in a successful attack, one's holdings increase from H to 2H; (2) the probability of successful attack is .50; (3) everyone is risk neutral, and is thus concerned only with the expected payoffs of alternative strategies; and (4) the probability of successful attack and defense are independent. The payoff matrix for this "state-of-nature" game can be represented as follows: (See Figure 5).

Given the above payoff structure, the expected value to individuals of playing the "state-of-nature" game of "attack and defend" is equal to the sum of the values of each outcome discounted by the probability of its occurrence. Because the probability of successful attack (or defense) is .5, the probability of each outcome, which involves both an attack and a defense

---

[11]   G. Calabresi and D. Malamed, "Property Rules, Liability Rules and Inalienability: One View of the Cathedral," *Harvard Law Review*, vol. 85 (1972): pp. 1089–1128.

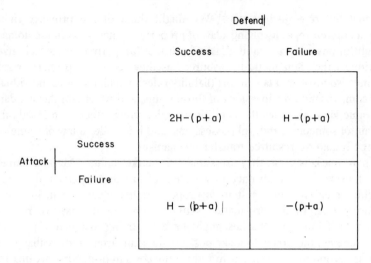

Figure 5: Attack and Defend

element, is equal to the product of the probabilities of each, or .25. The expected payoff of the game can be calculated as follows:

1. Let $C = p + a$
2. $E_v = .25 (2H - C) + .25 (H - C) + .25 (H - C) + .25 (-C), =$
3. $E_v = (.50 H - .25C) + (.25 H - .25C) + (.25H - .25C) + (.25C) =$
=
4. $H - C$
5. where $C = p + a$
    $E_v = H - (p + a)$

Suppose that there are increasing economies of scale in the joint production of protection; that is, the cost per unit of producing n units of protection is less than that of producing $n - 1$ units.[12] The marginal cost of providing protection, i.e., of establishing a property rights scheme, will decrease as protection is provided for more individuals. Let's label the per-unit cost of protection charged to each person Θ. If $(p + a) > \Theta$ for any i, as it must be if we assume linearly increasing economies of scale, each person stands to save the difference in costs by agreeing to a property rights scheme.

There is an inefficiency in the pre-market state of nature remediable by providing a property rights scheme that recognizes certain possessions as rightful and enforces claims in regards to them. Because the property rights scheme is capable of improving the lot of everyone by saving unnecessary

[12] It is doubtful that there can be indefinitely increasing economies of scale. Consequently, the argument works only for groups of certain sizes.

protection costs, we might think of the pre-market state as inefficient in the standard welfare-economic sense.[13]

There are gains to be had by overcoming the suboptimality of the pre-market system of nonrightful holdings. The way to do so is to create a property rights scheme. Provided the costs of providing protection cooperatively are less than the costs of doing so individually, the property rights scheme is in each person's rational self-interest. Thus, we should expect individuals to seek an agreement to provide the necessary good. On the other hand, provided exclusion is impossible (which it probably is not), or costly and inefficient (which it probably is), each person has an incentive to be a free-rider – to enjoy the savings in protection costs made possible by a property rights scheme, without incurring any of the costs of provision. Thus, we should expect problems of rational defection, as in the Prisoner's Dilemma, to surface. Once again, this time in the context of overcoming pre-market market failure, we are faced with the two basic problems in finding a cooperative solution to a market failure situation. These are the problems of reaching an agreement and of enforcing compliance.

Pre-Market Market Failure and the Problem of Compliance.   In the section on market failure and thin market contractarianism, I devoted some attention to the problem of compliance. The point I emphasized was that, defection, not compliance, is the rational strategy in the collective goods context. I argued from that to the need for a coercive mechanism, i.e., a state, capable of enforcing agreements to cooperate. I did not ask whether the state could itself emerge as the outcome of a rational bargain. But that is precisely the question we must face now.

The property rights scheme not only makes markets, including perfectly competitive ones, possible. It also constitutes a legal order – set of enforceable claims and the institutions to vindicate them. In asking, then, whether a property rights scheme can emerge by rational bargaining, I am asking whether the agreement to have a legal order is self-enforcing, or whether, instead, enforcing the agreement to have an enforcement mechanism itself presupposes such a mechanism.

The only agreements that demand compliance are self-enforcing; and an agreement is self-enforcing if compliance is the dominant strategy for each person. More typically, there are incentives to defect from whatever agreement one has made. This is especially true in public goods

---

[13] My claim is not that for each person in the state of nature the rational strategy is to engage in both attack and defense strategies. Instead, my claim is the weaker one – given the assumptions of the argument, for those who engage in both attack and defense, the expected payoff of doing so is $H - (p + a)$. These individuals have an incentive to collectively provide protection, provided the costs of doing so are less than $(p + a)$ for each. Others in the state of nature may seek membership in the coalition that provides protection on other grounds.

cases; and this is the way in which the Prisoner's Dilemma problem of defection surfaces in the public goods context, particularly, in the context of trying to create a property rights scheme. Rational bargaining may be necessary, but it is not sufficient to overcome pre-market market failure.

The problem is that no adequate enforcement mechanism in the pre-market market setting exists; the very point of the agreement is to put into place such an enforcement mechanism. In short, the problem is this: because the agreement to create a legal order, whatever its benefits, and however they are to be distributed, is not self-enforcing; it must be coercively enforceable by an already-existing coercive mechanism. But the object of the agreement is to create that mechanism precisely because in the pre-market state of nature setting no such instrumentality exists. Consequently, while it is possible to demonstrate the rationality of political association as necessary to overcome pre-market market failure, it may be impossible for individuals acting as rational utility maximizers to bring about what each recognizes to be in his rational self-interest, i.e., a legal order.

Pre-Market Market Failure and the Problem of Rational Agreement. This point is familiar and it is common to attribute it to Hobbes. I want to take up a part of the problem that has received a good deal less attention: securing agreement on the gains rational political cooperation makes possible. For if we assume that compliance could be enforced, there remains the question of exactly what the terms of the agreement would be. Indeed, there is a sense in which the problem of reaching the agreement and specifying its terms is more fundamental than is the problem of enforcing it. Suppose we could specify the terms of an agreement to produce and divide the gains made possible by overcoming pre-market market failure. Then we might argue as follows. If there is a state (or enforcement mechanism) – even if its emergence could not be reconstructed as the result of a series of rational, utility-maximizing choices – it could resolve the pre-market market failure problem in a particular way: namely, according to the terms of the agreement reached by rational bargainers in the pre-market market context. So, even if rational choice theory cannot provide an account of the actual *emergence* of political institutions, it might nevertheless provide an account of the contingent rationality of political association (that is, a theory about why the move from anarchy to polity is rational) and an account of the specific conditions or principles of rational political association (that is, a specification of the outcome of the rational bargain that takes place in order to overcome pre-market market failure).

The problem of securing agreement, however, is a good deal more difficult than one might suppose, and in the remainder of this section I want to discuss some of the formidable obstacles to securing meaningful rational agreement in the pre-market bargaining context. In exploring the bargaining problem, I want first to call the reader's attention to a point I made in the previous section in connection with ordinary market failure: namely, that in overcoming market failure through cooperation it is necessary to integrate considerations of wealth distribution and efficiency. The point takes on additional significance in the context of bargaining to overcome the suboptimality of pre-market interaction. The argument in the section on market failure warranted the conclusion that the nonintegration thesis does not apply in cases of market failure. Here a stronger inference is warranted. The issue is market success, not market failure. Market success is possible only if pre-market market failure can be overcome by an agreement to a property rights scheme. Putting such a scheme into effect is a collective-action problem that requires bargaining over the division of the gains made possible by an exchange economy. Bargaining to realize the conditions minimally necessary for competitive equilibrium requires the joint pursuit of efficiency and wealth distribution. Therefore, even the conditions of perfect competition logically presuppose the necessity of integrating efficiency and wealth distribution. In short, while there is no denying that we can distinguish between efficiency and wealth distribution, that feature of competitive markets is simply irrelevant to the kinds of problems that on the market model make political association necessary. In the market model, failures to achieve efficiency may motivate political cooperation; solving the problem of inefficiency, however, requires attending to both efficiency and distributive aspects of the problem.[14]

Let's set this point aside and return to the problem of securing an agreement on the division of the gains obtainable by a property rights scheme. These gains are of two sorts: (1) the savings made possible by jointly providing protection; and (2) the gains made possible by perfect competition – indeed, even the gains associated with the most rudimentary forms of exchange.

To explore how difficult reaching agreement might be I want first to focus in some detail on the problem of capturing and dividing the *savings* that will emerge by taking advantage of increasing economies of scale in the joint provision of protection, thus setting aside for the moment the much more complex problem of settling on a property rights scheme to secure the *gains* from exchange. Any person thinking about what share of the savings it would be rational to accept should take notice of the following problem. Suppose there are no defection problems, and suppose that the property

---

[14] My original interest in this project grew out of my work in law and economics. Advocates of the economic approach to law typically claim that the law should seek to promote both efficiency and wealth distribution, but they give no foundation for that claim. The market-contractarian account of rational political association provides the missing foundation.

rights scheme is in place. Further, suppose that, once in place, it enforces whatever division of the savings in protection costs everyone has bargained for.[15]

Let's inspect more carefully some of the salient properties of any property rights scheme. First, because it is a public good, the property rights scheme includes everyone. Still, its membership consists of two classes: providers and consumers. All providers of the public good are consumers as well; but not all consumers are producers. First, let Θ be the per-unit cost of producing and providing protection. The tax imposed on any consumer in order to raise revenue sufficient to provide protection can be set below, equal to, or above Θ. The providers can price discriminate. Let B equal the total cost of providing protection. Provided the revenue raised by the tax equals B, what each person can be taxed depends on the value to him of the costs of attack and protection. No person has an incentive (individually) to leave the coalition, provided his tax share is less than the sum of protection and attack costs. For each person, provided $(H - \Theta) > (H - C)$, the coalition remains rational. Because the tax enables price discrimination, it has a built-in redistributive capability. Moreover, though cooperation in the form of a joint effort to provide a public good (in this case, an enforceable system of property rights) is in each person's rational self-interest, it does not follow that everyone is equally advantaged – in either absolute or relative terms – by cooperation. The collective rationality of the coalition, in other words, can be maintained even if its fruits are differentially distributed. This redistributive aspect of the property rights asociation derives from its capacity to tax individual subscribers differentially; the only constraint on the extent of differentiation is that for each person the value (H minus the tax on him) must be greater than (H minus C for him).

This argument assumes a *balanced budget*: that is, the total costs of provision are equal to the total revenue collected. This assumption is too strong. If we assume that the providers of the property rights system constitute a monopoly within a particular geographic sphere, then they can tax to an extent greater than that minimally necessary to provide the good. The tax on *each* subscriber, then, will approximate the cost to him of his second-best option, namely providing the good by himself, (p + a), or in concert with others. Because we assume economies of scale, such a tax will lead to revenue in excess of that needed to provide the public good. The budget surplus means that, in addition to a public goods element in the state budget, there will exist a "redistributive" element as well. Moreover, redistribution will go from consumers (who are not themselves providers) to providers. Providers are, therefore, also members of what we might think of

---

[15] The following argument was much influenced by several discussions with James Buchanan.

as a sharing coalition. The additional proceeds from the tax are distributed among the members of this coalition in order to reduce the costs to each of the public good. In the extreme case, the public tax revenues will offset the full costs of providing the good to members of the sharing coalition.

Each subscriber to the property rights scheme has an incentive to remain in the coalition, provided the tax he incurs is less than the cost of providing the good himself or in concert with others. The same is true for the entire subgroup of subscribers who are not themselves members of the sharing coalition. The only constraint on the absolute level of public tax is set by the costs individual subcribers would have to incur to provide the public good on their own or in concert with others outside the sharing coalition.

The maximum dollar value of the redistributive component of the public tax is the sum of the differences between the per unit cost of providing the public good and the cost of each subscriber's second best alternative. Where exit is costless, the total is the sum of the differences between the marginal costs of providing the good within the coalition and the marginal costs of providing it either alone or in concert with others.

There are obvious incentives to seek membership in the sharing coalition. It is rational for individuals to spend real resources in order to pursue a piece of the redistributive budget. (This is the essence of rent seeking.) Membership in the sharing coalition reduces the costs of the public good, and as a consequence it increases the marginal costs of providing the good for those outside the coalition. One question is whether members of the sharing coalition have an incentive to minimize the size of the coalition, that is, to keep others out. The answer is surprising.

Provided additional members do not reduce the share of the redistributive surplus going to existing members, existing members will be indifferent to increases in the size of the coalition. If the total redistributive budget remains constant, the benefits of the coalition decrease to existing members. Moreover, by increasing the absolute number of individuals in the sharing coalition, there is a reduction in the number of those subscribers who must bear the additional tax burdens. The costs of increased membership, then, must fall on the ever-decreasing number of those who remain outside the coalition; and their tax burden must increase to provide the public good and to maintain the shares existing members of the coalition already receive. As it happens, taxes on those outside the coalition can increase to the extent to which the cost of providing the good on their own increases. Because the group outside the sharing coalition decreases in size, and because there are economies of scale in the production of the public good, individual and group costs increase. Thus, taxes can increase accordingly. Provided the increase in taxes is sufficient to offset new memberships in the sharing coalition, membership increases, taxes increase, and the overall institution remains rational. Only when the costs of exit and self-provision are less than the adjusted tax rate, thereby making exit rational, will the sharing coalition cease growing, or will the entire institution become unstable.

Any individual contemplating whether or not to accept a particular division of the gains must be aware that whatever he agrees to is very likely to be undermined by price discrimination, monopoly taxation, the existence of a redistributive element in the budget, and the subsequent rent-seeking behavior it encourages. The rent-seeking dimension of the problem is especially interesting. First, rent-seeking may simply nullify the substance of an agreement, by destabilizing it or by substituting distributions quite different from those originally agreed to. Moreover, because rent seeking involves the expenditure of real resources on nonproductive uses, it is inefficient.

Theoretically, the purpose of agreement is to overcome market failure and to promote efficiency in a way that secures agreement on the division of its fruits. But if the provision of the public good is by a monopoly – as it must be if the good is "the legal order" – then we have something to learn by switching our mode of analysis from "public or rational choice" to "public finance". What we have to learn is discouraging. If there is a redistributive component in the budget – and indeed, there are likely to be at least two different ones – rent seeking becomes a rational strategy. But rent seeking may render the terms of the agreement otiose, and to the extent potentially productive resources are employed to seek a larger share of the distribution budget, it is inefficient.[16]

In light of these sorts of considerations, it is hard to believe that individuals will reach a *meaningful* agreement, even on the savings made possible by taking advantage of economies of scale in the provision of protection. Because of what the future holds, once the property rights scheme is in place, the pre-market bargain is likely to be superseded almost immediately by strategic manipulation and rent-seeking behavior. Let me be blunt. The point of the bargain is to distribute and make possible gains associated with an efficient provision of protection. The net effect, however, of the dynamic mechanism and incentives put in place is to promote inefficiency and to undermine the terms of the original agreement. So even if bargaining is successful, in the sense that agreement is reached, it may turn out that the terms of the bargain are meaningless and the purpose of the bargain left unfulfilled.

[16] Here is one argument for constitutional constraints on budgets that goes in the opposite direction from the standard one. Usually, those who advance the cause of a constitutional amendment want to limit spending to collected revenues. The argument here is to restrict collected revenues so they do not exceed the sum of provision and administrative costs necessary to provide optimal levels of public goods.

The problem of securing a meaningful agreement does not get any easier if we focus on allocating once and for all a set of property rights thereby defining the core and the gains competition makes possible. Perfect competition results in a core solution to exchange – a Pareto-optimal allocation of resources that is Pareto-superior to the origin. Making possible the conditions of perfect competition is in each person's rational self-interest. If the other conditions of perfect competition are satisfied, then the establishment of a property rights scheme will guarantee that market behavior leads to the frontier. The location on the frontier that obtains from perfect competition is entirely a function of the *ex ante* allocation of property rights. It may be rational to seek to establish a system of property to fill the gap between the suboptimality of the pre-market market and the optimality of a perfectly competitive market. But the agreement to do so depends crucially on agreeing upon an *ex ante* distribution of property rights. Every mutually advantageous property rights system possesses the Pareto-optimality and Pareto-superiority properties. But which scheme any person would rationally assent to is a function, not only of the fact that he can secure gains from trade he otherwise would have been unable to (or which would have been extremely costly to secure), but of his expected *share* of the gains from trade under alternative property rights schemes. This may be just another way of making a point I have made elsewhere in another context: except at the margins, every Pareto-improvement involves potential surplus as well as the potential for efficiency; and so, embedded in all institutional arrangements that provide the opportunity for mutual gain is a bargaining game over relative shares.[17] The fact that gains are potential does not mean they will be realized, or even that rational people will take the first steps towards their actualization by reaching an accord on their division. Let's explore the problem more deeply. We will need to make two distinctions: one between alternative formal theories of the rational bargaining process and the other between two conceptions of the bargaining problem.

We have two options in thinking about the bargaining process over property rights. First, we might imagine this bargaining game as settling once and for all the allocation of property rights – except as those rights might be redistributed through post-bargaining contracts. We might alternatively imagine it to be an initial bargaining game settling on a distribution of property rights that will be in effect over a specified period of time, but subject to continual renegotiation. According to the second option, bargaining over property rights is subject to continual renegotiation; in the first, bargaining is a one shot deal.

Next, it is possible to characterize this and other bargains formally. There

---

[17] J. L. Coleman, "Economics and the Law: A Critical Review of the Foundations of the Economic Approach to Law," *Ethics*, vol. 94 (1984), pp. 649–679, especially pp. 664–667.

are currently any number of axiomatic treatments of rational bargaining. The most well-known is the extended-Nash/Zeuthen theory. Its most serious challenger is the Kalai/Smorodinski/Gauthier account. Nash bargaining is bargaining from threat advantage; the unique rational solution to any bargaining problem is that distribution of the gains that produces the greatest product of the utilities of the parties to the bargain. According to Gauthier, the unique solution to any bargaining game is given by the principle of minimax relative concession.[18] There is no need to explore the details of the various theories, for two reasons. First, even though axiomatic theories of bargaining each claim to provide a unique result for the bargaining problem, there is, in fact, no one theory of rational bargaining. In each case, only one principle of bargaining satisfies the axioms; but even slight changes in the axiomatic characterization of the problem yield a different "unique" solution to the problem. This result is important because it means we cannot legitimately impose a formal structure on the bargaining problem and thereby generate a unique solution to it.[19]

Secondly, the problems of rational bargaining that I want to focus on, e.g., strategic behavior and rent seeking, plague any dynamic bargaining process. Even if there were a unique solution to the bargaining problem, the problems I draw attention to would surface and render agreements inefficient or unstable. Because it does not matter which formal model we use, I will treat the bargaining process as proceeding along the lines suggested by the more widely-known Nash/Zeuthen account.

Consider, in Nashian terms, the one-shot-deal conception of the bargaining problem. In extended Nashian bargaining, a noncooperative game is embedded within the cooperative or bargaining game. The noncooperative game establishes the parties' relative threat advantages. Bargaining commences from this point of noncooperation, and, in the event negotiations fail, this is the point to which the parties return. The allocation of the cooperative surplus is in this model a function of the relative strength of the parties' threat advantages. Persons of relatively weaker threat positions run the risk of entering an agreement, which, though it makes them better off relative to the status quo, does not make them as well off, relatively speaking, as others who enjoy a greater threat advantage. A person in a relatively weaker position, however, is not without options. He can hold out. Gaining his assent to the bargain might be worth something to those of stronger threat advantages, who might themselves have more to gain by securing agreement. The longer the delay, the more real resources are wasted and the greater the risk of a decrease in the gains securable by cooperation. In short, in the hopes of inducing those possessing greater threat advantages to give up some

---

[18] D. Gauthier, *Morals By Agreement* (Oxford University Press, forthcoming 1985).
[19] For a contrasting view, see Gauthier.

of their advantage, the least advantaged might hold out. By the same token, those with stronger threat values can seek to exploit their relative strength. Recognizing that the least well off are particularly vulnerable, the stronger may hold out, hoping to squeeze even more of the surplus. Both "sides" have incentives to hold out. But hold-out behavior can lead to inefficiency. No agreement may be reached. This is especially true in large groups. Indeed, in large groups the problem of misrepresentation or strategic behavior is more formidable. Even if agreement is eventually reached, the expenditure of resources to improve one's relative position through hold-out behavior or rent seeking may mean that the outcome of the agreement is *not* efficient.[20]

Moreover, as Ned McClennen has pointed out to me, agreement that results from the physics of threat advantage bargaining is not underwritten by genuine consensus. So, even if Nashian bargaining succeeds in producing an agreement to create a property rights scheme, those who are relatively disadvantaged by the agreement will seek to destabilize it by engaging in post-contractual rent-seeking behavior. As the discussion of the properties of property rights schemes illustrates, there are ample opportunities for rent seeking. In Nashian bargaining, hold-out behavior may make agreement impossible, or if successful, inefficient. On the other hand, since Nashian bargaining is not based on genuine consensus, even if it is successful, the agreement may not endure. Moreover, whatever agreement is reached, those who feel they are exploited will seek to destabilize the agreement, and there is ample opportunity for them to do so. This problem is not significantly met by other theories of bargaining – even those like Gauthier's, in which rational bargaining secures outcomes that have the appearance of being fair or impartial. The reason is that rent-seeking behavior is motivated by self-interest and will occur regardless of the perceived fairness of the terms parties bargain to.[21]

The Buchanan model of continual renegotiation is problematic as well. The motivation for it seems clear and well founded. Individuals may be unsatisfied with the deal they originally make, and if there are no opportunities for renegotiation, they will try to destabilize or undermine the terms of the original bargain. Continual renegotiation attempts to keep the existing agreement reasonably stable. There are several problems here. First, renegotiation by itself does not guarantee that those who received the

---

[20] Alternatively, one could argue that the outcome is efficient because it has secured everyone's consent, whether or not it is efficient in the standard economic sense. This is Buchanan's view. For a discussion of its motivations and its problems, see below, "Unanimity as Efficiency."

[21] The claim here is that even a fair bargain is subject to rent-seeking efforts. That is because self-interested actors abide by fair bargains only if they view the fairness of the bargain as working to their advantage.

short end of the stick the first time will do better the next. Indeed, if continued rounds of bargaining involve Nash-bargaining, i.e., from relative threat advantage, the outcome of each round of bargaining continues to entrench relative disparities in threat advantage. Renegotiation does not guarantee an improvement in the status of those dissatisfied the first time around. But if individuals are aware of the need to improve their relative threat advantage for the upcoming bargain – and if their threat advantage is determined by their initial threat advantage plus the gains achieved by the existing agreement – then both those with weaker and stronger advantages have incentives to manipulate the first agreement. In that event, the continual renegotiation alternative simply collapses into the one-shot deal. If, however, renegotiation continually begins from a new initial bargaining position, and thus ignores the relative advantages secured under the previous bargain, it may have negative incentive effects, and, in any case it is grossly inefficient. Why not just negotiate one time, from what we might think of as a *fair* starting point, thereby reducing envy and providing the possibility of genuine consensus.[22] Finally, if continual renegotiation proves successful, it turns out to be entirely redistributive, providing no gains in efficiency. The point of continual renegotiation, after all, is not to overcome inefficiency but to redistribute the stakes. In that case rational political association is in fact a zero-sum game. Surely, such an alternative is inefficient, and therefore self-defeating.

Rational cooperation, in sum, is necessary to overcome market failure in the market contractarian theory of political association. Market failures are of two sorts: standard market failure and pre-market market failure. Examples of the first sort include attempts to provide privately basic medical research and national defense. The property rights scheme itself is an example of the latter. In seeking to overcome market failures of both types, cooperation is rational. Rational cooperation has three features relevant to the relationship between politics and economics. First, rational cooperation has strongly integrated efficiency and distributive elements. Thus, the nonintegration thesis is unhelpful, misleading, and perhaps false. Moreover, where rational cooperation takes the form of political association, politics is both productive and redistributive. Thus, Thurow's view of politics as purely redistributive, or the welfare economist's view of social choice as consisting

---

[22] Even then it is not clear that fairness of the point of departure suffices to stabilize bargains. Indeed, I want to go so far as to say that bargaining – even from a fair status quo point – will yield stable outcomes only if the parties already have a sense of fairness or a commitment to the ideal of fairness. It is a further question whether commitment to the ideal fairness or to being bound to one's bargains can itself be grounded on the rational self-interest of bargainers.

only in efforts to identify an economy's bliss point once the frontier is reached, are fundamentally mistaken.[23]

Second, in order for rational cooperation to succeed, an agreement, usually on the division of the cooperative surplus, must be achieved; and third, compliance with the agreement must be widespread. In this part of the essay, while I have discussed the more well-known problems of compliance, I have sought primarily to focus on problems in obtaining stable, meaningful, and enduring agreements. The problem of securing agreement in any bargaining circumstance involving large numbers of persons and a cooperative surplus are formidable. In the case of putting a property rights scheme or legal order in place, they may be insurmountable. The problem of compliance is less significant in the case of standard market failure where we legitmately assume that a coercive mechanism already exists. The problem of compliance may be insurmountable, however, in the pre-market setting, where no enforcement mechanism exists and where the very point of bargaining is to reach an accord to put such a mechanism in place. If that bargain is not self-enforcing, it may be impossible to give a rational choice or market account of the emergence of rational political institutions. If I am right, however, the more basic problem is that the terms of any such agreement are radically indeterminate. Efforts to make them determinate by imposing a Nashian bargaining model on the process may fail to make the outcomes more determinate. If they do, moreover, they may do so only at the expense of making the agreement less stable and secure.

The Unanimity Rule

Thin market contractarianism is the view that political association is a rational means to overcome market failures. Thick market contractarianism is the view that political association is a rational means to overcome both market failure and pre-market market failure, thus making possible the conditions of market success. In both conceptions of rational political association, politics has both productive and redistribute dimensions. Rational political association might then be viewed as a mixed bargaining game, the outcome of which specifies the conditions of political association.

To say that the terms of rational political association are specified as the outcome of rational bargaining is not to say that all political decisions are to be resolved by bargaining. That depends on whether, in either constitutional or post-constitutional bargains, bargainers would agree that the best way to overcome a particular market failure is by bargaining. It is perfectly plausible that rational bargainers seeking to overcome market failures owing to externalities might prefer a tax, subsidy, or liability approach to a bargaining

---

[23] A. Feldman, *Social Choice and Welfare Economics*.

or Coasean approach; or that bargainers in a public-goods context might agree to implement a demand-revelation mechanism,[24] rather than try to settle on the level of provision by simple majority vote.

The bargainers are seeking a mechanism that will secure an efficient allocation of resources and that divides the gains in a way that secures the agreement of all. The mechanisms open to rational bargainers in their efforts to overcome market failure include: bargains, social choice or collective decision rules, demand revelation or incentive compatible mechanisms, taxes or subsidies, and the property rule/liability rule transaction structure.

One of the options open to rational bargainers is to agree to solve certain inefficiencies by adopting a collective choice rule, such as voting. In this section I want to explore the argument for one kind of collective choice rule, namely, unanimity. Unanimity is democratic in a particularly strong sense. Moreover, unlike majority rule, unanimity is connected to efficiency in supposedly obvious ways. Its efficiency property alone makes unanimity attractive to rational bargainers seeking to overcome market failure. Its democratic features might be attractive to those aiming for stable or enduring agreements. Finally, unanimity is conceptually connected to the idea of the market, in particular to the concept of liberty of exchange. It is, therefore, the social choice rule naturally suggested by a commitment to the market pardigm.

Not without plausibility, advocates of unanimity have argued that the unanimity rule is both efficient and strongly democratic. Indeed, when leveled against the unanimity rule, the argument that collective choice rules are coercive because they impose policies on those who disagree with the majority decision is simply a nonstarter. Under the unanimity rule, no policy can be adopted if anyone votes against it. Furthermore, the unanimity rule appears to replicate in the political sphere, not only the efficient or optimal outcome of competitive markets, but the Pareto-improving character of free exchange as well. There are, I believe, at least four arguments for the unanimity rule suggested by these brief remarks, and in what follows I want to tease them out as best I can.

a.   *Unanimity, Public Goods, and Wicksell-Lindahl Taxes*
The paradox of public goods is that potentially they benefit everyone; and so providing them is in each person's rational self-interest. Nevertheless, if each individual acts to promote his rational sef-interest, it is virtually certain that less than the optimal number of public goods will be provided. The fact that public goods are potentially to each person's advantage, however, provides the basis for one argument for the use of the unanimity rule to

---

[24] For a fuller discussion of demand revelation mechanisms, see the special supplement to the Spring 1977 issue of *Public Choice*, vol. XXIX–2.

decide on the provision of public goods. This argument has its roots in the work of Knut Wicksell,[25] and it has been further developed by Erik Lindahl.[26] The basic idea behind what has been called the Wicksell-Lindahl tax is very simple. Because the provision of public goods is capable of making each person better off, there should be a way of providing and distributing their benefits and costs that can secure each person's agreement. There should exist, in other words, a public good/tax package tailored to each person which will secure his consent. In the aggregate, there is a relationship between the optimal provision of public goods and unanimity.

In the Wicksell-Lindahl scheme each person is asked to vote on a "tax package" applicable only to him. The tax package links a particular level of public good with a benefit tax. The purpose of the package is to match each person's marginal benefit from a public good with his marginal contribution to the costs of providing it. The point of matching benefits and costs follows from general equilibrium analysis of private goods: in optimal equilibrium, marginal private cost equals marginal private gain. The Wicksell-Lindahl scheme seeks to replicate in the realm of public goods what is essential to an efficient allocation of private goods: "linkage" of marginal benefit and marginal cost.

Each person has a demand schedule for public goods. As his tax share decreases, his demand for public goods increases. Theoretically, there exists an allocation of tax shares and units of the public good that meets with each person's approval. An illustration of this property of public good/tax packages is given in the following graph, originally given by Dennis Mueller.[27] (See Figure 6.)

The horizonial axis represents the levels of output of public good, G. The vertical axis represents A's share of the tax, T, necessary to provide the good at various levels. B's tax burden is equal to $(1 - A$'s share), for any level of provision. Both A's and B's demand for the public good is inversely related to their tax share: the lower the tax, the higher the demand.

The graph is complex in the following way. The indifference curves for A and B (labeled A_1, and B_1,) specify respectively A's and B's utilities in an economy *without* public goods: i.e., a private goods economy. Each point on the other indifference curves (A_2 through A_5, and B_2 through B_5) represents a preference for a mixture of public and private goods at various tax levels, given various budgetary constraints. C' is the contract curve. The difference between this graph and the standard Edgeworth box representation of a two-

[25] K. Wicksell, "A New Principle of Just Taxation," *Finanztheoretische Untersuchungen* (Jena: 1896).

[26] E. Lindahl, "Just Taxation – A Positive Solution," R. Musgrave and A. T. Peacock, eds., *Classics in the Theory of Public Finance* (New York: St. Martins, 1967), pp. 168–176.

[27] D. Mueller, *Public Choice* (Cambridge: Cambridge University Press, 1979), p. 29.

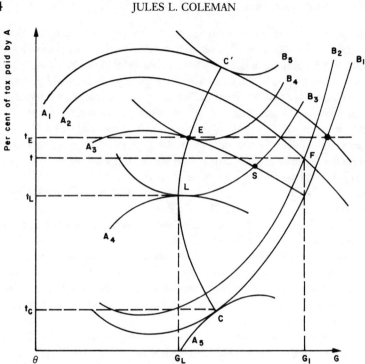

Figure 6   Wicksell-Lindahl Tax Scheme

person, two-commodity exchange economy is that in the standard case, A would prefer to be on an indifference curve further from the origin, whereas B would prefer to be on an indifference curve closer to A's origin: in contrast, in this graph, A prefers to be closer to his origin and B further from it. That is because as A moves closer to the origin his tax share drops; and as B moves further out from the origin his tax share declines.

We can say that the graph is *bounded* by the lens formed by the intersection of A's and B's indifference curves, A_1, B_1. Any level of provision of a public good is desirable for both A and B only if it promises to make both better off than they would be in the absence of public goods. The status quo point, then, is represented by the boundary A_1, B_1. A public good/tax package is Pareto-improving for A and B only if it is represented by a point that falls within the boundaries formed by the intersection of A_1, B_1, otherwise it is not.

Following Mueller, begin by assuming the relevant government agency offers to both parties a package that consists of a level of public good and a corresponding level of taxation necessary to provide the good. Either that offer falls within the lens formed by the intersection of A_1 and B_1, as it would if the government package was represented by F, or it does not. If the package falls outside the lens, either A or B or both will reject it. If the package falls within the lens, then both A and B will vote for the package, since at that level of taxation and public good both are better off than they would be in the absence of the public good.[28] F represents a Pareto-improvement, but it is not itself a point on the contract curve. Another tax package therefore is offered. Only tax packages offered that fall within the lens created by the intersection of A_2, B_2 are acceptable to both parties. Therefore, F represents the new veto point in the same way as the intersection of A_1, B_1 represented the original veto point. Only public good/tax packages Pareto-superior to it can secure the consent of both parties. One such package is represented by S. If S is offered, it is accepted and replaces F as the veto point. The process continues until a point on the contract curve is reached which is preferable to the previous veto point and cannot itself be improved upon. Such points fall on the contract curve and lie between E and L.

The Wicksell-Lindahl tax scheme appears to solve the public goods problem. It does so by replicating in the public sector the central features of exchange in the private sector: the linkage of marginal cost and marginal gain. Moreover, the process of securing an efficient or optimal level of public goods and public expenditures just described is based on giving each person a veto over all possible tax packages. The collective choice rule, then, that is employed to guarantee that the political process yields an optimal level of public goods is the unanimity rule. The argument from the Wicksell-Lindahl tax scheme is one argument for the unanimity rule based on its *efficiency*. It is not, however, the only argument for unanimity that relies on the relationship between it and Pareto-efficiency.

b. *Unanimity as Efficiency*
    James Buchanan is perhaps the most influential defender of the unanimity rule for collective choice.[29] He views himself, above all else, as a defender of unanimity on Wicksellian grounds. Even his severest critics, for example, Brian Barry, grant Buchanan this historical link to Wicksell.[30] I believe, however, that in an important sense Buchanan's conception of the relationship between unanimity and efficiency is not Wicksellian. The difference between the two views is important.

Buchanan's view is that unanimity is the *test* of efficiency. As I have argued

---

[28] The lens defines the range of Pareto-improving tax packages.
[29] Cf. J. Buchanan, *The Limits of Liberty: Between Anarchy and Leviathan* (Chicago: University of Chicago Press, 1975).
[30] B. Barry, Review of *Limits of Liberty: Between Anarchy and Leviathan*, in *Theory and Decision*, vol. 12 (1980), pp. 95–106, esp. page 96.

elsewhere, this claim is ambiguous because the term "test" may be given either an epistemic or a semantic rendering.[31] In the epistemic sense, unanimity is (perhaps the best) *evidence* of efficiency, but whether or not a state of the world is efficient depends on its satisfying some other criterion. In the semantic sense, to say that a state of the world is efficient is just to say that it has secured unanimous agreement. In this sense, unanimity is not simply evidence of efficiency; it is criterial of it. My view is that Buchanan is committed to the criterial, semantic, or ontological conception of the relationship between efficiency and unanimity, and not to the epistemic one. For Buchanan, unanimity constitutes efficiency: that is, unanimity is both necessary and sufficient for efficiency. Buchanan has accepted my characterization of his conception of unanimity and of its relationship to efficiency. Let's call Buchanan's view the *subjectivist* criterion of efficiency.

Given a loose reading, the subjectivist account of efficiency has some initial plausibility. Suppose one person vetoes a proposal. Then we can say that he does so because implementing the proposal would make him worse off. If no one vetoes a proposal – if a proposal secures unanimous agreement – then it makes no one worse off. Because it makes no one worse off it is efficient. Anything less than unanimity is inefficient. Not only is the argument plausible, it has happy consequences as well. If the point of political association is to mimic the perfectly competitive market by securing optimal allocations of resources, then one way to insure success in the political enterprise is to require unanimity. Unanimity entails efficiency; and efficiency is the goal. So one way of overcoming market failure is to get individuals to agree unanimously on policy recommendations.

What people agree to, however, may vary from what is in their rational self-interest. Presumably someone may be motivated by moral considerations to agree to a diminution in his well-being for the good of others. Unanimous agreement itself, even voluntary agreement, does not entail Pareto-efficiency in the usual sense. In the standard, welfarist conception of efficiency, a state of the world that makes someone worse off cannot be efficient. So there is no necessary connection between what people agree to, even unanimously, and what is Pareto-efficient or welfare enhancing.

The subjectivist theory of efficiency is not the one purportedly employed to demonstrate that the Lindahl-Wicksell tax scheme for public goods is efficient. Nor is the relationship between efficiency and unanimity in the Lindahl-Wicksell scheme the same as the one in Buchanan's argument for unanimity. In the tax scheme, the notion of efficiency is the standard one,

---

[31] J. L. Coleman, "The Foundations of Constitutional Economics," in *Constitutional Economics: Containing the Economic Powers of Government*, ed. Richard McKenzie (Lexington, Mass.: D. C. Heath and Co., 1984).

employing the common conceptions of rational self-interest, Pareto-superiority, and the core. The idea is that there exists a tax package for public goods tailored to each person capable of making each person *better off*, i.e., capable of increasing his welfare, and *therefore* capable of securing each person's consent. The package is efficient because it is welfare enhancing; and because it is welfare enhancing for everyone, each person will agree to it. Unanimity follows from efficiency, not the other way around. In contrast, in the Buchanan conception of efficiency, unanimous agreement constitutes efficiency, even if what people in fact agree to, say, in the allocation of public goods does *not* satisfy the Samuelson condition.[32] A state of the world that is efficient in the subjective sense need not be in the "objective," welfare sense. On the other hand, a state of the economy that is efficient in the Samuelson sense, and, therefore, in each person's rational self-interest, may not be unanimously agreed to, and, therefore, not efficient in the subjectivist sense.

These two arguments for the unanimity rule are based on two very *different* conceptions of efficiency and of the relationship between it and unanimity. Though Buchanan thinks of himself as above all else a Wicksellian, the differences between them may be more impressive than are the similarities. In Buchanan's argument for the unanimity rule, we infer efficiency from unanimity; in the Wicksell-Lindahl scheme we establish efficiency, then infer unanimity from it. In both cases, different conceptions of efficiency are at work. In both cases the inference may be unwarranted.

Once one appreciates the subjectivism of Buchanan's view, several serious problems emerge. The most pressing is the following. Return to the rational bargain. Suppose rational bargainers opt for a unanimity rule to overcome market failure. The problem is that there is no reason to believe that policy measures adopted by a unanimity rule are efficient in the sense in which market failures are inefficient. There is, in other words, no guarantee that a policy efficient in the subjectivist/Buchanan sense overcomes the market failure which is inefficient in an entirely different sense. But it was the very point of the unanimity rule that it held out the promise of solving the problem of market inefficiency.

The Wicksell-Lindahl scheme uses the useful sense of efficiency. The problem with it is that there is no reason to think that the scheme will actually lead to an efficient level of public goods. The reason is really quite simple. In order to secure an efficient level of public goods, the government needs consumers to reveal their true preferences for them. But each person has an incentive to withhold information. Therefore, the Wicksell-Lindahl scheme fails for the very same reasons private markets fail to provide optimal levels of public goods: inadequate honest information. If the good is

[32] See P. A. Samuelson, "The Pure Theory of Public Expenditure," *Review of Economic Statistics*, vol. 36 (1954), pp. 386–389.

provided, everyone has the opportunity to benefit from it. So each person's rational strategy is to understate the benefit to him of the public good, and hope, thereby, to benefit from its provision without incurring the full marginal costs of provision. In both the Lindahl-Wicksell and Buchanan arguments for the unanimity rule, the connection between efficiency and unanimity is a good deal less persuasive than advocates of the unanimity rule would have us believe.

There are two final points to be made about the unanimity rule and efficiency, both based on the fact that unanimity leads to strategic behavior. One consequence of a unanimity rule is that an individual may hold out in hopes of forging a better deal. Strategic behavior plagues unanimity and promotes inefficiency. Holding-out wastes real resources. So there is at least one clear and uncontroversial sense in which unanimity may lead to inefficiency. The irony here is that critics of majority rule claim it is inefficient, and it is;[33] but turning to unanimity need not obviate the problem of inefficiency.

The fact that the unanimity rule is subject to stragetic behavior implies a much deeper objection to it. Either the unanimity rule fails to secure efficiency or it is otiose; it is either unnecessary or ineffective. The argument is this. Where unanimity leads to efficiency, as in the idealized Wicksell-Lindahl scheme, it does so because individuals willingly *reveal* their preferences for public goods at various tax levels. Where it fails, it does so because individuals withhold pertinent information. But notice that the unanimity rule in the Wicksell-Lindahl context succeeds under precisely those conditions necessary for the optimal private provision of the public good. On the other hand, the unanimity rule approach fails precisely where, and for the same reasons, the private market fails in the provision of public goods.[34] The unanimity schemes have the same incentives that create private market failures, i.e., strategic manipulation. On the other hand, a unanimity rule works when individuals do not act strategically – when instead they reveal their true preferences for public goods. But under those conditions, a unanimity rule of collective choice may be otiose since the market itself can secure an efficient allocation of public goods. In short, it appears that no unanimity rule can rest on what seems its most promising foundation: its alleged connection to efficiency, or its capacity to overcome market failure.

---

[33] The inefficiency of majority rule is neatly discussed in Mueller, *Public Choice*, esp. pp. 31–47.
[34] I have a conjecture that I argue for in *The Market Paradigm*, and it is a follows: All institutional mechanisms for solving the public goods problems – from Lindahl-Wicksell taxes to Groves-Ledyard incentive-compatible mechanisms – are subject to problems precisely analogous to those that arise in the private provision of public goods. Therefore, they also tend to solve the public goods problem under the same conditions the private market does, i.e., iteration or honest preference revelation.

c. *The Argument from Liberty of Exchange*
The unanimity rule replicates the exchange aspect of the competitive market in two ways. First, in a competitive market, exchange is voluntary. No one is required to exchange unless he chooses to do so. Let's refer to this property of markets as "liberty of exchange." The unanimity rule of collective choice is liberty of exchange *writ large*. Just as in the market no one is compelled to exchange, the unanimity rule of collective choice guarantees that no person is required to commit his resources to public measures he disapproves of.

There are at least two arguments for liberty of exchange and, therefore, at least two arguments for the unanimity rule of collective choice that embodies it. The first argument appeals to its "prospective" value; the second to its "retrospective" value. In markets, rational exchanges are made only if they are mutually advantageous, that is, Pareto-superior. Only unanimity guarantees that no person is made worse off by collective policy. Unanimity duplicates the *Pareto-superiority* aspect of market exchange. Liberty of exchange guarantees Pareto-superiority. Unanimity does so as well – and for the same reasons.

There is a difference, however, between liberty of exchange and Pareto-superiority that surfaces both in market exchange and in the unanimity rule of collective choice. The former is connected to the idea of autonomy; the latter to welfare, well-being or utility. It may be irrational to agree to be made worse off, but it is not logically incoherent to do so. Because markets embody liberty of exchange, they may pave the way for Pareto-improvements; Pareto-superiority, however, is not a logical consequence of the liberty of exchange component of markets. Pareto-superiority follows from the conjunction of liberty of exchange and the assumption of rational self-interestedness, not from the former alone. The same applies to the unanimity rule. Unanimous agreement entails neither Pareto-optimality nor Pareto-superiority. This is the point I made above, and it is made by others as well.

One might respond to this objection as follows: in the same sense in which market behavior *reveals* one's preferences for commodities, voting reveals one's preferences for outcomes. Consequently, if exchange is efficient because it is preference maximizing, so should be unanimity. Unanimous agreement in the voting context is Pareto-improving.

The problem here is that, under conditions of perfect competition, market behavior is a *reliable* index of preference, voting behavior is not. The reason is that, under conditions of perfect competition, there is little, if any, room for strategic behavior. In the voting context – especially under a unanimity rule – opportunities for strategic behavior are manifest. There is just too much room between a person's vote and his honest preference for outcomes in the voting context to infer either Pareto-superiority or Pareto-optimality from any voting rule – even unanimity (and even assuming rational self-interestedness).[35]

In free markets, no individual is required to give up that to which he already has a legitimate claim. The unanimity rule provides each person with a veto over any policy that imposes net costs on him or anyone else. This feature of the unanimity rule is usually discussed favorably, in the context of bargaining over the terms of the *constitutional contract* specifying the conditions of the move from anarchy to polity.

Individuals come to the *constitutional contract* (or in my terms, to the bargain to solve the problem of pre-market market failure) with a set of holdings. In terms of the extended Nashian bargaining model, these pre-constitutional holdings constitute the threat advantage of each individual. The point of negotiations is to settle on the division of the gains made possible by cooperation. It takes place, in a Nash model, within the context of threat values secured noncooperatively. In any case, at the constitutional level no one is required to remit any of his or her pre-constitutional holdings. To say, however, that pre-constitutional entitlements are not up for grabs is not to say that those assets are frozen. Individuals may exchange what they have acquired pre-constitutionally. The key here is that any redistribution must be agreed to by those affected by it. In effect, each person has a veto over the transfer of his pre-constitutional entitlements. No one can obtain them other than by consent.

The liberty of exchange model suggests a way of securing pre-constitutional holdings against public measures that would encroach upon them, namely by constitutionally providing that in order to be adopted, policy measures must be unanimously agreed upon. While there is no way of separating (at the constitutional level) once and for all time objects in the domain of collective policy from those outside the domain, there exists in the unanimity rule a guardian of pre-constitutional holdings. Policy that encroaches on someone's pre-constitutional holdings (that fails, at least in that person's eyes, to confer sufficient offsetting benefits) is subject to veto. The unanimity rule is insurance that, once set, the domain of collective policy is properly maintained. This is the second way in which liberty of exchange, both in the market and in the unanimity rule of collective choice, is thought to be morally desirable. Liberty of exchange has the alleged

[35] Because of the incentives for strategic behavior in the collective choice and cooperative contexts, economists have been driven to develop demand-revealing mechanisms that seek to solve the problem of demand revelation noncooperatively. An example of a noncooperative, demand-revelation mechanism is the second-bid auction. In a second-bid auction, the high bidder wins but he pays a price determined by the second highest bid. Therefore, he has no incentive to behave strategically. His best strategy is to reveal his true preference.

prospective virtue of insuring that exchange and the adoption of public policy based on exchange, i.e., unanimity, will be Pareto-improving; it also has the *retrospective* virtue of securing a distribution of holdings against forced transfers. But is this really a virtue of the unanimity rule and of liberty of exchange generally?

One objection to this line of argument is that unanimity may freeze, or at least entrench, what is in fact a very unjust distribution of pre-constitutional holdings.[36] In the thick version of market contractarianism, the allocation of initial property rights is the subject of a pre-constitutional contract necessary in order to solve the collective action problem of pre-market market failure. In the thick theory, the initial assignment of rights is itself the outcome of rational bargaining. It will not follow, however, even on the thick theory, that the alloction of property rights, and of the gains from trade made possible by them, is morally unassailable. That is because the allocation is the outcome of rational bargaining, and the rational distribution of resources that results from a bargain need not be a moral one.[37] So not even the thick theory of market contractarianism can insure that the application of the unanimity rule at the stage of collective action will lead to a just pattern of holdings. On the other hand, it does not follow that unanimity will entrench injustice. Since everything depends on the justice or injustice of pre-constitutional holdings, we might remain agnostic about whether the conservative features of unanimity are a good or bad thing. What we can say with confidence may simply not be helpful, and that is: if forced redistribution through public measures is desirable, then we are unlikely to achieve it under unanimity; whereas, if the existing patterns of distribution are desirable, then unanimity is a good device for protecting the patterns of distribution from distortion through the implementation of publicly-financed projects. This, of course, is a much weaker claim on behalf of unanimity than its defenders – who imbue the status quo with objective value[38] – have been prepared to advance.

The first argument for the liberty of exchange feature of unanimity seeks to connect free exchange to Pareto-superiority; the second seeks to connect it to the protection of a system of holdings. Both arguments are inconclusive.

---

[36] The problem is that the unanimity rule gives a special standing to the status quo. To see this, consider two allocations, R_1 and R_2. First, let R_1 be the status quo. Then, unless everyone agrees to R_2, R_1 obtains. Suppose, however, we treat R_2 as the status quo. Now unless everyone agrees to R_1, R_2 obtains. If R_1 is in fact the status quo, it obtains if not everyone agrees to R_2, even though, from another perspective – the vantage point of persons at $R_2 - R_1$ is not itself efficient. The only justification for giving R_1 a privileged status is the belief that it somehow emerged from a series of Pareto-improvements. In general we see no reason to hold such a belief.

[37] This is just the question of whether rational bargaining also provides a theory of "moral bargaining": whether, in my terms, market contractarianism can also yield a version of "moral contractarianism." I take this issue up in the final section of *The Market Paradigm*.

[38] Buchanan, *Limits of Liberty*, pp. 78, 82–83.

The first because free exchange is not necessarily Pareto-improving. The second because existing patterns of holdings are not necessarily worth protecting.

d. *Unanimity, Externalities and Moral Skepticism*

I want to close by considering an argument for the unanimity rule that is suggested both by liberty of exchange and by moral skepticism. The argument is as follows: suppose that collective choices are made by a rule requiring less than unanimous agreement, for example, simple majority. If politics is, as Thurow claims, a pure redistribution game, then majority voting would consist entirely in transferring wealth from the minority to the majority. It would also very likely turn out that social choices would cycle as everyone offered up splits of the social pie in efforts to become a member of the wealth-sharing majority.[39] In the redistributive game, it is very clear that anything less than unanimity would impose costs on members of the minority: costs that members of the minority had not in any obvious sense agreed to have imposed upon them. (Of course, in a pure redistribution game, a unanimity rule might have the undesirable property of freezing the status quo.) We can capture this aspect of voting rules that require less than unanimous agreement by saying that they impose "voting externalities." The claim that `ple majority rule, for example, imposes externalities is really just the claim that a policy adopted by some is coercively enforceable against all, including those who do not favor it. At some level this is just the claim that the minority is required to act for the collective good and against what they perceive to be their own interest. Without some further justification, this may be simply unjustified coercion. Externalities in this sense occur under any voting rule that requires less than unanimity. Externalities are coercive. Coercion is *prima facie* wrong, and wrong full stop unless an overriding justification for it can be found.

One kind of justification for imposing coercive externalities might be that the majority is simply *right* about what ought to be done on a given collective matter. If it is, or if majorities tend to be right, then imposing coercive externalities on minorities is justified.[40] Defenders of the unanimity rule might agree. Indeed, they might agree that moral knowledge about what is right is all that could ever justify imposing voting externalities. Unfortu-

---

[39] Consider a simple illustration of cycling, when a rule of simple majority is used for redistributive purposes only. Suppose A, B, and C are to split $10,000 among them. A and B form a winning coalition to omit C and split the $10,000 as follows: $7,000 to A (it was his idea), $3,000 to B. Now C offers B a different split, say, 6,000 to C, 4,000 to B. B accepts, and B and C are a winning coalition. Now A is left out, so he offers B or C a split favorable to either, and so it goes.

[40] See M. de Condorcet, *Essai sur l'Application de L'Analyse à la Probabilite des Decisions Rendues à la Pluraliste de Voix* (Paris: 1785).

nately, or so they often argue, this sort of argument does not work because objective moral knowledge is not attainable. Indeed, most defenders of unanimity, like Buchanan, are moral skeptics. Without moral knowledge, the best one can do is secure consensus. Consensus or unanimity is as close as we can come to objective moral truth – it may even be all that we mean by truth. Moreover, consensus precludes the imposition of nonconsensual external costs.

There is a good deal in this argument that is problematic. I want to consider three problems with it. First, it is questionable whether being on the losing side in a vote is equivalent to having an externality imposed upon one. This is plausible only if we assume that individuals always vote their *interests* rather than their *judgment* about what the correct public decision ought to be. Only if votes are expressions of preferences can it be even minimally plausible that a policy adopted contrary to a person's vote imposes external costs upon him.[41] Second, this argument from unanimity assumes that the only grounds for justifiably imposing externalities are either the consent of the party who suffers the externality, or the moral rightness of the policy in question. Since advocates of the argument we are considering deny the possibility of objective moral knowledge, the only option is consent. But consent as a condition for justifiably imposing external costs is equivalent to unanimity. Indeed, there is a sense in which consent does not justify imposing externalities, but logically precludes them. If I consent to having the costs put on me, then in making that decision I take into account the effects of those costs on me; I internalize the costs.

Though wholesale moral skepticism might lend itself to a unanimity rule, unanimity cannot rest comfortably on general moral skepticism. For if skepticism about moral truth is in fact correct, then the advocate of the unanimity rule who claims that it is wrong to impose external costs on others without justification is advancing a self-defeating argument. If we cannot know what is morally true, then we cannot know that it is wrong without justification to impose voting or other externalities.

But it need not be wrong to impose voting externalities, for several reasons. It is a mistake to believe that voting externalities can be justified if and only if adopting the policies that impose them can be shown to be morally right. First of all, voting externalities may be defensible provided that the collective decision-making procedures are themselves "fair." Fair procedures are compatible with mistaken results. Hence a fair procedure may justify the adoption of the policy and the subsequent imposition of

---

[41] Michael Trebilcock has pointed out to me that this objection may not be a fair one in the context of developing a market theory of collective choice in which we assume individuals act to advance the satisfaction of their interests.

voting externalities. Second, an unfair decision-making procedure may invalidate even a correct decision. However we conceive of this argument for the unanimity rule – as rooted in moral skepticism or in a theory about the conditions under which voting externalities can be legitimately imposed – it falls far short of the defense of unanimity we seek.[42]

Philosophy, University of Arizona

[42] See J. L. Coleman, "The Unsteady Foundations of Liberal Democracy" (unpublished manuscript).

RULE UTILITARIANISM, EQUALITY, AND JUSTICE

John C. Harsanyi

Utilitarianism and the Concept of Social Utility

In this paper I propose to discuss the concepts of *equality* and *justice* from a
rule utilitarian point of view, after some comments on the rule utilitarian
point of view itself.[1]

Let me start with the standard definitions. *Act utilitarianism* is the theory
that a morally right action is one that in the existing situation will produce
the highest expected social utility. (I am using the adjective "expected"
in the sense of mathematical expectation.) In contrast, *rule utilitarianism*
is the theory that a morally right action is simply an action conforming
to the correct moral rule applicable to the existing situation. The correct
moral rule itself is that particular behavioral rule that would yield the
highest expected social utility if it were followed by all morally motivated
people in all similar situations.

It is clear from these definitions that utilitarianism, in either version of it,
is a very simple theory because it tries to derive all moral values from one
basic principle, that of social utility. Yet, the history of utilitarian theory
shows that interpretation of this principle gives rise to some far-from-simple
conceptual problems – and also to many disagreements among utilitarians.
But this is really not surprising. Moral problems are notoriously complex and
difficult; and any philosophic theory that makes a serious attempt to come to
grips with them cannot fail to reflect these complexities.

More specifically, interpretation of the principle of social utility poses
problems of three different sorts. First, it poses some technical problems
about how to define social utility and, more fundamentally, how to define
individual utilities. Second, it poses some specifically moral problems about
the definition of social utility. Finally, it poses the problem of how to apply
the principle of social utility and, in particular, whether its application should
follow the act utilitarian or the rule utilitarian approach.[2]

[1] The author wants to thank the National Science Foundation for supporting this research
through grant SES77–06394–A02, administered by the Center for Research in Management,
University of California, Berkeley.
[2] Any moral decision, under either version of utilitarianism, is a *constrained maximization*
problem, with social utility as the maximizand. But the actual constraints of maximization are
different under the two versions of utilitarianism. An act utilitarian must try to maximize

Under the first heading, we have to decide whether individual utilities are cardinal and interpersonally comparable quantities so as to make their sum and/or their arithmetic mean mathematically well-defined. We have also to decide whether to define a person's utility function in terms of his preferences, or of his feelings of pleasure and pain, or of his mental states of "intrinsic worth,"[3] or any other criteria. All of these are technical problems which raise no difficult moral issues.[4]

More difficult are the specifically moral problems posed by the concept of social utility. For example, how much weight should we give to people's patently irrational and/or antisocial preferences? Indeed, how much weight should we give to their socially very desirable altruistic preferences? (If we assign positive weight to people's preferences for *other* people's welfare, then we give unfair advantage to individuals with many friends and relatives, who wish them well, over individuals who lack such support.) How much weight should we give to the preferences of people unable to find out whether their preferences have been met or not – such as dead people or, in general, people who cannot monitor the situation, for whatever reason? Is it ever morally permissible to do what we like to do, even if our action does not yield the highest possible social utility?

Notice that these moral problems are important, not only for utilitarian theory, but also for any other moral theory – even though utilitarian theory does bring them more clearly out into the open, simply because it operates at a higher level of analytical precision than most nonutilitarian theories do. Of course, it is all to the good that utilitarianism forces us to face up to these problems: we learn a lot about the nature of morality by trying to answer them.

Rule Utilitarianism vs Act Utilitarianism

Even though all of these are important problems, in my opinion the most important internal problem for utilitarian theory is the choice between act utilitarianism and rule utilitarianism. No doubt, act utilitarianism is the

---

social utility under the assumption that the strategies of all *other* utilitarians are simply *given*, independent of his own strategy. In contrast, a rule utilitarian must try to maximize social utility under the assumption that *all* utilitarians will always use the *same* strategy. See J. C. Harsanyi, "Rule Utilitarianism and Decision Theories," *Erkenntnis* 11 (1977), pp. 44–48. As a result, the alternatives will also be different under the two utilitarian theories. Under act utilitarianism, they will be alternative individual acts. Under rule utilitarianism, they will be alternative moral rules; in fact, as closer analysis would show, they are alternative comprehensive moral codes.

[3] G. E. Moore, *Principia Ethica* (London: Cambridge University Press, 1903), p. 17.

[4] For a discussion of these problems, see my *Rational Behavior and Bargaining Equilibrium in Games and Social Situations* (Cambridge: Cambridge University Press, 1977), Chapter 4; and "Rule Utilitarianism and Decision Theory," pp. 27–30.

simpler one of the two versions of utilitarianism. But rule utilitarianism seems to be closer to common sense morality and to our basic moral intuitions. Moreover, much more importantly, I will try to show that by following the rule utilitarian moral code, society will achieve a much higher level of social utility than it could achieve by following the act utilitarian approach.

To be sure, act utilitarianism has no difficulty in dealing with the moral problem of benevolence. Surely, it is obvious enough that we can increase social utility by helping other people or at least by not causing them needless harm. Yet, it seems to me that act utilitarianism cannot deal adequately with the moral problem of *justice* and with many related issues because it cannot deal adequately with the problems of moral *rights* and of moral *obligations*. For instance, suppose the government wants to take away my home in order to build a freeway through my property. Is this a morally justified action? (Note that I am not asking here about the constitutionality or the legality of such an action. I am asking about its *morality*.)

According to act utilitarianism, it is morally justified if it creates more utility than disutility. The government's action will create positive utility for the prospective users of the freeway, and for the workers and their employers who will build it. It will create a negative utility for me and my family, who will lose our home, and for the taxpayers who will have to pay for the new freeway, etc. According to act utilitarian theory, taking away my home is justified if the benefits accruing to the first group will exceed, *however slightly*, the sacrifices imposed on the second group.

Yet, this conclusion is clearly inconsistent with common sense morality, according to which the government's action violates my individual rights, and more specifically, violates my property rights to my home. (It also violates my personal freedom to live my private life without government interference.) Therefore, even if the government offered me reasonable compensation, expropriation of my home could be justified only if the balance of the resulting total utility over the resulting total disutility were quite substantial. If the government were unable to pay proper compensation, then only extreme social emergencies could possibly justify expropriation.

What position should a utilitarian take on this? Obviously, any moral code protecting individual rights will generate both social benefits and social costs. Therefore, a utilitarian must try to compare the benefits people will obtain on occasions when this moral code protects their individual rights, with the inconvenience they will suffer on occasions when this moral code restricts their freedom of action by protecting other people's rights against them.

I think it is very clear that, by any reasonable standard, the social benefits of such a moral code will greatly outweigh the undeniable social costs. That is to say, most of us will strongly *prefer* to live in a society whose moral code gives clear protection to individual rights, and does not permit violation of these rights, except possibly in some rare and rather special cases. In my opinion, this fact is the basic argument for rule utilitarianism.

The situation is much the same with respect to our moral obligations. According to common sense morality, we have some special obligations resulting from our family roles, our occupations, our friendships, and our other special social relationships. These special obligations will, most of the time, take precedence over other moral obligations. But a consistent act utilitarian must deny this.

For example, suppose I have to decide whether to spend a given amount of money on my own children's education or on supporting some other children in urgent need of financial help. According to common sense morality, I must spend this money on my own children's education – unless denying the money to the second group of children would create very extreme hardship. In contrast, an act utilitarian would have to say that I should give the money to the second group of children if their need for the money were slightly greater, *however slightly greater*, than my own children's needs were – that is, I should give it to this group of children if they could be expected to derive slightly more utility, *however slightly* more utility, than my own children would derive from it.

Once more, a rule utilitarian must, by and large, side with traditional morality. In all known societies, there is a division of labor among adults in looking after the children of the community. This division of labor has considerable social utility because, if all adults had to look after all children, it would be virtually impossible for them to find out the various children's individual needs, and it would be virtually impossible for them to develop close emotional ties with individual children.[5]

The specifics of this division of labor are different in different societies. For example, in some societies, the mother's oldest brother is the principal person in charge of the children. Of course, in our own society looking after children is normally a responsibility of the two parents. But, in any case, the special relationship between a group of children and the relevant adults can be preserved only if this relationship normally takes precedence over most other social obligations. In contrast, if we followed the act utilitarian approach and permitted other – in some sense, perhaps momentarily more urgent – moral obligations to take precedence, this special relationship could not survive.

To put it differently, we must distinguish between local optimality, in the sense of maximizing social utility by each individual action we may take, and

[5] Harsanyi, "Rule Utilitarianism, Rights, Obligations, and the Theory of Rational Behavior," *Theory and Decision* 12 (1980), p. 128.

global optimality, in the sense of maximizing social utility by the moral code we adopt and by the entire system of moral rights and moral obligations this moral code brings into existence. Act utilitarianism focuses on local optimality, whereas rule utilitarianism focuses on global optimality. In some situations, local and global optimality pull in the same direction. But in all situations where they pull in different directions, we have to give preference to global optimality, which means adopting the rule utilitarian approach.

To put it still another way, the main difference between rule utilitarianism and act utilitarianism lies in the fact that the former recognizes, while the latter denies, the logical dependence of justice on the existence of suitable moral rules that define people's moral rights and moral obligations. Unlike some contemporary act utilitarians, John Stuart Mill clearly understood this relationship. After arguing that justice first meant conformity to positive legal rules, he wrote that later

> ... the sentiment of justice became attached, not to all violations of law, but only to violations of such laws as *ought* to exist, including such as ought to exist, but do not.[6]

Mill here obviously refers to moral laws.

Let me illustrate the actual working of the rule utilitarian approach in more specific terms, using the example of promise-keeping. Suppose that A promises B to do X for him but does not deliver on his promise. According to act utilitarianism, this breach of promise will be morally wrong only if it creates more total disutility than total utility. Of course, the main utility created by the broken promise is the utility A derives from not implementing a presumably burdensome obligation. In contrast, the main disutilities created by A's action are:

(1) The disutility to B of losing the promised physical benefit, and the extra disutility to him of having his expectations of obtaining this benefit utterly disappointed.

(2) The disutility to society as a result of decreased public confidence in future promises when people learn about this breach of promise by A.

Note that normally disutility (2) will be negligibly small because one act of promise-breaking is unlikely to have any noticeable effect on public confidence in promises.

Consequently, for an act utilitarian, the basic question is whether A's utility gain by breaking his promise exceeds B's utility loss. If it does,

---

[6] John Stuart Mill, "Utilitarianism," *Utilitarianism, Liberty, and Representative Government,* ed. Ernest Rhys (New York: Everyman's Library, E. P. Dutton and Co., 1926), pp. 43–44, quoted in J. Narveson, *Morality and Utility* (Baltimore: Johns Hopkins University Press, 1967), p. 148.

however slightly, then A's breach of promise is morally justified. In contrast, a rule utilitarian must ask the question, "Which particular moral rule about promise-keeping would yield the highest social utility?" Note that a rule utilitarian must judge the social-utility implications of any proposed moral rule on the assumption that, if this moral rule were adopted, this would automatically become public knowledge.[7] Therefore, in judging any proposed moral rule, he must always ask the question, "What would be the effects on people's expectations, incentives, and behavior, if they knew that this was the moral rule adopted for a given class of situations?"

Consequently, under rule utilitarianism, the moral rule about promise-keeping must be chosen in such a way that it will maximize social utility by striking the right balance between two classes of social interests. On the one hand, there is the interest of the *promisee* in obtaining the promised performance and in avoiding disappointment of his expectations by non-performance. There is also the interest of *society* in maintaining public confidence in promises. If the proposed moral rule permitted too many easy exceptions from promise-keeping, the promisee's interests would receive insufficient protection. Moreover, public confidence in promises would be significantly impaired (because people would know how lax this moral rule about promise-keeping actually was). This would be very undesirable because a good deal of social cooperation crucially depends on the credibility of promises – in fields ranging from commercial credit transactions to private agreements about where and when to meet, etc.

On the other hand, consideration must be given also to the promisor's interest in being morally released from his promise, when fulfilling it would cause him undue hardship. If the moral rule about promise-keeping permitted too few exceptions, the promisor would too often be saddled with excessively burdensome obligations.

Presumably, there will be a moral rule maximizing social utility by permitting just the right set of exceptions from promise-keeping. To be sure, it will often be a matter of difficult personal judgment whether a given situation does or does not represent a permissible exception under the rule utilitarian criterion. As I have argued elsewhere,[8] in practice it is often quite difficult to decide what specific moral rule, with what particular list of exceptive cases would in fact maximize social utility. Hence, the best course of action for a rule utilitarian moral decision maker will often be to defer

---

[7] Presumably, under *any* moral theory, we would have to assume that moral rules will be made publicly known to enable people to comply with them. But under rule utilitarian theory there is an additional reason for assuming that moral rules will be publicly known. For, in principle, every individual can compute what set of moral rules will yield the highest social utility.

[8] J. C. Harsanyi, "Some Epistemological Advantages of the Rule Utilitarian Position in Ethics," *Midwest Studies in Philosophy* 7 (1982), pp. 395–396.

to the social customs existing in his social environment (for example, as to permissible exceptions from promise-keeping) – unless he has strong reasons to believe that such conformity to these social customs would be definitely contrary to social utility.

Yet, even though there may often be practical difficulties in deciding what specific list of permissible exceptions to a given moral rule would in fact maximize social utility, I think it is very important from a philosophic standpoint that rule utilitarianism does provide at least a conceptually clear theoretical criterion for the set of morally permissible exceptions.

Let me draw three general philosophic conclusions from this discussion. First, in many cases rule utilitarianism and act utilitarianism will yield very different practical moral implications. In particular, as we have seen, rule utilitarianism will protect people's moral rights and their special moral obligations in a much wider range of cases, and will permit their infringement in many fewer exceptional situations, than act utilitarianism will. By the same token, rule utilitarianism will permit many fewer exceptions to the moral obligation of keeping our promises – or to that of gratitude to a benefactor, or to that of telling the truth, etc. – than act utilitarianism will. This should finally put to rest the surprising claim, sometimes made even by very distinguished moral philosophers,[9] that rule utilitarianism and act utilitarianism are equivalent as to their practical moral implications.

Second, it is *not* true, as some act utilitarian philosophers have claimed,[10] that rule utilitarianism amounts to "rule worship," in the sense of irrationally requiring observance of a moral rule even in cases where deviating from this rule would yield higher social utility. (At least, this is certainly not true about the version of rule utilitarianism that I am defending.) To the contrary, as we have seen, rule utilitarianism requires us to choose that particular set of permissible exceptions to any given moral rule that will maximize social utility. The only important moral philosopher who can be justly accused of "rule worship" is Kant, who denied that there were *any* morally justified exceptions to our basic moral rules.

Finally, society will reach a much higher level of social utility by following the rule utilitarian moral code than it would reach by following the act utilitarian approach. As we have seen, this is so because it will be much better to live in a society in which all people, or at least all morally motivated members of society, respect other people's individual rights and their own

---

[9] See Richard B. Brandt, "Toward a Credible Form of Utilitarianism," *Morality and the Language of Conduct*, H. N. Castañeda and G. Nakhnikian, eds. (Detroit: Wayne University Press, 1963), pp. 120–123; D. Lyons, *The Forms and Limits of Utilitarianism* (London: Oxford University Press, 1965), *passim*; R. M. Hare, *Freedom and Reason* (Oxford: Oxford University Press, 1963), pp. 130–136.
[10] J. J. C. Smart, "An Outline of Utilitarian Ethics," *Utilitarianism, For and Against* (London: Cambridge University Press, 1973), p. 10.

institutional obligations, keep their promises, tell the truth on important matters, etc. (unless they have exceptionally important reasons not to do so). Such a society would be preferable to an act utilitarian society where people will disregard other people's rights and their own moral obligations whenever this is likely to yield slightly greater total utility than total disutility.

To put it differently, rule utilitarianism places itself on the high middle ground between act utilitarianism and various deontological theories. Like the latter, it takes the view that we cannot define a morally right action merely in terms of social expediency, which, by itself, would necessarily lead to a super-Machiavellian morality. Rather, the pursuit of social expediency must always be constrained by the deontological requirements of morality, such as observance of rationally chosen moral rules, and respect for a rational system of moral rights and moral obligations. On the other hand, rule utilitarianism agrees with act utilitarianism, that ultimately the rational justification of these moral rules, moral rights, and moral obligations must lie in their undeniable social utility.

In fact, rule utilitarianism is the *only* moral theory that can provide a rational explanation and justification for these deontological components of morality. Act utilitarianism cannot do so because the limitations of its conceptual framework prevent it from recognizing these deontological concepts as relatively autonomous elements of morality. On the other hand, deontological theories, of course, fully recognize their importance, but cannot provide any rational justification for them. For example, Prichard and Ross based their theories on the concept of moral duty but they could not explain where these moral duties are supposed to come from and why a rational person should care to discharge them. Likewise, Nozick built his theory on the concept of "entitlements," but never explained their logical basis and their morally binding force.[11]

Finally, contractarians like Locke, Rousseau, and Rawls tried to explain our moral and legal rules in terms of a hypothetical prehistoric social contract. But this social contract is obviously pure fiction and, therefore, cannot possibly explain real-life moral obligations. Indeed, even if this social contract had been a real contract concluded by our very remote ancestors many thousand years ago, it could hardly be morally binding, now, on the present members of our society.

But the decisive objection to this social-contract theory is that it is irredeemably circular. The hypothetical social contract, like *any* contract, would derive all of its moral binding force from the moral rule that contracts should be kept. Therefore, we cannot without circularity claim that this

[11] H. A. Prichard, *Moral Obligation* (Oxford: Oxford University Press, 1968); W. D. Ross, *Foundations of Ethics* (Oxford: Clarendon Press, 1939); R. Nozick, *Anarchy, State, and Utopia* (New York: Basic Books, 1974).

moral rule itself, and all other moral rules, owe their moral justification to this social contract in the first place.

Moral Values vs Other Human Values

Kant took the view that morality is the highest value of human life. A consistent utilitarian cannot share this view.[12]

The basic task of morality is to induce people to help other people in achieving their own objectives, which are in most cases *nonmoral* objectives, such as economic well-being, a good social position, health, friendship, love, knowledge, artistic experiences, etc.

Thus, in an important sense, morality is primarily a servant of many other human values, rather than itself the highest value. Moreover, even though no person can have a rich and well-balanced life without strong moral commitments, these moral commitments are less likely to occupy the center of the stage for him than are his work, his family and friends, and his intellectual, cultural, social, and political interests.

Of course, our moral duties must always take precedence over any other considerations. But this is true only in the trivial sense that we would not call anything our moral duty simpliciter had we not already decided that it has an overriding moral claim upon us. In contrast, our prima facie moral duties do not always take precedence over our nonmoral interests.

For example, if I make a promise, I will obviously have a prima facie moral duty to keep it. Yet, if breaking my promise would not cause any serious harm to the promisee, but keeping my promise would cause me a very substantial financial loss that I could not have foreseen when I made the promise, then it might be morally permissible for me to break my promise. This means that I might be morally free to give precedence to my financial interests over a prima facie moral obligation.

Likewise, a utilitarian cannot regard very high degrees of moral devotion always as unmixed blessings. Even less can he so regard high degrees of morally motivated devotion to idealistic political objectives.

Great devotion to one's moral values requires a willingness to make great sacrifices for them. Yet, as experience shows, people who are willing to make great sacrifices for their moral values are often equally willing to sacrifice other people to them. The unfortunate fact is that great devotion to high moral and political ideals may not be very far away from socially disastrous moral and political fanaticism. Robespierre was no doubt a man devoted to the highest moral principles.

---

[12] My argument in this section has greatly benefited from Professor Narveson's discussion of these topics (J. Narveson, *Morality and Utility*, pp. 34–37). But he may not agree with all that I will say.

Utilitarianism and Equality

As has often been pointed out, there are many different types of equality and of inequality. I will discuss only two: *equal consideration* for the interests of different individuals, and equality of social benefits for different individuals in terms of income, wealth, status, power, etc., which can also be described as *economic and social equality*.

The principle of equal consideration is a rather undemanding principle. All it requires is that, in dealing with different people, we should not provide rationally unjustifiable favorable treatment or unfavorable treatment for any one of them. This principle has a fundamental role in any version of utilitarian theory because it enters into the very definition of social utility: whether we define social utility as the *sum* or as the *arithmetic mean* of individual utilities, we must give equal weight to all individuals' utilities.

The principle of equal consideration is a direct corollary of one of the most basic general principles of rationality, viz., the principle of sufficient reason. Therefore, we may be tempted to conclude that the principle of equal consideration is morally binding on all human action. I do not think this is the case. For in some decisions we may have virtually unlimited moral discretion, and may be under no moral obligation to follow any objective criteria at all.

For example, it seems to me that if I pay my secretary out of my own private funds, and need a new secretary, I will be morally free to follow my own preferences in choosing among alternative candidates for the job. I will have no real moral obligation to give all candidates "equal consideration," or to use any specific criteria in order to select the "most deserving" candidate – though, of course, it will be morally praiseworthy if I do so.

In contrast, if I am acting as a public official, or even as an official of a large, or at least a moderately large, social organization, I will be morally obliged to make any major decision on general and rationally defensible criteria (even if I am under no *legal* obligation to do so). This is so because such officials are, in an important sense, agents of society as a whole and ought to follow the standards of fairness and of rationality of society in all major decisions, even in situations where a private citizen would not be positively required to do so.

I now propose to discuss *economic and social equality*. It seems to me that, for a consistent utilitarian, economic and social equality is *not* an intrinsic moral value. To be sure, other things being equal, a more equal distribution of economic and noneconomic benefits is always preferable to a less equal distribution. But the main reason for this lies in the law of diminishing marginal utility of money and of most other good things in life. Thus, greater economic equality is morally desirable mainly because a poor man, who is likely to spend any extra money on important necessities, is also likely to derive a much higher utility from an extra $100 than will a rich man, who is likely to spend any extra money on relatively unimportant luxuries.

For this reason, a utilitarian will favor government policies for a moderate redistribution of income and wealth. But he will have to counsel moderation, because society has a vital interest in maintaining people's incentives for hard work, for enterprise, and for developing their talents. Some redistributive policies may increase poor people's incomes by a few percentage points but may decrease the rate of growth in national income, possibly making these poor people actually much worse off a few years later than they would have been in the absence of these policies.

On the other hand, there are strong utilitarian reasons for opposing both extreme poverty and extreme wealth, especially extreme levels of inherited wealth. Extreme poverty not only causes physical hardships, but also tends to paralyze the intellectual and cultural life of its victims, and tends to poison their moral attitudes. Surprisingly enough, the intellectual, cultural, and moral effects of extreme wealth, especially of very great inherited wealth, are often much the same. In many societies, children of very rich families are seldom conspicuous by their intellectual, cultural, and moral accomplishments, nor by their ability to lead a happy and well-balanced life. Moreover, extremes of poverty and of wealth also tend to hinder proper operation of our democratic political institutions.

No doubt, many moral philosophers take issue with the utilitarian view that economic and social equality is not an intrinsic moral value. But if these philosophers were right, this would mean that, in a distribution of social benefits, a poor person (or an otherwise disadvantaged person) should be given priority over a rich person (or an otherwise more fortunate person) even if, for a given benefit, the former is not expected to derive a higher utility than the latter is. For easier reference, I will describe the moral value judgment contained in this last sentence as *statement A.*

I now propose to show in two examples that statement A would be an utterly unacceptable moral value judgment. I will need examples involving noneconomic benefits because, in a distribution of economic benefits, owing to the law of diminishing marginal utility, a poor person will almost always derive a higher utility from any given benefit.

Consider a distribution of a scarce lifesaving drug, or a distribution of scarce university admissions, when the available supply of either falls very much short of existing demand. Suppose that, in the case of the drug, we have to choose between a rich patient and a poor patient, both of whom badly need this drug. Suppose, also, that the rich patient is definitely expected to benefit more from the drug. Or suppose that, in the university admissions example, we have to choose between a rich candidate and a poor candidate, both of whom have the qualifications required for admission. Suppose, also, that the rich candidate is clearly better qualified and can derive a greater benefit from university education.

Then, statement A would imply that we should give the lifesaving drug or the university admission to the poorer person, even though the richer person would derive a greater benefit from it – except, perhaps, if this richer person would derive a *very much* greater benefit from the lifesaving drug or from the university admission. Yet, even if the richer person is expected to derive only a moderately greater benefit from the drug or from the university admission, he will have a stronger moral claim to it. It would be morally unjustifiable discrimination against him if he were denied the drug or the university admission merely because he happens to be rich.

Thus, I conclude that statement A is a completely unacceptable moral value judgment. Utilitarian theory is right to take the view that economic and social inequality is not an intrinsic moral value, and that it is morally wrong to discriminate against a rich or an otherwise fortunate person in order to reduce the difference between him and the poorer or otherwise less fortunate members of society.[13]

Utilitarianism and Justice

As I have argued earlier, society has a very important interest in having its members respect each other's basic rights and institutional obligations – in other words, in having its members observe the basic standards of justice.

Yet, this coin also has another side. Preoccupation with minor violations of our rights, real or apparent, and the widespread passion for litigation so prevalent now in the United States, are highly counterproductive social practices. Indeed, not only is it often socially preferable if people put up with minor injustices, instead of engaging in endless litigation, it is often socially *desirable* to have social institutions whose very success depends on having some "unfair" practices built into them.

For instance, the effectiveness of the free enterprise system (and even that of a socialist system) crucially depends on the fact that a successful business executive will be promoted and an unsuccessful one demoted. Yet, this is often "unfair," because this success or failure may be unrelated to the business executive's own effort and ability, and may be a matter of sheer luck. Likewise, in many parliamentary systems, a cabinet minister must take political responsibility for his subordinates' mistakes, regardless of whether he is really responsible for them by common sense criteria or not.

---

[13] Of course, there is a very strong case for remedial actions in favor of social groups unjustly treated in the past. But it is a more difficult question how far we may go in discriminating against people not belonging to these social groups, if these people have no personal responsibility for the unjust policies of the past.

In both cases, of course, it would be possible to promote or to demote the individual in question only after an inquiry determined how much responsibility he really had for the outcome. But such inquiries are costly, time consuming, and often quite inconclusive. Thus, there are good arguments for acting without any such prior inquiry.

More fundamentally, it is possible to argue that it is "unfair" to reward a person's superior performance by higher pay, higher prestige, and higher social status, if this performance is largely a result of his outstanding ability, rather than of his greater effort, or of his higher moral standards. But a utilitarian must fully support rewards based on performance because the alternative would destroy the incentives for gifted people to fully develop and use their talents to the benefit of society, and would encourage philistinism and hostility to excellence.

Again, it is hard to deny that proportional representation is the "fairest" electoral system, and the only one really "fair" to small parties. But this is not necessarily a convincing argument for proportional representation. From a utilitarian point of view, a question much more important than such "fairness" considerations is, "which particular electoral system is more likely to yield a stable and effective government, one able to take unpopular measures when they are called for on economic issues, on minority rights, on foreign policy and defense, etc.?" On this score, it seems to me that two-party systems, with the two parties from time to time alternating in government, have been in most cases far superior.

Conclusion

I have discussed the nature, and some of the internal problems, of the utilitarian point of view. In comparing act utilitarianism with rule utilitarianism, I have come down in favor of the latter, primarily on the ground that rule utilitarianism will yield a higher level of social utility because it requires wider respect for other people's rights and for our own special obligations. I have argued that, for a utilitarian, moral values will not be always the highest values of human life, and sometimes will have to yield precedence to other social values. I have also argued that, even though equality and justice (including fairness) are of fundamental importance from a utilitarian point of view, they cannot always be the decisive considerations for framing social policies.

School of Business Administration, University of California, Berkeley.

MORALITY, REASON, AND MANAGEMENT SCIENCE: THE RATIONALE OF COST-BENEFIT ANALYSIS

David Copp

The Problem

Economic efficiency is naturally thought to be a virtue of social policies and decisions, and cost-benefit (CB) analysis is commonly regarded as a technique for measuring economic efficiency. It is not surprising, then, that CB analysis is so widely used in social policy analysis. However, there is a great deal of controversy about CB analysis, including controversy about its underlying philosophical rationale. The rationales that have been proposed fall into three basic, though not mutually exclusive categories. There are *moralist* views to the effect that an acceptable CB analysis would provide, or contribute to, an *ethical* appraisal of proposed policies or projects. There are *rationalist* views to the effect that an acceptable CB analysis would contribute to the selection of social policies and projects that are "socially rational." Finally, there are so-called *management science* views to the effect that the purpose of CB analysis is to promote the achievement of objectives held by the policy maker, whatever they may be. Different positions are available within each of these categories. But there is also the possibility that CB analysis lacks *any* viable rationale. I will examine some of the major rationales for CB analysis in this paper, and I will suggest that the last view is close to the truth.

Given the disagreement about the rationale of CB analysis, and given the accompanying disagreements about its criteria and techniques, it is misleading simply to describe CB analysis as *a* technique for measuring *economic efficiency*. As things now stand, CB analysis is a *family* of techniques and approaches. Different theorists considering a social decision problem might take account of different sets of costs and benefits, might differ in their assignment of values to given costs or benefits, might discount future costs and benefits differently, and might weight and aggregate them differently. These differences might merely involve technical matters within the framework of an agreed-upon procedure. But they might also reflect differences of opinion regarding the objective of CB analysis itself, e.g., whether maximizing *economic efficiency* is the proper objective. In fact, many issues that appear to be simply technical ones turn on basic theoretical questions about the rationale. E. J. Mishan has pointed this out in connection with the dispute over how to value loss of life in a CB analysis. He suggests that the resolution of the dispute turns on "the basic rationale of the economic calculus used in cost-benefit analysis".[1] I suggest that this is true of a wide range of disputes in CB analysis.

The controversy about the rationale of cost-benefit analysis occurs in a political as well as in a technical context. There are economic concepts, criteria, and techniques that have been used for fifty years to assess the economic feasibility of projects such as airports and hydroelectric developments. Some economists think that these concepts and techniques are capable of more ambitious use, but other economists and many citizens question even in their current application. Much of the controversy is political, and it arises because people now see environmental, ethical, and aesthetic issues where before they saw mainly economic ones. This new set of concerns compromises the ability of CB analysis to resolve issues that used to be thought easily within its purview. So it might be argued that CB analysis has, at best, a minor role to play when issues other than efficiency arise, in other words, that it must retain normative neutrality. But an ambitious moralist view would suggest, to the contrary, that CB analysis ought to contribute to the resolution of moral disputes.[2] It is in this context that we find the debate about the underlying rationale of CB analysis.

Although CB analysis is a family of analytic techniques and approaches, there are at least two features that would be possessed by anything that we would describe in this study as a procedure of CB analysis.[3] CB analysis is a means of evaluating and ranking proposed social policies and projects; and it uses economic techniques to assign quantitative values (usually monetary values) to the different costs and benefits of various options for social choice, and to aggregate these values into a quantitative measure of each of the options. In the case of a properly designed procedure of CB analysis, this measure would genuinely reflect the relative desirability of various social policy options, and it would warrant being a factor, or, perhaps, even *the* factor, in a social decision among them. That is, a decision maker who decided on a matter of social policy while ignoring the results of a properly conducted and adequately designed CB analysis would deserve criticism. The problem we need to address can be characterized simply. *Is there an*

---

[1] E. J. Mishan, *Cost-Benefit Analysis: An Introduction* (New York: Praeger Publishers, 1971), p. 159.
[2] See David Copp and Edwin Levy, "Value Neutrality in the Techniques of Policy Analysis: Risk and Uncertainty," *Journal of Business Administration*, vol. 13 (1982), pp. 161–190.
[3] The notion of a *procedure* of CB analysis is vague, and "procedure" may not be the best word. The idea is that to specify a "procedure" would be to specify a property or properties to be measured by CB analysis, and a set of techniques for measuring that property or those properties.

adequate rationale for any procedure of cost-benefit analysis? This question can be broken down into three major component issues: (1) What property of the various options in a social decision problem is to be measured? (2) Would it be possible to devise a set of CB techniques to measure this property? That is, would it be possible to provide a quantitative measure of the relative degree to which the available options have the property in question, and to do so by aggregating in some way the monetary or other quantitative values assigned by economic techniques to the various costs and benefits of the options? (3) Finally, on what basis, or for what reason, should a decision maker prefer the option possessing the relevant property to the greatest degree? On what basis would the decision maker deserve criticism if some other option were chosen, or if the result of the CB analysis were ignored?

There may be more than one adequate approach; but there may be none. We will begin to deal with the issue by considering some of the answers that economists and philosophers have given to the three central questions. First, however, we need to consider the standard approach to CB analysis.

The Standard Approach, Objections, and Rationales

Despite considerable controversy about the basis of CB analysis, there is a standard view about the associated economic techniques and criteria. All of the costs and benefits of a project, to all of the individual members of the relevant society, are supposed to be taken into account, discounting future costs and benefits, ideally at the rate of time preference of each person concerned.[4] The benefits of a project to an individual are, in principle, to be valued at the maximum amount of money he would be willing to pay in order to have the project go forward. His costs are to be valued at the minimum amount he would be willing to accept as compensation for its having gone forward.[5] This is the concept of a "compensating variation" (CV). Here the notion of "willingness-to-pay" is used as an economic criterion of the magnitude of a cost or benefit, and economic techniques are used to estimate individuals' CVs for each cost and benefit of a project under evaluation. This is the theory, although in practice there often is insufficient data to enable a reasonable estimate of individuals' CVs for certain costs or benefits. Ideally, all costs and benefits are to be assigned a monetary value, positive or negative, and, in the simple case – where there is no uncertainty and where all costs and benefits are expected immediately – their values are added. The result is a measure of the expected net social gain or loss. A project is to be selected only if it is expected to yield a net gain. If a choice must be made

---

[4] See Robert Sugden and Alan Williams, *The Principles of Practical Cost-Benefit Analysis* (Oxford: Oxford University Press, 1978), p. 89; Mishan, *Cost-Benefit Analysis*, p. 159, n. 14.

[5] Mishan, *Cost-Benefit Analysis*, p. 159.

between competing projects, then, in the standard view, the project is to be chosen which will maximize the overall gain.

This "choice rule" is known as the *Hicks-Kaldor test*,[6] or the *potential Pareto-improvement criterion*. A Pareto improvement is an economic rearrangement that makes someone in the society better off without making anyone worse off.[7] A *potential* Pareto-improvement, however, simply creates the theoretical *possibility* of realizing a Pareto-improvement by the costless redistribution of money: an event produces a potential Pareto-improvement if it produces a net gain that *could* be distributed so that some persons in the society would be better off and none would be worse off, the rearrangement being assumed to be costless.[8] This is obviously compatible with some persons actually being made worse off, for it requires only a net gain *overall*. According to standard CB analysis, projects should be undertaken only if they produce potential Pareto-improvements.[9]

This approach to CB analysis seems to be the one most widely accepted by theorists,[10] and the one that is usually employed in practice. For instance, the Canadian Treasury Board paper, *Benefit-Cost Analysis Guide*, accepts the concept of a compensating variation as the appropriate criterion for valuing costs and benefits, and accepts the Hicks-Kaldor decision rule.[11]

There are well known problems with this standard approach. I will not explore these problems in any detail, but it will be helpful to discuss the most significant of them, because assessing these problems brings the issue of the rationale of CB analysis to the fore. Three areas of controversy require attention.

(1) The Range of CB Analysis. *Whose* costs and benefits, and *which* of their costs and benefits, should be taken into account in CB analysis, and with respect to *which* social decision problems. Different answers to these questions distinguish the three basic views about the rationale. If one's fundamental objective is to promote the rationality of social decisions from the point of view of our society, then it is presumably costs and benefits to our society, or to its members, that must be considered. But suppose the issue is the *moral* acceptability of social decisions. Then it is arguable that everyone's costs and benefits must be weighted equally, including members of future generations, and including the costs and benefits that we will receive in the future. From the *moral* point of view, costs are not to be given

---

[6] Christopher Nash, David Pearce, and John Stanley, "An Evaluation of Cost-Benefit Analysis Criteria," *Scottish Journal of Political Economy*, vol. 22 (1975), p. 126.
[7] Mishan, *Cost-Benefit Analysis*, p. 311.
[8] Mishan, *Cost-Benefit Analysis*, pp. 316–317.
[9] Sugden and Williams, *Principles*, p. 90.
[10] Nash, Pearce, and Stanley, "Evaluation," p. 130.
[11] Canada, Treasury Board Secretariat, Planning Branch, *Benefit-Cost Analysis Guide* (Ottawa: 1976), pp. 4, 13, and 31.

less weight simply because they will occur next year. Also, from the moral point of view, everyone's costs and benefits must be considered. Costs or benefits should not be ignored just because they will be incurred by people who are not members of our society. However, it is arguable that *some* costs and benefits *should* be ignored. For instance, Mishan suggests that *envy* is a cost that should be ignored in CB analysis.[12] Similarly, a CB analysis of a proposal to abolish the institution of slavery would presumably ignore certain costs and benefits to the slaveowners. We would hardly find it relevant to a moral appraisal of a proposal to abolish slavery that it would be financially costly to the slaveowners, for we would agree that the slaveowners have no right to the financial benefits they have secured. Clearly, the moralist and rationalist views have different implications for the issue of whose costs and benefits, and which of their costs and benefits, are to be considered in CB analysis.[13]

The management science view would have quite different implications. It would counsel that the costs and benefits of a proposed policy or project are to be identified, valued and weighted relative to the objectives of the decision maker.[14] Hence, it would seem that the costs and benefits of other individuals or groups within or without the society are to be considered if and only if they matter to the *decision maker*. Envy might find entry; the slaves' costs might be ignored; political costs to the government might have pride of place.[15]

Standard CB analysis considers only the costs and benefits of *persons*, that is, of *individual* members of the society concerned. However, a society includes groupings of persons, and an appraisal of the costs and benefits to such groups might sometimes yield results different from a CB analysis that restricted attention to costs and benefits incurred by persons. Philosophers and economists who subscribe to the view sometimes called methodological individualism may think otherwise, but the point is quite innocent, though important. The willingness to pay, or the compensating variation of a group, in relation to a particular group cost or benefit, might, in certain circumstances, differ from the sum of the CVs of its members, in relation to the same cost or benefit.

Consider a proposal to build a pipeline through an Indian reservation. Given their usual poverty and lack of education, individual members of the

---

[12] Mishan, *Cost-Benefit Analysis*, p. 313.

[13] Consider a CB analysis of a proposal to expand an international airport like Heathrow. Are everyone's costs and benefits to be considered, including those of foreign travellers, or just the costs and benefits of British subjects? See Richard Layard, "Introduction," R. Layard, ed. *Cost-Benefit Analysis: Selected Readings* (London: Penguin Books, 1972).

[14] Sugden and Williams, *Principles*, pp. 232–241.

[15] D. W. Pearce and C. A. Nash, *The Social Appraisal of Projects: A Text in Cost-Benefit Analysis* (London: MacMillan Press Ltd., 1981), p. 37.

tribe might be prepared to accept quite small sums of money in compensation for the loss of their share of the land. Even a relatively small amount might be quite important to them, at least in the short run. However, the tribal council could well have a better sense of the worth of the land, and of the need for the pipeline. Consequently, it might refuse to settle for anything less than an amount that exceeds the sum of the amounts that would be accepted individually by the band members in compensation for their individual shares. There then would be two amounts that could be selected as a measure of the social cost of building the line through the reservation. The choice between them would depend on one's views of the rationale of CB analysis.

CB analysis is best used with respect to problems that raise no ethical disagreement. As I said earlier, much of the current controversy about CB analysis arises because environmental, ethical, and aesthetic concerns are not easily brought within its purview. It would clearly be controversial to apply standard CB analysis to an issue such as whether to use diplomatic channels to protest the treatment of religious minorities in another country. So it may be best to restrict the application of the technique to areas that raise only economic controversy. The Canadian Treasury Board guide asserts, for instance, that "benefit-cost analysis is designed for a particular kind of problem, that of achieving efficient resource allocation when lumpy initial capital outlays are required and benefits accrue over extended periods of time."[16] When issues other than efficiency are involved, it is arguable that CB analysis should recede into the background.

This claim is compatible with the rationalist and management science rationales of CB analysis. But it is not compatible with the moralist view, at least not on the face of it. Moralist views may be more or less ambitious concerning the comprehensiveness of CB analysis, but they are defined by a concern to use it to contribute to resolving moral debate. It is interesting that the implications of the moralist view seem to imply the opposite of the claim I have just made. For, if it is admitted that a decision raises no moral issues, then on the moralist view, CB analysis would be expected to have nothing to contribute. For instance, a decision about the siting of a dam may raise no moral issues. It may be agreed that a dam must be built and that all of the options being considered are morally on a par. On the moralist view, one would expect CB analysis to have nothing significant to contribute to the decision. Yet experience suggests that this is just the kind of case where CB analysis techniques can contribute most effectively.

(2) Compensating Variations and Utility. A second area of controversy surrounds the notion that costs and benefits are to be valued at the amount

[16] Canada, *Guide*, p. 7.

of a person's corresponding compensating variation, defined in terms of willingness to pay (as explained above). A person's willingness to pay may be a poor measure of the accompanying variation in his *welfare*. The importance of this is that one may take the *rationale* of CB analysis to require that it measure the welfare effects of social projects and policies, typically the effects on *social welfare*, which is understood to be an aggregate of individuals' welfare. The idea that CB analysis is to measure social welfare is not uncommon. For instance, it is accepted both by Mishan and by the Canadian Treasury Board's guidebook.[17] The idea is suggested both by the moralist view of the rationale, given a utilitarian perspective on morality, and by the rationalist view, given a social welfare maximizing conception of social rationality. On either of these views, costs and benefits must be measured in terms of their effects on welfare.

There are at least three reasons why a CV may be a poor measure of individual welfare. First, one's willingness to pay for a commodity or amenity reflects one's *market power* as much as the strength of one's preference, or the impact on one's welfare.[18] A poor person may gain as much or more than a rich person, but be willing to pay less, because he is able to pay less. Willingness to pay is a function of income and wealth. Because of this, CB analysis based on the standard techniques may bias the selection of social policies and projects in favor of the better-off.[19] Second, because of lack of information, imperfect rationality, and so on, one's preferences – and so one's willingness to pay – may not accurately reflect one's welfare.[20] For these reasons, a greater CV need not indicate a greater change in welfare.[21]

Third, there may even be cases where a person has *no* CV, despite a change in his welfare, because he would not be willing to accept *any* amount of money as compensation for some project, policy, or decision that would affect him.[22] If a decision must be made of whether or not to build a life-saving medical facility, and if I will die unless it is built, then there may be no amount of money that I would be willing to accept as compensation for a

[17] See Mishan, *Cost-Benefit Analysis*, p. 6; and Canada, *Guide*, p. 9.

[18] Nash, Pearce, and Stanley, "Evaluation," p. 128.

[19] Kristin S. Schrader-Frechette, "Technology Assessment as Applied Philosophy of Science," *Science, Technology and Human Values*, Special Issue, Fall 1980, No. 33, pp. 36–37. See Mishan, *Cost-Benefit Analysis*, p. 356.

[20] Schrader-Frechette, "Technology Assessment," p. 39.

[21] Mishan officially defines a person's CV as "a measure of the money transfer necessary, following some economic change, to maintain the individual's welfare at its original level" (*Cost-Benefit Analysis*, p. 127). This definition presupposes the dubious assumption that every welfare change is equivalent to some transfer of money. But even ignoring this problem, the definition does not ensure that the magnitude of a CV accurately reflects a change in welfare. Income-related differences in the marginal utility of money mean that a greater money transfer will be required at a higher income level than would have been required at a lower income level, to compensate for a given change in welfare.

[22] Or because no money transfer would return his welfare to its original level.

negative decision. There is a loss of welfare, but since I am not willing to accept money as compensation, *I have no CV*. This is a life and death case, but others are imaginable. Suppose I am placed under house arrest, or made a slave because of my ancestry, or forced to listen to Muzak every hour of the day, or legally barred from reading along with others who share my hair color. In these cases again I may have no CV. This problem could be avoided by a restriction of CB analysis to cases where every party whose welfare is affected has got a CV. But whether this restriction is acceptable depends on one's view of the rationale of CB analysis.

An alternative to simply using CVs would be to devise CB techniques that measure costs and benefits in units of welfare or utility rather than in money.[23] Cost-benefit analysis would then aim directly to maximize the sum of individual utilities.[24] Except where there were no CVs, this suggestion could be implemented by weighting assigned monetary values by a factor that reflects the marginal utility of money. Unfortunately, the marginal utility of money likely varies from individual to individual as well as from income level to income level.[25] Therefore, it would be necessary to measure individual variations in the marginal utility of money. At a minimum, it would be necessary to estimate how the marginal utility of money changes with income. But Pearce and Nash claimed, in 1981, that attempts to estimate the income elasticity of the marginal utility of money required implausible assumptions, and they concluded that "this approach . . . appears inoperable."[26] Where, then, does this leave CB analysis?

The Canadian Treasury Board guide suggests that willingness to pay or to accept money as compensation is "the best available measure" of utility.[27] This may be so, and for this reason it may be that governments and agencies will continue to look to standard CB analysis techniques to help them to estimate the welfare effects of their projects and policies. However, they should realize that the resulting estimates may be quite poor when there is inequality of income and wealth, and when people have less than full information and perfect rationality. Of course, this is the case in all forseeable social settings, so CB analysis should be used with care if the objective is to maximize social welfare.

(3) *Potential Pareto-Improvements.* A third area of controversy surrounds this standard criterion for determining which projects and proposals are cost-benefit preferable. A common objection to the potential Pareto improvement rule is that it ignores the distributional effects of social

[23] I assume that "welfare" and "utility" are synonymous.
[24] Nash, Pearce, and Stanley, *op. cit.*, p. 127.
[25] Pearce and Nash, *Social Appraisal*, p. 26.
[26] *ibid.*, p. 27.
[27] Canada, *Guides*, p. 13.

decisions.[28] The *Pareto*-improvement rule requires that no one be made worse off in fact. However, this rule would be completely impractical, for "we know of no government decision that has ever brought a Pareto-improvement in welfare in its strict form."[29] The *potential* Pareto-rule avoids this difficulty, but at the cost of sacrificing intuitive appeal. While it is easy to be seduced by the thought that decisions should be approved which make some people better off, provided that they make no one worse off, it is harder to be seduced by the idea that decisions should be approved provided that they have net benefits that could be distributed in a way that makes no one worse off. This idea is compatible with many people actually being hurt a good deal, and those people may be from the less well-off groups in society.

There are two common responses to this objection. The first is to amend standard CB analysis. One would incorporate both "marginal utility weights," to take into account variations in the marginal utility of money, and "equity weights," to reflect some view about the morally preferable distribution of income and utility in society.[30] The second is to try to preserve standard CB analysis, despite the objections. One would distinguish between "allocation" and "distribution," restrict CB analysis to a concern with the former, and leave the problem of distribution to be assessed and handled by parties other than the CB analyst.[31]

The first response, that of incorporating equity weights, will seem most plausible to those with a moralistic view of the foundations of CB analysis. But there is no reasoned consensus on issues of distributive justice, and so the inclusion of equity weights would open an analyst to the charge of using CB analysis as "a purely normative device for representing one's ethical position."[32] For this reason, if one favored the use of equity weights, one might be tempted to move toward the management science rationale for CB analysis. If the aim is to assess projects by criteria supplied by the decision maker, then equity weights can be used as required by the decision maker. CB analysis can then be seen as a value free technique: it simply discovers the extent to which proposed policies and projects will meet previously specified objectives.[33]

However, even if there were agreement about distributive justice, or even if a given conception were clearly favored by the relevant decision maker, I

[28] See, e.g., Schrader-Frechette, "Technology Assessment," p. 35; Mishan *Cost-Benefit Analysis*, p. 318; Nash, Pearce, and Stanley, "Evaluation," p. 126–127.
[29] Nash, Pearce, and Stanley, "Evaluation," p. 126.
[30] Nash, Pearce, and Stanley, "Evaluation," p. 128; Pearce and Nash, *Social Appraisal*, pp. 31–37.
[31] Mishan, *Cost-Benefit Analysis*, pp. 136, 318.
[32] Layard, *Readings*, p. 42.
[33] See Sugden and Williams, *Principles*, pp. 234–241; and Pearce and Nash, *Social Appraisal*, pp. 35–37.

think it still would be an error to incorporate equity weights into CB analysis. Conceptions of justice relate primarily to the basic structure of social and economic institutions.[34] Therefore, since CB analysis is a method used to evaluate projects with only a limited effect on this structure, issues of justice are mainly outside its scope.[35]

The second strategy for responding to objections arising from concerns about distributive justice is to restrict CB analysis to a consideration of "allocative effects," and to leave it to the decision maker to take other effects into account as he sees fit. This proposal will seem least plausible to those with a moralistic view, for it suggests that CB analysis should leave ethical debates to the political forum.[36] I will return to this idea below.

This survey of some of the main criticisms of standard CB analysis will suggest, I think, why there is so much uncertainty surrounding its rationale. We have seen that CB analysis is a family of concepts, criteria, and techniques; and we have seen that the family can be understood to consist of one major matriarch, the standard view, and a number of offspring that represent attempts to avoid criticisms of the standard view. Associated with these concepts and criteria are various technical problems of implementation. What, then, is the underlying rationale of CB analysis?

Three Proposed Rationales

I have characterized three rationales offered in defense of CB analysis: the moralist position, the rationalist position, and the management science approach. There is room for variation within each school of thought. For instance, within the moralist position there can be differences arising from disagreement about ethical issues, and within the rationalist position, there can be differences arising from disagreement about the concept of rationality. Within all three positions there can be differences regarding the comprehensiveness of CB analysis. I believe there is a grain of truth in each. The relevance of CB analysis to social decisions derives from the special responsibility of the decision maker to decide social questions as it would be rational for the society to decide. This responsibility is sensibly viewed as an ethical responsibility.

A satisfactory account of the rationale of CB analysis would have two

---

[34] See John Rawls, *A Theory of Justice* (Cambridge, Mass.: Belknap Press of Harvard University Press, 1971).

[35] This argument is discussed in detail in my "The Justice and Rational Transparency of Cost-Benefit Analysis," forthcoming.

[36] Pearce and Nash suggest that there is no such thing as CB analysis without an equity weighting system. "A decision to adopt no weighting system is itself equivalent to adopting a particular value judgement, namely, that the existing distribution of income is optimal." *Social Appraisal*, (p. 34). I reject this suggestion in "The Justice and Rational Transparency of Cost-Benefit Analysis."

characteristics. First, it would explain why CB analysis is relevant to (certain) social decision problems on a basis that is independent of the particular characteristics of any given decision maker, such as whether he wants to use CB analysis. If the relevance of CB techniques turned simply on the desires, objectives, or directives of the decision maker, then a decision maker with suitably nonconformist desires could not be faulted for resorting, say, to a ouija-board rather than to CB analysis. Matters must be put on firmer ground than this. A satisfactory account of CB analysis would explain why any social decision maker who ignored the recommendations of an adequate procedure of CB analysis for appropriate kinds of social decision problems would be open to criticism. It would do so on the basis of the nature of this cost-benefit procedure. I call this the "objectivity constraint."

Second, a satisfactory account would explain why CB analysis is particularly relevant to *social* decision problems. I call this the "social constraint." There is no apparent problem in explaining the relevance of CB analysis in the private sector, where it is simply a form of financial analysis that involves assessing financial costs and benefits to an agent seeking to maximize net financial benefits. We are interested here in public sector uses of CB analysis, where a broad range of social costs and benefits is taken into account, including costs and benefits that are not purely financial, and where the decision is to be made *on behalf of society* as a whole. There are two senses in which a decision can be said to be on behalf of society. First, the choice of the decision maker may "constitute" a decision of the society, or be attributed to the society.[37] For example, it is the *United States* that is pursuing the space program. Second, the decision maker has the *responsibility* to decide with a view to the interests or welfare of the society as a whole. Our problem is to explain on what basis a decision maker with this role and responsibility deserves criticism if he ignores the results of an adequate procedure of CB analysis.

It may seem obvious that a social decision maker has a duty to take into account the results of CB analysis. Suppose I am a public official charged with deciding where to locate a hydro-electric dam, and suppose that I also must decide what sort of waterproof coating to use on the verandah of my house. My decision about the dam is *on behalf of* society as a whole, in at least the sense that it is my responsibility to make the decision with a view to the interests of the society. This implies a responsibility to take into account costs and benefits to the society as a whole, and to all categories of citizens in the society. I would be corrupt if I decided simply on the basis of costs and benefits *to myself*. However, in my private decision I have no special

---

[37] David Copp "Collective Actions and Secondary Actions," *American Philosophical Quarterly*, vol. 16 (1979), pp. 177–186.

responsibility to the society; I would not be corrupt if I restricted attention to my own costs and benefits; and I am even free to decide capriciously. The difference between the cases is not due simply to the scale of the two projects, for consider another example. Suppose a decision must be made about where to locate a new hospital. If a philanthropist is building the hospital, she is free to ignore the result of a CB analysis in a way that the government would not be if the government were building the hospital. It is not the philanthropist's *responsibility* to build a hospital, much less to build a cost-benefit effective one. She is free to place the building on a very expensive site where it will be prominent on the skyline. However, the government is responsible both for health care and for a wise budgeting of social resources. That is why CB analysis seems relevant to the government's decision in a way that it does not to the philanthropist's decision.

These cases suggest that CB analysis can be recommended to a social decision maker on the basis of his special responsibility. But this conclusion would be premature. Let us consider the three proposed rationales in more detail.

The Management Science View

The management science account meets neither of the two constraints we have just discussed. It fails the objectivity constraint because it fails to show that a decision maker would be liable to criticism for ignoring CB analysis, *unless* he already *wanted* to take it into account, or had other objectives that required him to do so. And it fails the social constraint because it does not distinguish between appropriate criteria for *private* decisions and appropriate criteria for *public* decisions.

Sugden and Williams accept the management science view, or the "decision-making approach," as they call it.[38] They distinguish between the role of decision maker and that of analyst, and agree that the former is entrusted to act on behalf of the community. The analyst's role is that of providing technical advice to the decision maker.[39] This much is common to all three views regarding the rationale of CB analysis. But Sugden and Williams go on to assert that CB analysis is to be seen "as a process of appraising decision problems in the light of objectives chosen by the decision maker." "The role of the analyst is to assist the decision maker in making choices that are consistent with his (that is, the decision maker's) objectives." In principle, at least, "any objective could be used." Moreover, CB analysis "can, in principle, be comprehensive; that is, it can produce unqualified recommendations as to how the decision-maker should act."

[38] Sugden and Williams, *Principles*, pp. 92–93, 235–241. Nash, Pearce, and Stanley call it the "management science approach." See "Evaluation," p. 130.
[39] Sugden and Williams, *Principles*, p. 230.

Costs and benefits are to be measured in units defined by reference to the decision maker's objectives, and they are to be aggregated in a way that measures net benefits and costs relative to those objectives.[40]

Nash, Pearce, and Stanley claim that "this is the most widely-expressed alternative view of cost-benefit analysis to the Hicks-Kaldor approach." They accuse other authors of confusing the two approaches in thinking that the management science view could be a basis for using the Hicks-Kaldor decision rule.[41] But it is they who are confused on this issue. After all, one *could* take the view that CB techniques can measure only the economic efficiency of proposals and policies, in the sense defined by the Hicks-Kaldor test. One could hold, moreover, that economic efficiency has nothing to recommend it except where the decision makers *want* to achieve it. On this view, the Hicks-Kaldor approach delimits what CB analysis can achieve; the basis for using the approach, when it has a basis, is that a decision maker wants it to be used. There is, then, no incompatibility between the management science position and the Hicks-Kaldor or potential Pareto-rule. The latter is an aggregation or choice rule; the former is an account of the *rationale* of using any such rule in CB analysis.

The problems with the management science approach can be quickly explained. The first concerns its recommendatory force. There is no guarantee that the usual economic techniques and criteria of cost-benefit analysis can be recommended to a decision maker, given the management science view. It is quite possible for a decision maker to have objectives that "are not easy to incorporate into the economic framework of cost-benefit analysis"; examples would be the objective of increasing racial harmony, or of preserving his own job security.[42] For this reason the management science approach may not be able to recommend the standard CB framework. But suppose one conceives of CB techniques as simply *any* techniques that maximize one's ability consistently and efficiently to achieve any set of objectives. This is a decidedly unorthodox conception, but we must concede that *if* this is the conception one has, then the management science approach can recommend so-called "CB techniques" to any decision maker for any decision problem, regardless of his objectives. However, on this conception, "CB techniques" cannot be *specially* recommended to social decision makers, and need not be *economic* techniques.

The second problem is that the management science view does not distinguish between appropriate criteria for the public choices of social decision makers, and appropriate criteria for their private choices. Sugden and Williams do acknowledge that a person can be "responsible for making

---

[40] *ibid.*, pp. 91, 235, 236, 237.
[41] Nash, Pearce, and Stanley, "Evaluation," p. 130.
[42] Sugden and Williams, *Principles*, pp. 237, 238.

decisions in the public interest," but they suggest that a CB analysis is to define costs and benefits in relation to the decision maker's objectives.[43] On this account, any *personal* objective of a public official, such as his objectives of keeping his job, is treated as on a par with the public interest. But if a distinction can be drawn between the public interest and the interest of the decision maker, or between social objectives and individual objectives, then it is certainly the former that a social decision maker has the responsibility to pursue, and it is certainly the former that a CB analysis of a social decision problem should take into account. Hence, we see that the management science view depends for its plausibility on the metaphysical view that society has no objectives or interests in its own right.

To be sure, there are philosophical problems involved in giving sense to the concept of society's objectives or interests. But we need not postulate a "group mind," whatever that would be, "over and above" the minds of individual persons. I believe that the fact that a collective entity, like a society, has a given objective is *constituted by* facts about the objectives of its members.[44] The semantic reduction of one set of sentences to another is not involved. Rather, to use another terminology, collective objectives are *supervenient on*, or *emergent from*, the objectives of individual persons in much the way that certain physicalists propose that our own personal objectives and mental states are supervenient on states of our body.[45] Of course, some groups or collective entities may in fact have no objectives, the goals of the members being too diverse; and in other cases there may be insurmountable epistemological problems that prevent our identifying the collective's goals. But some cases are perfectly clear. A *firm* may usually be assumed to have the goal of maximizing its profits. The management science view itself presupposes that a *government* can have objectives when the government is the decision maker.[46] If it is intelligible for collectives such as these to have objectives, it presumably is also intelligible for a society to have objectives. I will return to this issue.

The errors of the management science view can be illustrated in the case where CB analysis is used in the private sector. The relevant objectives are those of the *firm*, not those of the corporate decision maker himself. The rationale of CB analysis in the private sector is not to help corporate managers achieve their own objectives.

I suggest that the management science view seems plausible to some

---

[43] *ibid.*, p. 91.
[44] See Copp, "Collective Actions and Secondary Actions."
[45] For relevant discussion, see Richard Boyd, "Materialism Without Reductionism: Non-Humean Causation and the Evidence for Physicalism," forthcoming. See also, Jaegwon Kim, "Supervenience and Nomological Incommensurables," *American Philosophical Quarterly*, vol. 15 (1978), pp. 149–156.
[6] Sugden and Williams, *Principles*, p. 238.

theorist as a result of reasoning along the following lines. It is not proper for an analyst to impose his own view of the objectives to be pursued, or of the aggregation or choice rule to be employed in an analysis of a decision problem. The decision maker has the responsibility of selecting the objectives and criteria; the analyst only works for the decision maker.[47] This is well and good, but not relevant. The problem of *imposition* does not arise, for the decision maker can always choose to ignore a set of recommendations. Moreover, the analyst presumably can be asked or told to use any set of objectives and criteria that appeal to the decision maker. What we are trying to determine, however, is whether there is a basis for *recommending* CB analysis to a decision maker in the context of certain *social* decision problems, a basis that is independent of his own objectives.

The Moralist Position

The moralist view implies that CB analysis is to be recommended because it will aid the decision maker in reaching an ethical evaluation of proposals under consideration. However, *everyone* has a duty to reach ethically acceptable decisions, while not everyone has the responsibility to consult CB analysis. Perhaps it can be shown that CB analysis is specially suited to contribute to the making of ethically acceptable *social* decisions. But unless this can be shown, the moralist view has not isolated a basis for criticizing social decision makers who fail to consult CB analysis, as opposed to private individuals who fail to consult it.

The moralist view is based on a confusion that can be illustrated with an analogy. It is the duty of a deckhand on a ship to swab the decks. This may be a duty of no great moral import, but it can be regarded as a moral duty that derives from a voluntary undertaking to perform the job. A knowledge of preferred deck-swabbing techniques, therefore, becomes relevant to the moral acceptability of the deckhand's behavior, but this is not because of the nature of the techniques *per se*. It is because of the person's special responsibility. The relation of CB analysis techniques to the responsibility of social decision makers is somewhat similar. Recall the case of the philanthropist and the hospital. CB techniques vary in their relevance to one's morally acceptable decision making because their relevance depends on one's responsibilities.

A utilitarian need not disagree. To be sure, my argument depends on the idea that one's moral responsibility is not simply the duty to maximize social welfare, as measured in CB analysis. Otherwise, the philanthropist and the government official would be in exactly the same position from the moral point of view. However, most utilitarians attempt to find a place both for the

---

[47] *ibid.*, p. 235.

special responsibilities of people who have taken on roles, and for the notion of philanthropic action beyond one's moral duty. Moreover, utilitarianism concerns the maximization of *utility*, or the maximization of the overall total of welfare, not just, as in CB analysis as it is generally conceived, the maximization of the *monetary* surplus in *one's society* of benefits over costs. For these reasons, my argument does not require the rejection of utilitarianism.

It remains tempting to regard CB analysis as a method of moral appraisal. The promotion of social welfare seems to be *a* duty that we have, if not the only one, and CB analysis purports to appraise social options for their potential contribution to social welfare. Even in the case of the philanthropist, where the promotion of social welfare is supererogatory, its moral relevance is shown precisely by its being supererogatory.

Layard apparently believes that CB analysis is potentially a method of *comprehensive* moral analysis.[48] This view is made somewhat plausible by the formal similarities between CB analysis and consequentialist moral theories like utilitarianism. If our sole moral duty is to maximize utility, as simple utilitarianism implies, and if CB analysis aims to assess projects and policies for their contribution to utility, then CB analysis would seem to be utilitarianism applied to social decision problems. However, many people hold that there are moral constraints on the pursuit by society of social welfare, constraints implied by considerations of distributive justice and by individual rights and liberties. In order to claim moral comprehensiveness for CB analysis, therefore, one would have either to deny that there are any moral constraints on the maximization of social welfare, or to claim that CB analysis can take into account all such constraints. But we have been given no reason to accept the latter claim, and the former is a matter of considerable philosophical debate.

Mishan claims that there is a broad moral consensus in society on two propositions that can be said to form a "virtual constitution": Pareto improvements are to be sought; and distributional changes are to be sought when there is near-unanimity that the changes would represent an improvement.[49] He thinks that the major features of CB analysis rest on this virtual constitution; in particular, CB analysis is "linked with" the notion of a Pareto improvement in that the decision rule of CB analysis is the *potential* Pareto improvement rule.[50] However, Mishan's view is puzzling. If the Pareto rule is sanctioned by a consensus, then the *potential* Pareto rule is not, for a social innovation can satisfy the latter while conflicting with the former.

---

[48] Layard, *Readings*, pp. 9, 11.
[49] Mishan, *Cost-Benefit Analysis*, pp. 310–311.
[50] *ibid.*, p. 316.

The potential rule would not command the intuitive assent commanded by the Pareto rule itself. Consequently, even if Mishan is right about the virtual constitution, he is wrong about standard CB analysis finding its basis in the virtual constitution. Moreover, Mishan rests his account on certain moral views, not because he is willing to defend them *per se*, but simply because of his belief that there is a consensus. A consensus does not guarantee truth or even plausibility. So if Mishan's account shows that there is an ethical basis to the enterprise, the fundamental basis presumably is a duty on the part of a social decision maker to respect a social consensus.

To the extent that CB analysis evaluates projects in terms of social welfare, or to the extent that, say, economic efficiency contributes to social welfare, and to the extent that one believes that everyone has a duty to promote social welfare, to that extent one may believe that CB analysis can contribute to the moral acceptability of anyone's decisions. But CB analysis may be of special relevance to the ability of social decision makers to meet *their* moral responsibilities, even if in itself it has no moral relevance. This can be so if the responsibility of a social decision maker is a moral responsibility to promote social welfare, or social rationality, or what have you, and if CB analysis can contribute to this responsibility.

Social Rationality

If CB analysis can be recommended to a decision maker on grounds independent of his own objectives, and if it can be specially recommended to *social* decision makers, this is due to the responsibility carried by anyone in that *role*. This responsibility may be a moral responsibility although it may be legal or organizational. In any case, the nature of the duty is due to the nature of the *role* of a social decision maker.

Consider the analogy of a firm. A corporate decision maker decides on behalf of the firm. That is, he is to decide on the basis of the *objectives of the firm*. This is not to deny that he has an independent moral responsibility, even if the firm itself has no moral objectives. *Every* agent, including the firm and the corporate decision maker, has a moral responsibility to decide and act in morally appropriate ways. However, this is not part of a corporate decision maker's *special* responsibility. His special responsibility is to implement the firm's objectives: *viz.*, in the usual case, the objective of profit maximization.

On an instrumental view of rationality, if the special responsibility of the corporate decision maker is to decide on the basis of the objectives of the firm, then his special responsibility is to decide in a way that would be rational for the firm. His special responsibility is to eschew maximizing his own expected utility in favor of maximizing the expected utility *of the firm*. Given that a firm typically aims ultimately to maximize its profits, the economic framework of CB analysis can obviously be of assistance to corporate decision makers in this pursuit. Alasdair MacIntyre has said that in the case of the firm, "the norms of rationality . . . are such that the cost-benefit analysis yields the essential normative form of argument."[51]

The most plausible rationale for CB analysis in the context of social decision problems is, I think, parallel to the rationale I have sketched for corporate decision problems. A social decision maker is to decide on behalf of society; he is to decide in a way that would be rational for society to decide. His general moral repsonsibility is additional to this special responsibility carried by his role. On an instrumental view of social rationality, this special responsibility can be characterized as the duty to maximize expected social utility. If CB analysis can be recommended specially to social decision makers on a basis independent of their own objectives, it will be on the basis of their special responsibility. Of course, if it can be recommended to them on this basis, then CB analysis must be able to contribute to the social rationality of their decisions. We will consider its ability to do so after a brief digression.

This account will be challenged on metaphysical grounds. It will be said that society is not an entity; that if it is an entity, it is not an agent with objectives and preferences; that there is no such thing as a ranking of social states from society's point of view; and that the notion of a rational choice for society is unintelligible. I want to say, first, that if these objections are well taken, then so much the worse for the idea that CB analysis has a rationale that underwrites its recommendation to social decision makers. But the objections are not well taken.

It cannot be doubted that we regard many collective entities as agents with objectives and preferences, whose choices can be assessed for rationality. The university and the department are favorite targets of professors. The government is a favorite target of journalists. Historians so regard states, political parties, government administrations, etc. Economists take families to be "rational preference maximizers like individual consumers," and take firms "to make decisions relative to information available to them and to be subject to criticism depending on whether the decisions are intelligent given their aims."[52] We have similar views in our ordinary life, feeling no metaphysical concerns as we argue whether, for instance, Dome Petroleum took a reasonable risk in the Beaufort Sea. None of this *proves* that a collective entity can be an agent that makes choices, and whose choices can

---

[51] Alasdair MacIntyre, "Utilitarianism and Cost-Benefit Analysis: An Essay on the Relevance of Moral Philosophy to Bureaucratic Theory," in *Values in the Electric Power Industry*, edited by K. Sayre (Notre Dame, Indiana: Notre Dame University Press, 1977), p. 219.

[52] Isaac Levi, "Conflict and Social Agency," *The Journal of Philosophy*, vol. 79 (1982), pp. 231–232.

be assessed for rationality. Yet this the belief is as intelligible as it is useful in historical, journalistic, economic and everyday theorizing. If the belief implies a kind of "organicism," then so be it.[53]

Perhaps, however, there is a special problem in the case of *society*. Firms and governments have authoritative decision procedures, the results of which can be attributed to the entity in question as *its* decisions or preferences. But a society as such, as distinct from the state that may embrace it, does not have an authoritative decision procedure in this sense. At least it *need* not. Families similarly may lack authoritative decision procedures. But we can attribute choices to a family when there is near-unanimity, or at least unanimity among the adult members. A society rarely reaches near-unanimity. But when it does, few would have difficulty attributing to it a preference. The more typical case, though, is that the members of society have conflicting preferences for society. Still, the fact that unanimity is *possible* shows that *social choice* is possible on the same basis as familial choice.

Of course, Kenneth Arrow's famous impossibility theorem is a serious threat to the idea of a social choice.[54] Arrow argued that a social preference ranking cannot depend on the rankings of social alternatives by the members of society unless, at the same time, it fails to satisfy several important and reasonable conditions. One of these is a "nondictatorship" postulate, according to which a social welfare function is not to be based solely on the ranking of social alternatives by one individual alone.[55] Another is the "independence of irrelevant alternatives" condition, according to which the social preference between social alternatives is to be "determined solely by the preferences of the members of the community as between [those alternatives]."[56]

It is obvious that this essay is not the forum for a discussion of Arrow's theorem. Moreover, I do not reject the idea that a society's preference ranking of social alternatives depends on the attitudes taken toward those alternatives by the members of society. However, the independence of irrelevant alternatives postulate rules out an appeal to anything but the members' orderings of the social alternatives in defining the social preference. For instance, it rules out an appeal to interpersonal comparisons of utility, and it rules out an appeal to the members' attitudes toward decision procedures. As for the former, it certainly is not obvious that there is no basis for interpersonal utility comparisons, although there is no doubt

[53] See *ibid.*, pp. 232–236.
[54] Kenneth Arrow, *Social Choice and Individual Values*, second edition (New Haven: Yale University Press, 1963).
[55] *ibid.*, p. 30.
[56] *ibid.*, p. 23.

that serious epistemological difficulties often stand in the way of our determining how different persons' utilities actually do compare.[57] It may well be that the threat of Arrow's theorem can be handled.

In conclusion, if CB analysis has a basis that underwrites its recommendation to social decision makers in particular, independently of their own objectives, then the basis is in the special reponsibility assumed by social decision makers along with their role. This responsibility is, I suggest, to decide among social alternatives on the basis of society's objectives, with a view to maximizing social welfare, and thereby with a view to the social rationality of their decisions. CB analysis has a basis insofar as it can contribute to the social rationality of social decisions. Its having a basis depends on the intelligibility of the notion of social rationality. But so too does the notion of the special responsibility of social decision-makers. And I think that the notion is intelligible.

The Adequacy of CB Analysis Procedures

The question that remains then is whether there are CB analysis techniques that could contribute to the social rationality of decisions. Is there a property that can be possessed by an option for choice in a social decision problem, a property that can be ascertained or measured by CB analysis techniques, and a property the possession of which in sufficient degree would ensure or contribute to the social rationality of the choice of that option? I will restrict attention to the standard techniques of CB analysis.

If economic efficiency is a property measured by standard CB analysis techniques, then the answer is affirmative. There are many cases where the economic efficiency of a choice would be a factor in assessing its rationality. But even if CB analysis measures economic efficiency, CB analysis of a social decision problem would not *determine* the socially rational choice. Social welfare does not consist simply in maximizing the surplus of economic benefits over economic costs. In certain cases, moreover, society may rationally ignore economic efficiency. Finally, in certain cases, a society may be *morally* obligated to forego economic efficiency. There are occasions when a society should sacrifice some of its own economic welfare in order to contribute to human rights or social welfare in some other society. For all of

---

[57] On interpersonal utility comparisons, see: Harsanyi, *op. cit.*, pp. 15–20; Charles R. Plott, "Axiomatic Social Choice Theory: An Overview and Interpretation," *American Journal of Political Science*, 1976, 20, pp. 511–596; Richard Brandt, *A Theory of the Good and the Right* (New York: Oxford University Press, 1979), chapter xiii; and John G. Bennett, "The Problem of Interpersonal Comparisons," unpublished. On attitudes toward decision procedures, see my "Do Nations Have the Right of Self-Determination?" in Stanley G. French, *Philosophers Look at Canadian Confederation* (Montreal: Canadian Philosophical Association, 1979), pp. 71–95.

these reasons, CB analysis is at best a *contributor* to social decisions, and a contributor in a *restricted* set of cases.[58]

However, two serious concerns remain, one conceptual and one political. First is the conceptual problem of distinguishing economic from non-economic costs and benefits. The former are relevant to the measure of economic efficiency, the latter are not. The classic issue that illustrates the problem is the dispute regarding the costing of the loss of life. Loss of life is not simply an *economic* cost, least of all to the victim and his family, and neither is the *risk* of death an economic cost. But there is an associated set of economic costs, and these should be taken into account in a measure of the economic efficiency of a program that envisions the loss of some lives. Mishan is right to say that, from the perspective of CB analysis, if a method of "measuring the loss of life" were "satisfactory on economic grounds," the fact that it had morally untenable implications "would not, of itself, provide any reason for rejecting it."[59] That is, it would not provide any reason for rejecting its use in a measure of the *economic efficiency* of the program in question.

In standard CB analysis, the cost of a risk of death is measured by the willingness of potential victims to accept compensation for the increased risk. But their willingness reflects their feelings about the loss of security, and these feelings are not *economic* costs, even though they may have economic consequences. Hence, the victims' willingness to pay does not measure an economic cost to them. It also does not measure an economic cost *to society*, for even if the project is approved in CB analysis, the chances are that the potential victims will not *in fact* be compensated by the society. Similarly, if prisoners are deprived of their right to practice their religion, theirs is not an *economic* loss. They may be willing to accept financial compensation, but there is no reason to think that their willingness to do so adequately measures the cost to them or to society. Similarly, the loss of an aesthetically pleasing view is not an *economic* loss, though it may have economic consequences. The problem, then, is how to *distinguish* noneconomic costs and benefits from economic costs and benefits, and how to *value* the

[58] We have so far ignored the Scitovsky paradox (Mishan, *Cost-Benefit Analysis*, pp. 319–321; Pearce and Nash, *Appraisal*, pp. 28–29). The paradox turns on the twin facts that the introduction of a project can have distributional effects, and that potential Pareto improvements are assessed relative to a given economic state of affairs. Because of these facts, the *introduction* of a project may achieve a potential Pareto improvement relative to the status quo, while the *elimination* of the project would achieve a potential Pareto improvement relative to the state of affairs that would result from its introduction. Obviously, in such a case, the economic efficiency of the project, or its cost-benefit effectiveness, relative to the status quo, would not be a sufficient reason for introducing it.
[59] Mishan, *Cost-Benefit Analysis*, p. 156.

latter.[60] Willingness to pay is not always an adequate or appropriate measure. In those cases where it is not, standard CB analysis would not actually assess economic efficiency.

One might propose that CB analysis should take into account only *financial* costs and benefits, or effects on the financial objectives of members of society. However, a CB analysis restricted to financial efficiency would not be suited for the decision problems it is meant to handle. For some costs and benefits that are plausibly regarded as economic, such as certain spillover effects of economic activity, and certain benefits of public works, may not appear in anyone's financial accounts:

> In many cases, the outputs of public investment projects are provided free of charge to the public. Benefit-cost analysis then requires that dollar values be imputed to these outputs. . . . Similarly, . . . the inputs of projects [may] not have market prices. . . . Furthermore, market-determined prices of inputs and outputs sometimes may not reflect true social costs and benefits.[61]

The distinction between economic and noneconomic costs and benefits is most plausibly drawn in terms of an *efficiency objective*, an objective of achieving an efficient allocation *of resources*. The Canadian Treasury Board guide specifies this as the objective for CB analysis.

> Efficiency or allocative benefits are these favorable consequences of projects which represent opportunities to increase production or consumption; the allocative costs are the opportunities for production and consumption foregone because of projects undertaken.[62]

If efficiency objectives are taken to be definitive, then CB analysis will focus on "the determination of the effects of public projects on total physical production possibilities and consumption opportunities, given the existing stock of resources in the economy."[63] However, the adequacy of this conception depends on how consumption and production are understood. If, for instance, the loss of religious liberty is regarded as the loss of a "consumption opportunity," then it may inappropriately be regarded as an economic cost. Thus, much rests on the notion of *physical* production and consumption. Moreover, standard CB analysis techniques do not uniquely measure economic efficiency even on this conception of it. The willingness-to-pay criterion can assign a monetary value to certain noneconomic costs

---

[60] The problem of how to assign a monetary value to *noneconomic* costs and benefits in CB analysis is much discussed. The present issue is how to value *economic* costs and benefits.

[61] Canada, *Guide*, p. 5.

[62] *ibid.*, p. 8; see also p. 3.

[63] *ibid.*, p. 8.

and benefits, or to certain *nonefficiency* costs and benefits, such as the loss of religious liberty and the risk of death. So, even if we define economic efficiency in terms of allocative objectives, we have shown that standard CB techniques do not simply measure economic efficiency.

One might respond that standard CB techniques measure the amount of money one would have left over as profit or loss if one implemented a project, and collected from or gave to each individual a dollar amount equal to his compensating variation. Call this the "virtual profit" of the project or policy.[64] There can be no doubt that the virtual profit of projects is what CB analysis *would* measure if *all* effects for which *anyone* has a compensating variation were taken into account. But what is the significance of this concept? As we have seen, greater virtual profit does not necessarily mean greater economic efficiency; it does not necessarily mean a greater contribution to social welfare, or to welfare aggregated over society; it need not represent greater desirability from the point of view of society, for a social preference function would more plausibly track social welfare than virtual profit; and it does not necessarily represent greater opportunities for future social investment, for the CVs typically are neither collected nor paid out. For all of these reasons and others, the significance of a measure of virtual profit for the rationality of a social choice is quite unclear. Thus, virtual profit lacks *rational transparency*. I think it would be best if CB analysis aimed to measure economic efficiency rather than virtual profit.

The second concern about the adequacy of CB analysis is political. There is a potentially serious source of distortion in CB analysis if ambition on the part of CB analysts, combined with an enthusiasm for quantifying, leads to attempts to quantify in dollar terms factors that resist being adequately measured in this way. Attempts to quantify such factors in a way that makes them comparable to straightforward economic costs and benefits can be detrimental. It can mean that CB analysis, or certain applications of it, fail not only to measure economic efficiency, but fail to measure any other conceptually distinguishable and rationally transparent property of the options for choice. As a result, it can make it impossibly difficult to interpret the significance of CB analysis. And, given a mystique that attaches in certain circles to quantified, apparently scientific results, it can hinder decision makers in their attempts to make socially rational choices.

Let us conclude. The issue has been whether there are any adequate procedures of CB analysis. We have found a basis for recommending to social decision makers the use of techniques that may assist them in reaching decisions that are socially rational. The rationale is that they have a responsibility as *social* decision makers to promote the social rationality of

---

[64] This term, and this response to my position, were suggested by Robert Binkley.

their projects and policies. However, it is not clear that CB analysis can be recommended on this basis. To be sure, some cost-benefit studies may be well designed and well conducted, and they may be extremely useful. But the recommendation of CB analysis techniques *per se* is another matter. They could be recommended if they measured the economic efficiency of social options. However, standard CB analysis techniques do not measure economic efficiency the way a yardstick measures length. Even so, if used appropriately, they may measure economic efficiency, but they can be used otherwise. And they typically are used in such a way that they measure no rationally transparent attribute of social options. Finally, because of the political problem I mentioned, standard CB analysis cannot in general be recommended to social decision makers as a means of enhancing the social rationality of their decisions. Nor can any proposed non-standard CB techniques be recommended. The problem is not that the standard techniques need to be amended to take into account social objectives in addition to economic efficiency; it is that they cannot even be relied upon to measure economic efficiency. Strict guidelines need to be imposed to ensure that *efficiency* costs and benefits are measured, and measured appropriately. However, in the absence of guidelines of this sort, we must conclude that the standard procedures of CB analysis, as well as the suggested non-standard procedures, lack an adequate rationale.[65]

Philosophy, Simon Fraser Univrsity and University of Illinois at Chicago

---

[65] This essay was presented to the University of Waterloo Conference on Philosophy, Economics, and Justice, May 21, 1983. Robert Binkley was commentator. I would like to thank him, and the many others who contributed to the discussion, for their helpful remarks. I would also like to thank Edwin Levy for many useful discussions of CB analysis.

CONSISTENCY IN THE VALUATION OF LIFE:
A WILD GOOSE CHASE?

E. J. MISHAN

As Sir Thomas Browne solemnly observed in his Religio Medici, "Heresies perish not with their authors but, like the river Arethusa, though they have lost their currents in one place, they rise up in another." So too with the economist's valuation of life, the heresy being that – without seriously challenging the current concept of subjective valuation of changes in risk – economists have regressed to the once-persistent belief that it bears some quantitative relation, if not to expected earnings, at least to the utility of expected earnings or capital or consumption. This old-tyme recipe for estimating the value of a human life – notwithstanding the ornate convolutions and occasional intellectual effronteries to be found in the more recent versions – is much like that for calculating the value of a two-week honeymoon for a loving couple by reference to their anticipated outlays (including foregone earnings) plus perhaps an allowance for the probability of non-consummation owing to frigidity in either.

The figure arrived at on this conception of relevance bears no logical relation whatever to the money value that would be placed on the anticipated honeymoon experience by the enamored couple measured, say, by the sums necessary to persuade each of them to forego the event.

In this connection, three recent models for calculating the worth of a human life are worth mentioning: in order of technical sophistication, that of Usher (1971), that of Conley (1976) and that of Arthur (1981).[1] It would be

---

[1] See D. Usher, *An Imputation to the Measure of Economic Growth for Changes in Life Expectancy* (National Bureau of Economic Research, New York, 1971); B. C. Conley, "The Value of Human Life in the Demand for Safety," *American Economic Review*, vol. 66 (March 1976), pp. 45–55; W. B. Arthur, "The Economics of Risks to Life," *American Economic Review*, vol. 71 (March 1981), pp. 54–64. Arthur's criticisms of the compensating variation method of calculating life are unconvincing. In particular, his statement that both earlier human capital models and compensating variation (CV) methods both entail "partial equilibrium approaches that ignore the chain of wider economic transfers set up through society when life is lengthened" is quite misleading. Cost-benefit analysis is, of course, an exercise set up within a partial context as, indeed, is his own model – differentiating such approaches, that is, from a Walrasian general equilibrium model. Moreover, contrary to his allegation, the CV method – stemming as it does from the normative maxim that each person himself places a value on the given change (including a change in the risk of death or accident) – is in no way limited in covering the range of consequences, even though there may well be difficulties in the actual estimation of each of a variety of effects or externalities.

tedious to give a summary description of the construction of these models, which are, however, worth ploughing through for the intellectual diversion afforded by misguided ingenuity, though also for the examples they provide of the proliferation of journal articles today which bear eloquent testimony to the current crises in economic theory: much too much technique chasing far too few ideas. But for my purpose we need not summarise such articles. In any case all of them, including a number of other ambitious models such as those of Cook and Graham (1977), Jones-Lee (1980), and Keeney (1980), which involve neither expected earnings nor direct willingness to pay, run into an insurmountable methodological obstacle – which becomes evident once we consider that such models are *not* those of positive economics. Using such models, that is, we do not attempt to forecast how one observable magnitude will respond (over time) to movements in other economic variables. Thus, since there manifestly is no market in human lives (or human deaths), the economist is constrained to determine how the saving or loss of a human life *ought* to be valued, generally for the purpose of guiding allocative decisions![2]

To be more specific, since the introduction of a project often entails an increase in the number of lives saved, or lost, to say nothing of non-fatal injuries, the net benefit of the project cannot be evaluated unless the economist may 'correctly' attribute a value to this sort of change. Since the

---

[2] See P. J. Cook and D. A. Graham, "The Demand for Insurance and Protection: The Case of Irreplaceable Commodities," *Quarterly Journal of Economics*, vol. XCI (Feb. 1977), pp. 143–156; M. W. Jones-Lee, "Maximum Acceptable Physical Risk and a New Measure of Financial Risk Aversion," *Economics Journal*, vol. 90 (Sept. 1980), pp. 550–568; R. L. Keeney, "Evaluating Alternatives Involving Potential Fatalities," *Operations Research*, vol. 28 (Jan./Feb. 1980), pp. 206–224. It must be confessed that economists take sly pleasure when they are attacked for asserting that a finite value can indeed be placed on a human life and, which is probably more provoking to prevailing democratic sentiment, that a rich man's life is worth more then a poor man's life. For we can then explain patiently to the indignant layman that the evaluating economist is not addressing himself to philosophical or transcendental questions. He is aware, for example, that a casual interpretation of the gospels suggests that, if anything, the life of a rich man is worth less than that of a poor man – especially when account is taken of the rich man's tenuous prospects of entering the Kingdom of Heaven.

But once we agree to abide by the money value that people themselves put on the goods and bads they have commerce with here on this earth, the existence of a normal income effect assures, *ceteris paribus*, that the higher a person's income the higher the value he will place on his life – or, rather, the more he will pay for a given reduction in the risk of death. For accepting some *increase* in the risk of death, on the other hand, the answers provided by economic theory are less certain, and become ever more uncertain as the increase of that risk becomes larger.

Again, the question of whether the value placed on any given change of risk (from which currently the value of a statistical life is calculated) varies in any systematic way with age cannot be answered by economic theory as theory, only by investigation – unless, of course, we surrender to the recidivist propensities condemned above and calculate the value of a human life by reference, *inter alia*, to his expected future earnings, and to his utility to the rest of society, if any.

economist, in effect, is to explain how he believes human life in the above circumstances *ought* to be valued he is perforce operating within the field of normative economics. Considerations of consistency therefore require his abiding by the standard normative procedure: in particular, he is bound by the maxim that the preferences and the valuations of the individual himself alone are to count.

Thus, as distinct from the methodology of positive economics, the proper test of an allocative proposition of the preference of a community, or of a net benefit figure, entails a calculation of the preferences or the valuations (revealed or expressed) of the individuals concerned. If this much is conceded, it follows that the authors of the above papers are faced with a dilemma. To illustrate, each of such models yields a crucial magnitude, say Q, from which (given other data or assumptions) the value of life can be deduced or, at least, set within bounds.[3] Now in order to test the figure for value of life produced by such a model, it is necessary to have some independent estimate of the value of life – which as indicated implies recourse to the individual's subjective valuation, in accordance with the basic maxim of normative economics. The test therefore requires a calculation of the individual's compensating variation for the gain or loss of life or, rather, for some pre-determined gain or loss in chance of survival. No other test is possible. But once we perform the required test – once, that is, we have calculated the individual's compensating variation by reference to revealed or expressed values – we have no need for the aforementioned sophisticated model. For by reference to the figure revealed by our direct test, we are compelled either to reject the model or not to reject the model. And where we do not have to reject the model, we should save time and effort by simply deriving the value of life by the direct test.

I would not want to appear too rigid however. I would readily grant that if a new model for calculating the worth of a human life not only survived the direct test but also yielded other important implications then, provided these implications successfully met empirical tests also, the model would not be redundant. But the new models mentioned above are not of that type. They address themselves entirely to the value of life,[4] and, as stated, they persist in conceiving this value as deriving in some way from expected earnings or consumption over the future.

Once we agree that such models can be tested only by reference to the subjective valuations of the individuals themselves, they are unacceptable for

[3] Thus Q would be H^T in Conley's 1976 paper, WE in Arthur's 1980 paper, and RL in Jones-Lee's 1980 paper.

[4] To be sure, the paper by Jones-Lee (1980) also introduces the concept of maximum acceptable risk. But he cannot obtain it from his RL figure. He must discover it from direct estimates, or guess at it, or else accept it as a residual from a direct estimate of his $\Delta v/\Delta p$ – always assuming he can also place a reliable figure on his RL.

another reason. Significantly, it is a reason that applies also to the now-familiar calculations of life which are derived directly from estimates of the revealed or expressed compensating variation for a change in risk. For whatever the age and material circumstances of the person, it transpires that there cannot, in the nature of economic behaviour, be a unique value of his life – nor of any 'statistical life' for that matter, always allowing that our individuals are rational and fully informed about the import of the change in risk. Indeed, as we indicate below, the value of life calculated in this way for a given individual can be any figure from zero to infinity according to the magnitude of the change in the existing risk of a particular kind of death. It is of auxiliary interest only that for any specific risk-change this calculated value of life alters also with the type of death envisaged, and also with the way in which that risk is translated into casualties.

II

In view of my scepticism also of the new models purporting to estimate the value of life taking as the crucial datum revealed or expressed preferences, let us turn our attention wholly to the analysis of the subject's willingness to pay for a reduction in some existing risk of death, or his willingness to accept compensation for an increase in that risk. The exposition can be simplified by ignoring all relevant externalities[5] and by concentrating on the risk of a specific sort of death without in any way restricting the essential logic.

The basic idea in this more recent and popular alternative method of calculation can be summarised in the equation

$$V = \frac{v}{r} \tag{1}$$

where V is the calculated value of life, and v is the compensating variation for elimination of the existing risk r – all on a *per annum* basis.

More frequently, however, the formula used is

$$V = \frac{\Delta v}{\Delta r} \tag{2}$$

where Δr is the risk-reduction (or risk increase) from some existing level of risk, and Δv is the corresponding compensating variation – again on a *per annum* basis.[6]

---

[5] For a classification of these externalities, the reader is referred to my, "Evaluation of Life and Limb: A Theoretical Approach," *Journal of Political Economy*, vol. 79 (July 1971), pp. 687–705.

[6] For those economists who have never given this matter much thought, either equation can be made plausible by simple example. In equation (2) for instance, suppose that the existing risk of death is 10 percent per annum, and person A is willing to pay as much as $5,000 to reduce this risk to 9 percent. It follows from equation (2) that Δr, being $1/100$, and Δv, being $5,000, the value of life V must be equal to $500,000. This value for V may be rationalized as follows:

The art of the economist who adopts this seemingly more acceptable approach is directed to estimating the change in risk in some particular occupation or activity and, by recourse to revealed preference (market or experimental data) or expressed preference (questionnaire techniques) to estimate the corresponding individual compensating variations.

Bearing in mind that we are to illustrate the implications of this sort of economic calculation of human life abstracting from externalities and focussing on the annual risk of a specific sort of death to which a group of people is collectively subject, it is appropriate to choose a person A that is in all relevant respects representative of the group. In particular, the compensating variation (CV) he offers for risk-elimination or risk-reduction is to be supposed equal to the mean average of the CVs of the entire group. Following this obvious simplification, the economist intent on calculating the value of a statistical life for the group in question comes up against three problems which we take up in the three following sections.

First, for the rational individual, assumed also to have the Hicksian ordinal behavioral characteristics, a uniform valuation of life using the above formulae is not possible: it necessarily varies with the level of risk and its change.

Secondly, although the ranges of a risk-change that are available from economic data are usually so narrow as to warrant expectation of constancy in the resultant figure for the value of life, the most astonishing discrepancies have appeared in published and manuscript form. However, these seeming discrepancies could conceivably be rational, or else partly or wholly 'irrational' (arising, that is, from inconsistencies in individual orderings).

Thirdly, even if the first difficulty could somehow be circumvented, and the second resolved, a statistical value of human life determined for any particular set of circumstances is not a datum suitable for allocative economics. Employment of such datum can lead to erroneous conclusions.

III

For a given age, pecuniary circumstances, temperament, expectations, etc., constancy in person A's valuation of life requires, from equation (1)

1,000 persons identical to A would, between them, be willing to pay $5,000 times 1,000 or $5 million per annum to reduce the existing collective risk by one percent per annum. Such a reduction would result, however, in an expected saving per annum of 10 lives. The value of each life saved per annum is, therefore, equal to $5 million divided by 10, or $500,000 as stated. It is common to talk of this value of $500,000 as the value of a *statistical* life, inasmuch as the particular lives saved cannot be determined in advance.

It may be noted in passing that the simplifying assumption of identical individuals is unnecessary. Each of these 1,000 individuals could have a different CV for the reduction of the same risk to 9 percent. Provided that the aggregate of their CVs is equal to $5 million, the value of a statistical life to this group continues to be equal to $500,000.

above, that v and r vary in direct proportion; i.e., v/r = a constant V, or

$$v = V.r \dots (0 \leqslant r \leqslant 1) \dots \tag{1a}$$

This simple linear relation is represented in Figure 1 below where v, the compensating variation for risk-*elimination* is measured vertically and r, the expected risk of death is measured horizontally form the origin. For example, when r is equal to 1/5, person A is shown to be willing to pay up to $100,000 to eliminate this risk entirely.

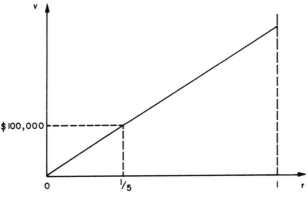

Figure 1

If we now regard the broken vertical line above the point $r = 1$ as a vertical axis about which we can swivel the horizontal axis through an angle of 180° we produce Figure 2 below (the broken line in Figure 1 becoming the solid vertical line in Figure 2, the solid vertical line in Figure 1 being eliminated in Figure 2). Thus, the same linear relationship between v and r now takes on the more familiar economic form of an indifference curve corresponding to a given level of a person A's welfare.

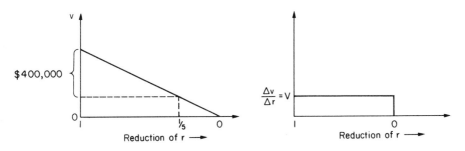

Figures 2/2a

Moving rightward along the horizontal axis we now measure as a good the *per annum reduction* of risk of death – or, if we prefer, the per annum increase in the chance of survival s, where s = (1-r) for $0 \leq s \leq 1$. I shall, however, continue to measure r along the horizontal axis.

The distance v o (measured downward) along the vertical axis represents the maximum annual sum that person A is willing to pay for the total elimination of *certain* death. The height of a point along the straight-line indifference curve to the right of the v intercept would show the smaller sum that person A would, at most, be willing to pay for the total elimination of the corresponding *risk* of death. It follows that the reduction of height in moving rightward from the intercept v to this point measures the largest sum that person A would pay for the corresponding *reduction* of risk (from certain death, that is, to the particular risk in question).

For example, the point q on this straight-line indifference curve indicates that person A is prepared to pay up to $400,000 per annum for the opportunity of transforming, within the relevant time span, the existing state of certain death to a probability of death of one in five. *Per contra*, a movement along this indifference curve to a point that is to the left of q would show the additional income that person A will require in order to induce him to accept additional risk.[7]

The first derivative of equation (1a) is $\frac{dv}{dr} = V_{Constant}$, a relation that can be represented by Figure 2a (the horizontal curve being drawn, by economic convention, above the horizontal axis with the incremental symbol $\Delta v / \Delta r$ replacing the derivative dv/dr).

Constancy of valuation of A's life that is invariant to changes in risk of death clearly requires a straight-line indifference curve as drawn in Figure 2, and, therefore, also a horizontal *marginal* indifference curve (or compensated demand/supply curve) from r = 0 to r = 1. If, for example, we suppose V to be constant at $500,000, then for the Δv of, say, 10^{-6} the corresponding Δv remains unchanged at 50 cents irrespective of the position of Δv within the interval $0 < r < 1$.

Obviously this construction is highly implausible notwithstanding its implicit assumption by economists seeking to attribute some average value to human life by reference to equation (2). Certainly it violates the accepted convexity assumption; the assumption, that is, of diminishing rates of substitution. In this connection, it will be instructive to consider briefly, first the area about the vertical intercept of the indifference curve, and then the area about the horizontal intercept.

In fact, indifference curves between income (or wealth) on the vertical axis and survival (1-r) on the horizontal axis have generally been drawn so as to be

---

[7] Following the Hicksian definitions, the compensating variation for a given increment of risk is equal to the equivalent variation for the *removal* of that increment of risk.

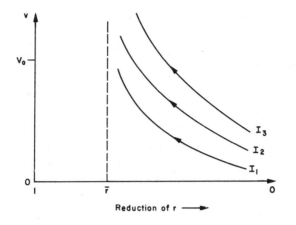

Figure 3

asymptotic to the axes (certainly to the vertical axis) or, rather, asymptotic to a vertical line set at some distance $\bar{r}$ to the right of the vertical axis proper, as illustrated in Figure 3. The implicit assumptions of this familiar construction, however, are (1) that person A is *being compensated* for bearing additional risk (the movement contemplated being in the direction indicated by the arrowheads in the Figure), and (2) that, irrespective of person A's initial level of welfare, there is no sum large enough to induce him to bear a risk as great or greater than $\bar{r}$.[8]

If we accept the first assumption, the second is plausible enough. I should guess that for all but the most reckless or desperate, the critical $\bar{r}$ is well below ½. (I have not yet met a colleague who would honestly agree to accept any sum of money to enter a gamble in which, if at the first toss of a coin it came down heads, he would be summarily executed.)

If we now turn to the horizontal part of the indifference curve, we can be sure – whether we draw the curve with compensating or equivalent compensation in mind – that it is not asymptotic. In either case, as the risk approaches zero, the sum Δv for a small change in risk, Δr, eventually becomes zero.

---

[8] Consistency requires that the area between the vertical axis and the line that is vertical through $\bar{r}$ remain blank. For should we begin instead on the vertical axis at a point v_0 – indicating the individual's income along with the certainty of death – then whatever the terms presented to the individual for reducing the risk of death, he will either remain where he is at v_0 or else he will choose a point (along the terms-of-trade line from v_0) which is right of the vertical line through $\bar{r}$. He cannot, that is, choose a point to the left of $\bar{r}$ since such a point would then be on an indifference curve that is to the left of $\bar{r}$, and any set of indifference curves to the left of $\bar{r}$ not only violates the assumption about the critical nature of $\bar{r}$ but must also cut the asymptotic indifference curves to the right of $\bar{r}$ in Figure 3, thereby violating the consistency axiom.

In the equivalent variation case (where A pays to reduce risk), however, we should bear in mind that in the limiting situation in which the initial situation facing A is certainty of death, the operation of the budget effect (as indicated above) implies that Δv becomes zero after r^*, which point may be well above an r of zero. Even in the compensating variation case, in which the indifference curves are properly drawn asymptotic to a vertical line through $\bar{r}$, as in Figure 3, they will touch the horizontal axis at a point before $r = 0$. This occurs simply because person A is assumed to conceive of some magnitude of risk so small as to be negligible. And this must be the case for a wide range of activities associated with any style of life that is not eccentric. In fact, it would be hard to identify those production or consumption activities of modern man that carry a risk of death as low as, say, 1 in 10 million. In any event, if person A is correctly informed that the use of a step-ladder exposes him to an annual risk of death of one in ten million, and he chooses to ignore it, the corresponding Δv is equal to zero. In the event, the value of life V, calculated from equation (2), is also equal to zero.

Taking the example a step further, it follows that, in a population so large that 50 million people each year use step-ladders, the annual expected loss of 5 lives arising from step-ladder usage has necessarily, by this method, to be valued at zero – a conclusion that is, as we know, abhorrent to economists of the Broomian persuasion.[9]

IV

We turn, finally, to that part of the indifference curve corresponding to observed or suggested changes in risk from some existing risk-level within which economists seeking to derive a statistical value for life are effectively operating. Beginning with some existing annual risk of death, the magnitude of r – let us say a *reduction* in the existing risk of death – is often taken to be within the range 10^{-3} to 10^{-6}.

The values attributed to a statistical life by economists basing their calculations either on revealed or expressed preferences are so various as to excite mirth even among professionals. To my knowledge, the lowest of these calculated values of life (in 1980 dollars) is about $15,000 in Needleman (1980) for roofing workers.[10] The figure produced by the Thaler and Rosen (1976) study, based on 1967 data, average about $200,000, or more than twice that amount in 1980 dollars.[11] Of the several other

[9] See J. Broome, "Trying to Value a Life," *Journal of Political Economy*, vol. 49 (February, 1978), pp. 91–100; and subsequent comments in the same journal, vol. 12 (October 1979), pp. 259–262.
[10] L. Needleman, "The Valuation of Changes in the Risk of Death by Those at Risk," *Manchester School*, vol. XLVIII (September 1980), pp. 229–256.
[11] R. Thaler and S. Rosen, "The Value of Saving a Life: Evidence from the Labour Market," Discussion Paper 74–2, Economics Department, University of Rochester, (1974).

calculations made, the highest mean valuation of life, about $10 million, was that derived by the questionnaire method from a rather limited sample by Lee-Jones (1976).

It is natural for the conscientious economist, disturbed by such outlandish discrepancies, to subject such studies to scrutiny; to examine both the data used and the assumptions made in arriving at the figures for the valuation of a statistical life. A part of Needleman's (1980) paper is most persuasive in revealing how difficult and tricky it can be to isolate a pure occupational risk premium from existing sources of classified data, and also the extreme sensitivity of the calculated valuation to some critical and arbitrary assumption – as, for instance, in Blomquist's (1979) study, which uses 40 per cent (!) of the wage rate as the appropriate value of time in estimating the worth of the average eight seconds of time per journey needed to put on and remove a seat belt.[12]

The discrepancies in calculated value of life from studies of expressed preference alone are no less alarming. And they are sure to arouse suspicion, revealing, as they do, a marked negative relation between Δr and the resultant V.

The more suggestive examples of the latter method of calculating the value of life, V, are found in Mulligan's 1977 paper and that by Frankel (1979), the findings of which are summarised below:[13]

	Reduction in Risk of Death (Δr)	Calculated Life Value (V) (in 1980 U.S. $)
Mulligan:	10^{-3}	$ 62,000
	10^{-4}	428,000
	10^{-5}	3,576,000
Frankel:	10^{-3}	$ 57,000
	10^{-6}	3,370,000

It is hard to resist the temptation to surmise that individuals have some difficulty in grasping the import of risk-reductions of that order of smalls. Introducing a hypothetical limiting case in which the individuals concerned cannot apprehend the import of a risk reduction smaller than one thousandth, as a result of which the average sum offered for a risk reduction

[12] G. Blomquist, "Value of Life Saving: Implications of Consumption Activity," *Journal of Political Economy*, vol. 87 (June 1979), pp. 540–558.
[13] P. Mulligan, "Willingness to Pay for Decreased Risk from Nuclear Plant Accidents," Working Paper No. 3, Energy Extension Program, Penn-State Univ., Nov. 1977; M. Frankel, "Hazard, Opportunity, and the Valuation of Life," Preliminary Report, Economics Department, University of Illinois (November 1979).

of one thousandth, say $50, remains the same also for any smaller risk reduction, we should (using equation (2)) derive the following correspondence between Δr and V.

Δr	V
10^{-3}	$ 50,000
10^{-4}	500,000
10^{-5}	5,000,000

On this hypothesis, we come up with results that are not too different from those actually calculated by Mulligan (1977).

The hypothesis has to be taken seriously. Indeed, in my 1971 paper, I recognized the possible difficulty of people in grasping the 'distance' of large numbers, or their reciprocals, in consequence of which they tend both to overestimate their chances of winning a lottery and their risk of suffering damage. For example, if a lottery offers a 1 in 10,000 chance of winning a prize of $10,000, they would be willing to pay more than one dollar to enter the lottery since, subjectively speaking, their chance of winning appears to them to be much better than one in a thousand. *Mutatis mutandis*, if the risk of a house catching fire during the year is also 1 in 10,000, their apprehension of the risk is greater than that; possibly more like one in 1,000.[14]

An unavoidable agendum for further research in determining the compensating variation for risk reduction, at some given level of risk, is that directed toward discovering just what part of the subject's Δv figure corresponding to a specified Δr figure of 10^{-3}, 10^{-4}, 10^{-5}, or less, is *irrational*; attributable, that is, to a failure of imagination to cope consistently with magnitudes below a certain order. It may transpire that for the operational levels of risk-change currently associated with contemplated policies or projects – as also for the risk-changes that have been used in existing economic studies – the subject's Δv figures are completely irrational; implying that they remain the same irrespective of the Δr magnitude. If, on the other hand, the subjects were indeed able to assess risk-changes of that order with perfect rationality, there would be – if the indifference curve were approximately linear along the relevant range – a direct proportional relation between Δr and Δv.

[14] My 1971 paper suggested, in passing, that this fact of life can explain why the individual both gambles and insures without invoking the utility hypothesis advanced by Friedman and Savage (1946).

One testable (and distinguishable) implication of my suggested hypothesis is that people would prefer to enter ten lotteries, each having a one in 10,000 chance of winning a prize X, to the opportunity of entering a single lottery having a one in 1,000 chance of winning the same prize X. Another would be that people who would pay no more than $100 to fully insure their homes against a one in 1,000 risk of destruction by fire, would be willing to pay more than $10 to fully insure their homes against a one in 10,000 risk of the same fire hazard.

It is, however, important to take precautions, when faced with the results of such studies as those of Mulligan and Frankel cited above, against *assuming* that people are responding irrationally over those ranges of Δr. If, for example, an *existing* risk of death per annum of 1 in 500 can be reduced either by a Δr_1 of 10^{-3} for which person A would pay a Δv_1 of $100, or reduced by a Δr_2 of 10^{-4} for which person A would pay $60, we are *not* at liberty to assume any irrationality – even though the respective calculations of a statistical life, V_1 and V_2, are $100,000 and $600,000. For it is not impossible that the relevant portion of the indifference curve is markedly curvilinear.

Irrationality is certainly present,[15] however, if person A is willing to pay $60, not only for an initial risk-reduction Δr_2, but also for subsequent risk-reductions equal to Δr_2. More generally, in the above example, he is irrational if he is willing to pay ten consecutive sums for ten consecutive risk-reductions, all equal to Δr_2, that in aggregate *exceed* $100. For in that case, by using two different procedures, person A can be seen to choose two different Δv figures – $100 in the first experiment, more than $100 in the second – for exactly the same risk-change of Δr_1 equal to 10^{-3}.

On the other hand, person A is *not* behaving irrationally if he is willing to pay as much as $60 for an initial risk-reduction of Δr_2, but so much less for each of nine successive Δr_2s that the total he is willing to pay at most for ten successive risk-reductions of Δr_2 comes exactly to $100 – this $100 being the most he offers, in our example, for a single risk-reduction Δr_1 equal to 10^{-3}.

V

Finally, in order to illustrate the sort of error that can arise in any allocative exercise by recourse to a figure for the value of a statistical life, it is clearly appropriate to assume that person A has a consistent ordering of valuations over the relevant range of risk changes. Let us suppose, therefore, that with an existing risk of, say, 1 in a hundred, person A's Δv_1 for a risk-reduction Δr_1 of $1/500$ is $1,000 (which yields a value of life of V of $500,000) whereas for a risk-reduction Δr_2 of only $1/1000$, his Δv_2 is $800 (which yields a value of life V_2 of $800,000). As required, however, person A is quite consistent in his risk valuations since, moving from the existing risk of $1/100$ to $8/1000$ – a Δr_1 of $2/1000$ – he is willing to pay $1,000; whereas

---

[15] Where there is a small likelihood of removing the subject's irrationality – manifest over the required magnitudes of Δr – from some existing level of risk, the economist may wish to experiment with larger magnitudes of Δr in the attempt to discover some range of consistent Δvs. If, over such a range, the Δvs vary (approximately) in direct proportion to the Δrs, the persistent economist might take the liberty of extending this proportionality to the smaller changes in Δrs that are actually involved in the project under scrutiny. The Δvs so calculated would have to be regarded, however, as an upper limit.

for moving from this same existing risk of 1/100 to 9/1000 – a Δr_2 of only 1/1000 – he is willing to pay \$800. Thus, for a first risk-reduction of 1/1000 he will pay \$800, and for a further risk-reduction of 1/1000 he will pay only \$200.

With these data we now consider a whole community of A persons[16] that is faced with the choice of two types of technically feasible alternative projects. Project I reduces the collective risk of death for one million people by Δr_1 (by 2/1000) at a total cost of \$1 billion, whereas project II reduces the collective risk of death for the same one million people by Δr_2 (by 1/1000) for a total cost of \$0.6 billion. In neither case, we suppose, are there any benefits other than the reduction of these risks.

A properly conducted cost-benefit analysis finds in favor of project II being adopted. For each of projects such as I, which reduces risk by Δr_1 (2/1000) for one million people, confers a total benefit of (1 million times \$1,000), or \$1 billion, for a cost of exactly \$1 billion. Each of projects, such as II, on the other hand, reducing risk by Δr_2 (1/1000) for one million people, confers a total benefit of (1 million times \$800), or \$0.8 billion, for a total cost of \$0.6 billion, yielding a benefit-cost ratio of 4/3.

If therefore a budget of, say, \$3 billion is available to spend on reducing this particular risk of death, the conclusion of a cost-benefit analysis would propose 5 type-II projects to yield an aggregate benefit of \$4 billion, rather than 3 type-I projects that would yield an aggregate benefit of only \$3 billion for the same \$3 billion cost.

To the economist who chooses instead to operate with a valuation of a statistical life, this result would not be apparent and, indeed, would seem unacceptable. First of all, by reference to equation (2), he will be faced with a seeming inconsistency: the data above yield him two valuations of life, a V_1 of \$500,000 and a V_2 of \$800,000. If he is to make a calculation for these two projects by calculating benefits in terms of lives saved he has to choose one or other of these two valuations of life – or, some valuation between those of V_1 and V_2. But whatever the value of life he finally decides to adopt, he will reject the conclusion of the cost-benefit analysis; indeed, he will reverse it.

Thus, thinking in terms of lives saved, he will point out that if the available \$3 billion is spent on 5 projects of the II-type (as recommended in the cost-benefit analysis) the expected total saving in lives will be (5 million times 1/1000) or 5,000 lives saved *per annum*. In contrast, if the \$3 billion is spent instead on 3 projects of the I-type, the expected total saving in lives will be (3 million times 2/1000) or 6,000 lives saved *per annum*. Whatever the figure

[16] It is, perhaps, unnecessary to repeat that this simplifying condition is not essential. It is sufficient if the aggregate of the Δvs for the one million people affected by the risk reduction Δr_1 comes to \$1 billion, and by the risk reduction Δr_2 comes to \$0.8 billion.

used for the value of a life, then, more lives will therefore be saved if the $3 billion is spent entirely on I projects. Consequently, aggregate benefits are higher investing the $3 billion in I projects rather than in II, contrary to the findings of the cost-benefit analysis.

There is no paradox in these contrary results. By reference to the axiom basic to all evaluative techniques, which requires the economist to respect the value placed by the individual on the change in his own welfare resulting from the introduction of the policy or project in question, the latter calculation made by treating as benefits the *value of lives saved* will be in error. By the same token, the former calculation which treats the benefits to the community as no more than the value to it of the collective *reduction in risk* will be correct.

Sticking to his last, that is, the evaluating economist is compelled to recognize that, in the last resort, the benefits at issue are not those of saving life *per se*; they are those of reductions in risk. And the benefits from such risk-reductions have to be valued according as they are perceived by the individuals so affected.

Thus, in the above example, each of the A individuals is willing to pay $800 for an initial reduction of 1/1000 in the annual risk of death. But he is willing to pay no more than $200 for a subsequent reduction of this risk of 1/1000. This fact is overlooked in the valuation-of-life approach. As a result (i) an initial risk-reduction of 1/1000 for each of two A individuals is no different (in its effect on lives saved) from the alternative (ii) an initial risk-reduction of 2/1000 for a single individual A. There is, however, indeed a big difference between alternatives (i) and (ii) where there is a direct valuation of the sorts of risk-reduction involved. In (i), the total benefit enjoyed by the two A individuals is $1,600, whereas in (ii) the total benefit enjoyed by the single A individual for the same amount of risk-reduction is only $1,000. It follows, therefore, that for the same $3 billion outlay, installing 5 projects of the II kind, which make 5 million A persons better off by $4 billion (5 million × $800), confers greater benefits on this society – as measured by society's willingness to pay – than installing 3 projects of the I kind, which make no more than 3 million A persons better off by only $3 billion (3 million × $1,000). And this is true even though, in the event, the expected saving of lives only would actually be greater in the latter case.[17]

---

[17] Notwithstanding the standard format of economic evaluation, method I – in which the benefits are calculated in terms of the value of (statistical) lives saved – is not a genuine cost-benefit analysis. It is equivalent, rather, to a cost-effectiveness analysis. It is a ranking of the alternative projects by reference to the least cost of saving a statistical life – plus a proviso, however, that for a project to enter the lists, the cost per life saved must not exceed its value.

VI

In conclusion, I have sought to establish the following propositions all of which argue against attempts by economists to put a value on human life.

1. That a value of life calculated in the main from models of expected (utility of) lifetime consumption, income, production, reproduction, and so forth – more generally from any model that disregards the individuals' revealed or expressed preference (in respect of risk-changes) in favour of more accessible economic data[18] – no matter how technically impressive, could be accepted only if it were vindicated by a test that, in any evaluative context, had reference ultimately to the subjects' own valuations. But since we have first to be satisfied with the value of life derived from such a test before we may accept or reject the findings of a more elaborate model, such necessary test renders the model itself superfluous.

2. However, it also transpires that it is *not* possible to determine some average workaday value for human life for any given population, or for that matter, a unique value for a statistical life by reference to the compensating variation measure of the individual's own subjective valuation for a given risk-change – even allowing that the economist normalizes for age, income, family circumstances, and all other relevant characteristics. This is simply because the crucial $\Delta v/\Delta r$ ratio varies, *inter alia*, with the level of risk r, with the magnitude of Δr, with the interpretation placed on Δr and also, of course, with the specific sort of death envisaged.[19] In particular, a valuation of life derived from the $\Delta v/\Delta r$ ratio will vary from zero (for small enough levels of r

---

[18] Passages such as the one below in Arthur, "Risks to Life," p. 64, are revealing:

A change in the pattern of the mortality schedule, it was shown, should be assessed by the difference it makes to expected length of life, production, reproduction, and consumption support; loss of life should be assessed by the expected opportunity costs of lost years, production and reproduction, less support costs.

Clearly, there is no social sanction – more precisely, no sanction from the basic axiom of economic evaluation – in the word "should" as used above. The "should" can be intended only to refer to conclusions that are to be inferred from the model as elaborated by the author.

[19] A given Δr is itself open to a number of alternative interpretations. For example, an increased annual risk of one in 1,000 of a specific sort of death could mean (a), an expected increase of $n/1000$ deaths annually for a community of n individuals affected by the project in question, there being no way of discovering in advance the exact number of deaths that will occur in any future year. This has been the interpretation of Δr as used in the text. Alternatively, however, the same Δr could refer to (b), a situation in which each year *exactly* $n/1000$ deaths will occur. Again, this same Δr could be used to express (c), the expected destruction each year of a community of, say, 10,000 people within a region containing 1,000 such communities. (In this connection, see Keeney, "Equity and Public Risk," *Operations Research*, (May/June 1980); and M. W. Jones-Lee, M. Hummerton, and V. Abbot, "Equity and Public Risk: Some Empirical Results," *Opinion Research*, vol. 30 (January/February 1982), pp. 203–207). People will not, in general, be indifferent as between these three alternative interpretations of the same Δr.

and Δr) to infinity (for large enough levels of r and Δr). And there is no justification for the economist choosing to derive his valuation from any one of an unlimited number of such ratios.

3. Although for required or measurable magnitudes of Δr effective linearity of the indifference curve might obtain, so producing a constant valuation of life V, it so happens – providentially in my opinion – that for the cases being studied by economists such constancy does not emerge. In fact, in all studies where very different Δr measures have been used, the $\Delta v/\Delta r$ (and therefore also the V) has varied inversely, and quite remarkably, with the magnitude of Δr. Such studies suggest that, in addition to the possible convexity of the indifference curve over the particular range of Δv variation, individual consistency breaks down for small orders of Δv. Testing for such consistency at operational magnitudes of Δr is therefore necessary.

4. Not only is the search for a usable value of human life – even where all the economic circumstances of the population are known and the particular risk specified – a search for a green mare's nest, persistence in employing the concept can seriously vitiate the evaluation of projects that save or destroy lives. As indicated in section V, a calculation of social benefits (or losses) made by translating the value of risk-changes into values for a statistical life can, in quite plausible instances, lead both to error and to a misranking of alternative projects.

For these reasons I propose that economists give up the search to discover a value for human life, or for a statistical life in any specific circumstances, and, in order to avoid error, to restrict their investigations of those projects or policies that, *inter alia*, affect life and limb to deriving consistent estimates only of compensating variations for the relevant changes in the specific risks associated with the particular projects in question, these alone being are the pertinent benefits or losses.

Economics, London

Note: At the author's request, this piece has not been edited.

THE VALUE OF LIFE FOR DECISION MAKING IN THE PUBLIC SECTOR*

Dan Usher

The Ministry of Transport is planning for the construction of new roads in its territory. Many projects are being considered, and the Ministry needs to identify the worthwhile projects for which the benefits exceed the costs. Among costs and benefits are the expense of constructing the road, the time saved by motorists using the new road rather than some other road, the time saved through the reduction of congestion on other roads, and the expected increase or decrease in the number of deaths due to traffic accidents. I am concerned in this paper with the last item on the list. It is, of course, difficult to estimate fatalities accurately, but this difficulty is neither unique nor central to our problem. The problem is how best to place a monetary value on fatalities, so that the expected number of fatalities can be compared with other costs and benefits in deciding whether to build a road. However chosen, the monetary value of fatalities for use in this context is what the economist means by "the value of life." The term is almost a joke, a bit of gallows humor to exorcise the ghoulishness that inevitably clings to analysis of life and death in monetary terms.

The problem is unavoidable. The road will be built or it will not be built, and a decision either way is a statement about the value of life. If the total cost of the road is $5,000,000, if the benefits in time saved amount to $4,000,000, and if there is an expected reduction of four deaths from traffic accidents, then a decision to build the road implies a value of life of not less than $250,000 per life, while a decision not to build implies a value of life of not more than $250,000.

We must distinguish between statistical and actual lives. A statistical life is saved when the mortality rate of a group of people is reduced sufficiently that one less person will die than would otherwise be the case, as when each of 1,000 men experiences a decrease in his mortality rate from .01 to .009. If each man would pay up to but not more than $250 to bring about that decrease in his own mortality rate, then the 1,000 men together would pay up to $250,000 and we say that the group collectively places a value of $250,000 on the saving of one statistical life. An actual life is saved when the

* Thanks to Jack Mintz for comments on an earlier draft.

identity of the beneficiary is known before the lifesaving expenditure is made. The distinction is important for the motivation of lifesaving expenditure. If it costs $250,000 to save Esther's life, and if she cannot obtain that sum herself, then her life depends on the good will, decency, generosity, or prior commitment of her community. If it costs $250,000 to save a statistical life, then the interest of each member of the community is the same, and the life will be lost or saved on purely selfish considerations, according to whether each man's value of life is greater or less than $250,000. This statement will have to be modified to some extent as we proceed. The point here is that value-of-life calculations are about the saving of statistical lives.

We might object that life is too precious to weigh against mere dollars in such calculations, but we cannot translate that objection into rules for the Ministry of Transport to follow. To refuse to compare lives and money is not to treat life as infinitely precious. It is to treat life as worthless, for roads would then be built regardless of lives lost or saved. Nor can we seek to minimize the number of lives lost in traffic accidents. The entire national income is not large enough to finance a policy of reducing fatalities in every possible way, regardless of the cost.

There is an inescapable trade-off of mortality rates for time or money in our personal lives, as, for instance, when we install a smoke detector in the house, but not one for every room, or when we fasten safety belts for some but not for all rides in the car. There is a similar and equally inescapable trade-off of lives for money in the public sector in the financing and administration of road-building, medicine, environmental protection, and above all, national defense. The government must trade lives for money on our behalf, and we want it to do so on more or less the same principles that we adopt in our personal lives.

Most of this paper will examine the difficulties with the concept and measurement of the value of life. The concept will disintegrate somewhat as we proceed, measures will become fuzzy, and the reader may begin to wonder whether it might not be best to recognize the importance of lifesaving in a general, nonquantitative way without reference to a value of life in money terms. There are three reasons why it may be important for the public sector to choose a specific numerical value of life, even if the number itself has to be chosen arbitrarily to some extent.

First, lives may be wasted, thrown away without compensating advantage, if no single value of life is recognized in public sector decision making. One department of the hospital is administered by a sensible, frugal doctor who is careful not to waste the taxpayers' money. He refuses to purchase a machine that costs $1,000,000 and would in all probability result in the saving of 100 lives. Another department is administered by a doctor whose mission it is to save lives regardless of the cost and who hires extra nurses at an average cost of $50,000 per nurse as long as an extra nurse has a one in ten chance of saving a patient's life during the year. Never mind, for the moment, whether the hard-hearted or the soft-hearted doctor is correct in his implicit assessment of the value of life. The point is that they cannot both be right. The purchase of the machine coupled with hiring twenty fewer nurses would save 100 lives in one department at a cost of only 2 lives in the other, and at no extra expense to the hospital. Any specified value of life between $10,000 – the implicit value of life of the hard-hearted doctor – and $500,000 – the implicit value of life of the soft-hearted doctor – would avoid the anomaly automatically, while values outside these limits would impose frugality in both departments or neither. I am not asserting here that a death is a death is a death. There may be many reasons why one death is more to be avoided than another; one disease may strike the young and healthy, while another may strike those who are old and soon to die of some other disease. I am asserting that distinctions among deaths should be based on something more substantial than our unwillingness to calculate.

Second, in matters of life and death, as in all other matters, the public sector should act to make the average citizen as well-off as possible. This implies that there be a relation – not necessarily an identity, as we shall see – between the individual's value of life and the value of life implicit in public sector decision making. It is difficult to see how such a relation can be maintained, without at the same time designating an exact numerical value of life for decision making in the public sector.

Third, a numerical value of life – a number chosen by the government and employed by all departments for projects involving the saving or losing of lives – is a defense against the emergence of (quite literally) life-and-death conflicts among people in different regions or social classes. In the building of roads or hospitals, the life of a randomly-chosen resident of city A may count for more (or less as the case may be) than that of a randomly-chosen resident of city B, depending on the influence at the center of their representatives, unless some reasonably objective procedure is employed to ensure that lives are counted equally. Citizens may be in broad agreement about the value of life to be employed in public sector projects where the losing or saving of statistical lives is involved and where each citizen is implicitly trading his tax dollars for changes in *his* mortality rate. Should the government fail to specify a unique value of life for all public sector decisions, it becomes a vital interest of people in every county, age group, or circumstance to use all available means to persuade the government to undertake projects in which their life expectancy is increased at the expense of the community as a whole. Potential unanimity among voters may give way to "tragic choices" if the public sector is too squeamish to specify a value of life, or if the refusal to do so is a device by which one group gains advantages not open to everyone else.[1]

The case for a single, nationwide value of life in public sector decision making is similar in many respects to the case for a single, nationwide discount rate, and that case grows stronger with every increase in the influence of the public sector in the economy. To be sure, there is no universally accepted value of life, in Canada or in any other country today. Public sector decision making is on that account less efficient and more acrimonious than it needs to be. Despite the diversity of estimates of the value of life to be discussed below, I believe that the literature on this topic has created a pressure toward uniformity that has contributed to efficiency and harmony in public sector decision making.

The organization of the paper is as follows. I begin with an examination of the meaning of the term "value of life" in the literature of economics, with special emphasis on the distinction between statistical and actual lives. Next, I look at evidence on the value of life as manifested in behavior in life-threatening situations. A value of life is implicit in the premium for undertaking dangerous work and in the usage of safety devices such as smoke alarms and seat belts in cars. I also consider how people differ in their personal values of life and how a social value of life might incorporate the value one man places on another man's life. Then, I look at public valuation with special emphasis on whether the public sector should value lives equally or according to the valuation of the person at risk. Finally, I try to come to terms with an objection to the use of a value of life in cost-benefit analysis. One cannot help being concerned that there is something immoral about the enterprise, that it is wrong to trade lives for money. I try to examine the basis for this concern, to determine when it is justified and when not.

The Meaning of Life

(a) *Alternative definitions of the value of life.* The term "value of life" or "value of a man" has been used in a variety of contexts and with a corresponding variety of meanings. Contrast our example of road-building in the opening paragraph of this paper with the situation of a man who is deciding how much insurance to buy. Suppose his object in buying insurance is to see to it that his family would be financially no worse off if he dies than if he lives. The appropriate amount of insurance would then be the difference between

---

[1] A tragic choice is a choice that society finds intolerable, though it must be made all the same. A choice is tragic when something of great importance – the right to bear children, the right to live, or the requirement to bear arms in the defense of one's country – has to be assigned to some but not to all citizens. See Guido Calabresi and Philip Bobbit, *Tragic Choices* (New York: W. W. Norton & Co., 1978).

the present value of his earnings over his life and the present value of his portion of the family's consumption. The result of this calulation is sometimes referred to as "the value of a man," a not unreasonable usage of the phrase.[2]

The value of life in the context of road-building or other projects affecting mortality rates and the value of life in the context of the purchase of insurance are not two measures or two interpretations of the same concept; they are two distinct concepts that happen to share the same name. This has been a source of much confusion in the literature where the "willingness to pay" approach and the "human capital" approach are often contrasted, as though the approached object, whatever it might be, were the same for both. The earliest studies of the value of a man were attempts to ascertain the right amount of insurance, and there has been a tendency to treat estimates of the present value of consumption, gross income, or net income as measures of the value of life appropriate for cost-benefit analysis. The complexity of this issue is compounded by several considerations: the value of life (defined as the amount of money I would pay to avoid a small probability of death divided by the probability itself) would normally be expected to increase with the present value of income or consumption; there are assumptions on which the present value of the stream of consumption is a lower bound to the value of life; the present value of the net income of the person at risk *is* relevant for cost-benefit analysis; and my concern for the welfare of my family may be a component of my value of life. I will discuss these issues presently. For the moment, the important consideration is that the value of life and the present value of consumption or earnings are conceptually and empirically distinct.

The present value of earnings may also be relevant in determining awards to victims of crime or negligence, where the purpose of the award is to preserve the victim's standard of living. The value of life, on the other hand, is the appropriate concept for adjustments to the measure of economic growth of nations to account for changes over time in age-specific mortality rates. The evaluation of programs of birth control is somewhat more complicated because a social value is placed on the nonexistence of a potential being. Our concern here is not with any of these matters. It is exclusively with the saving or losing of lives in public sector projects associated with such matters as the provision of medical care, public works, or protection of the environment.

---

[2] See, for instance, Louis Dublin and Alfred Lotka, *The Money Value of a Man* (New York: Ronald Press, 1930). Dublin and Lotka were quite explicit in asserting that the purpose of their calculation was to determine the appropriate amount of insurance. The same kind of calculation has been employed – inappropriately in my opinion – to determine the value of life for cost-benefit analysis. See Dorothy Rice and Barbara Cooper, "The Economic Value of Human Life," *American Journal of Public Health*, 1967, reprinted and updated in Steven Rhoads, ed., *Valuing Life: Public Policy Dilemmas* (Boulder, Colorado: Westview Press, 1980).

It is also useful to distinguish between (1) the value of my life to me, (2) the value of my life to you, and (3) the value of life in cost-benefit analysis. If I am subject to a one in a thousand chance of losing my life and if the risk can be eliminated by the payment of a certain sum of money, the value of my life to me is what I would pay to eliminate the risk (multiplied by 1,000). Its value to you is what you would pay to eliminate the risk, a sum that would only be positive if your concern for my welfare takes precedence over your interest as the inheritor of my share of the assets of the nation. The value of life in cost-benefit analysis is what we collectively would pay to save the life of a randomly-selected person.

(b) *Categories of lives saved or lost.* What we have in mind when we speak of a decision to save a statistical life is that we pay a certain sum to save a randomly-chosen person. If we undertake the transaction, we may never know which one of us has been saved. If we do not undertake the transaction, we shall have no time or opportunity to change our minds, once the victim is identified. Road safety fits this pattern quite well. Medical care fits the pattern less well, for we may have the opportunity to treat the disease after the patient has fallen ill. A decision not to provide artificial hearts requires us to watch the death of someone whose life might have been prolonged, if we were prepared to pay the price, though we did not know who the patient would be when the decision was made. The distinction is between the saving of a statistical, never-to-be-identified life and the saving of some unknown person who will in time be identified. The latter is always the more painful choice, and the implied value of life in public sector decision making might be correspondingly higher.

Both variants of statistical lives are distinct from (1) the Doctor's dilemma where a choice must be made between two potential victims because society has the means to save one but not both, and (2) the unique event where the decision to save or not to save cannot be made before the victim is identified, as when a trapped mountain climber can be rescued at great expense. The Doctor's dilemma and the unique event involve the saving of actual lives and require altruism or principles of just conduct on the part of the decision makers, while both varieties of statistical lives can be dealt with by enlightened self-interest.

Among the four cases – the saving of statistical, unidentified lives, the saving of statistical, identified lives, Doctor's dilemma, and the unique event – the first is, in a sense, the easy case. The others are progressively more problematic. Value of life calculations are most useful in the easy case, where the identity of the victim is unknown until it is too late to influence his fate. The easy case is, I believe, the common case in cost-benefit analysis. It includes virtually all decisions about traffic safety, protection of the environment, the release of dangerous substances into the upper atmosphere, and a great deal of medical expenditure, including such decisions as whether to equip a mobile first-aid team to treat heart attacks. There are instances in which it is impossible or unappealing to decide matters of life and death according to calculations of cost and benefit, but the existence of hard cases is no reason for not dealing with the easy cases easily. Specification of a value of life for statistical, unidentified lives does not make the hard cases any harder, and the failure to employ a common measure of the value of life makes easy cases difficult.

(c) *The justification for calculations ex ante.* I have been assuming that risks are to be assessed in the public sector *ex ante* rather than *ex post*. This point of view has recently been called into question:

> A project is going to kill someone. As yet she does not know; to her the project only appears to increase slightly her chances of dying. For the sake of the project's benefits she and everyone else would, were they to have a vote, accept it unanimously. Of course, if she knew what was going to happen to her she would veto it at once. Now, actually, there is to be no vote and the government is deciding. Can it justifiably accept the project on the grounds that a unanimous vote would have done so? I think not (though it might on other grounds, depending on the full circumstances). The government knows that the vote would have turned out that way only because the voters are not fully informed. It also knows that, had they been fully informed, the vote would not have been unanimous, and it knows this, notice, even if it knows no better than anyone else just whom the project will kill; whoever it is, he or she would certainly have voted against it. If the government's decision is to be modeled on a hypothetical vote, it cannot be justified to model it on a hypothetical ignorant vote when the outcome of a hypothetical informed vote is equally predictable. An informed vote is a better model than an ignorant one.[3]

The premise in this quotation is that no project is acceptable unless the winners can compensate the losers, where winners and losers are identified after the event and not merely in anticipation of the event. The victim is dead. She can no longer be compensated with money. The "compensation test" must fail.

---

[3] John Broome, "Trying to Value a Life," *Journal of Public Economics*, vol. 9 (February 1977), pp. 91–100. See also the comments by Buchanan and Faith, Jones-Lee and Williams, and the reply by Broome, in *Journal of Public Economics*, vol. 12 (October 1979), pp. 245–265. Buchanan and Faith's defense of the use of a value of life in cost-benefit analysis is that "The only test for Pareto-superiority of one project over another lies in the expressed or revealed unanimity of all persons affected by the alternatives. The Wicksellian unanimity test incorporates the Pareto-superiority criterion and the cost-benefit test, when properly conceived and applied." Buchanan and Faith are right, in my opinion, and Broome is wrong.

The *ex post* compensation test does indeed fail, and I would argue – contrary to the spirit of the quotation – that it is a poor test on that account. Paradoxical as this may seem, it is not the case that knowledge is always better than ignorance, that "an informed vote is a better model than an ignorant one." Suppose that a project is going to kill someone, that the net value of all benefits less all other costs is $300,000, and that the common value of life is $500,000. As long as the identity of the victim is unknown, the community will vote *unanimously* not to undertake the project. If the name of the victim were known and if the victim's assets were insufficient to enable him to bribe the community to do otherwise, the community will vote *almost unanimously* to undertake the project, for everyone but the victim himself has an incentive to proceed. If the identity of the victim were unknown but could be revealed, the community would vote unanimously, and would pay up to $200,000, not to have that information revealed. Ignorance is preferable to knowledge whenever risks can be pooled.[4] Everyone can agree to compensate the victim with money when the harm is not lethal, and to desist from acts that will cause lives to be lost when the net benefit falls short of the value of life, as long as the identity of the victim is unknown.

Ex post unanimity is a useless criterion in an uncertain world because someone is going to lose out whatever we do. If we build the road, Mr. A will die in a traffic accident. If we do not build the road, Mr. B will die in a traffic accident. We may not know the identities of A and B when the decision is made, but we must discover the identity of one of them eventually. Both building the road and not building the road must be rejected on the *ex post* compensation test, for neither party can be compensated for the loss of his life. Action requires some other criterion.

We are always confronted with risk, including the risk of losing our lives. The best we can do is to seek the most favorable prospects, knowing full-well that any course of action may turn out disastrously. Similarly, in cost-benefit analysis we try to establish rules that make a randomly-selected person as well-off as he can be in the long run, knowing full-well that no set of rules can ever be best for everyone *ex post*. *Ex ante*, the benefits of a project to the survivors may compensate for a small extra risk of death that the project entails, or a small reduction in the risk of death may be worth the cost. No other comparison is possible.[5]

---

[4] There is now a substantial literature on the question of when knowledge is socially advantageous and when it is not. See Jack Hirshleifer, "The Private and Social Value of Information and the Reward for Inventive Activity," *American Economic Review*, vol. LXI (September 1971), pp. 561–574, and J.M. Marshall, "Private Incentives and Public Information," *American Economic Review*, vol. 64 (June 1974); pp. 373–390.

[5] For a good introduction to the theoretical literature on the value of life, see Joanne Linnerooth, "The Value of Human Life: A Review of Models," *Economic Inquiry*, vol. XVII (January 1979), pp. 52–74. Much recent work is discussed in K. W. Jones-Lee, ed., *The Value of Life and Safety* (Amsterdam: North-Holland Publishing Company, 1982).

Measuring the Value of Life

(a) *A table of estimates*. Ideally, one would estimate the value of life by asking people what life is worth: "What would you pay to avoid playing Russian roulette when the barrel of the gun contains 999 blanks and one live bullet?" "What would you accept to drink the contents of a cup when there is a one in a thousand chance that it is poison?" If the answer to these questions is $500, then the value of life is half a million dollars.

There are obvious practical difficulties in trying to determine the value of life by asking questions of this sort. People may be quite mistaken in their predictions of what they would do if the situations described were for real. The manner of death may influence the answers. An aversion to playing games with life and death may lead subjects to claim that they would pay more to avoid these risks than they would if the risk arose more naturally, as in decisions among alternative modes of transport. Individuals may find it difficult to reason about small probabilities.

In practice, the value of life must be inferred from situations where people buy or sell small risks of death as part of ordinary economic activity. Inferences as to the value of life can be gleaned from evidence about the rates of hazard pay and the corresponding risks to which one would be subjected, about occupational mortality rates and wages in different occupations, about the cost of smoke detectors and their effects in reducing the risk of getting caught in a fire, about the choice of driving speed in circumstances where each increase in speed is a trade-off between the saving of time and the risk of accident, about when people wear safety belts, and so on. The value of life which cannot be observed directly must be cunningly inferred from evidence of individual behavior. A list of recent estimates is contained in the accompanying table.

Table 1

Estimates of the Value of Life*

(original data converted to 1982 Canadian dollars; figures are in thousands)

From the Labor Market

1.	correlation of wages and mortality rates among occupations	481
2.	correlation of wages and mortality rates among occupations	632
3.	correlation of wages and mortality rates among occupations	1,496
4.	correlation of wages and mortality rates among occupations	3,200
5.	correlation of wages and mortality rates among occupations	6,000
6.	hazard pay	170

From Consumption Activity

7.	the purchase of smoke detectors	175
8.	speeding on highways	305
9.	the decision to wear a seat belt	593
10.	house values and environmental risk	616

* Sources for Table 1 are:

1. A. Dillingham, "The Injury Risk Structure of Occupations and Wages," Ph.D. Dissertation, Cornell, 1979;
2. Richard Thaler and Sherwin Rosen, "The Value of Saving a Life: Evidence from the Labour Market," in N. Terleckyj, ed., *Household Production and Consumption*, N.B.E.R. Conference on Income and Wealth, 1975;
3. C. Brown, "Equalizing Differences in the Labour Market," *Quarterly Journal of Economics*, vol. 94 (February 1980), pp. 113–134;
4. C. A. Olson, "An Analysis of Wage Differentials Received by Workers on Dangerous Jobs," *The Journal of Human Resources*, vol. 10 (Summer 1981), pp.165–185;
5. W. K. Viscusi, *Risk by Choice* (Cambridge: Harvard University Press, 1983), p. 105;
6. Lionel Needleman, "The Valuation of Changes in the Risk of Death by Those at Risk," *The Manchester School*, vol. 48 (September 1980), pp. 229–254;
7. R. Dardis, "The Value of Life: New Evidence from the Marketplace," *American Economic Review*, vol. 70 (December 1980), pp. 1077–1082;
8. D. Ghosh, D. Lees, and W. Seal, "Optimal Motorway Speed and Some Valuations of Life and Time," *The Manchester School*, vol. 43 (June 1975), pp. 134–143;
9. Glen Bloomquist, "Value of Life-saving: Implications of Consumption Activity," *Journal of Political Economy*, vol. 87 (June 1979), pp. 540–558; and
10. P. Portney, "Housing Prices, Health Effects, and Valuing Reductions in Risk of Death," *Journal of Environment Economics and Management*, vol. 8 (January 1981), pp. 72–78.

Technical problems in employing market information to estimate the value of life are discussed by Glen Bloomquist in "The Value of Human Life: An Empirical Perspective," *Economic Inquiry*, vol. XIX (January 1981), pp. 157–164, and by Steven Landefeld and Eugene Seskin in "The Economic Value of Life: Linking Theory to Practice," *American Journal of Public Health*, vol. 72 (June 1982), pp. 555–565. In item 6, Needleman estimated the value of life for roofing workers, steel erectors, and scaffolders in the U.K. to be 8,000, 17,000, and 46,000 respectively. The figure in the table is a simple average of the three, converted to 1982 Canadian dollars. Needleman's estimates are considerably lower than the other estimates based on data from the labor market. Two possible explanations are that the wage rate in the U.K. is substantially below the wage rate in the U.S. and that hazard pay is typically received by those who are less risk averse than the work force as a whole.

The estimates vary considerably, as one might expect, for they refer to different groups of people, situations, and times, and they also reflect different hypotheses of the investigators. Taken as a whole, they suggest that the value of life might be somewhere between half a million and a million dollars. That is good enough, for any arbitrarily-chosen number within that range will do the job of rationalizing public sector decision making. There are unlikely to be many projects that would be accepted when the value of life is set at $1,000,000 but rejected when the value of life is reduced to $500,000. Major anomalies would be eliminated. A project that is sensitive to variations in the value of life within the range is a marginal project in any case.

(b) *The Variability of the Value of Life.* An obvious question presents itself. Does the variation in the estimates of the value of life reflect our limited capacity to measure a single true value out there in the market, or does the variation in the estimates reflect a variation among people in their values of life? Do people differ in their value of life according to age, wealth, health, occupational status, or the idiosyncrasies of taste? Measurement error is likely to be substantial for so elusive an object as the value of life, but there may be more involved.

The natural starting point for the analysis of this question is the observation that the value of life is a price, a trade-off between reduction in mortality rates and money. It is characteristic of most prices that they are the same for everyone in the market. The price of butter, for example, is the same for young and old, rich and poor, people who love butter and people who do not. The grocer who tried to charge a premium to those of his customers who liked butter best would soon lose those customers to his competitors. If the price of life were like the price of butter, the value of life would be the same for everyone, though the amounts of safety purchased would not. If that were so, then differences in the estimates of the value of life would have to be attributed to measurement error alone.

There is, however, an essential difference between the price of life and the price of butter, a difference that can be explained best by a brief digression into considerations of international trade. In trades between countries, two polar types of goods can be identified: *traded goods* like watches or rice that "in principle" have the same price everywhere (just as butter has a unique price to all buyers in any given market); and *untraded goods* like haircuts that have different prices in different places because they can only be consumed where they are produced. An Englishman, without leaving London, can buy rice grown in Thailand, but he cannot buy a haircut in Bangkok. The relative price of watches produced in England and rice produced in Thailand will differ somewhat between London and Bangkok because of international transport cost but prices become progressively closer together as transport cost and other impediments to trade diminish. In the limit, the relative price of watches and rice will be the same in both places. The relative price of watches and haircuts will never be the same.

A similar distinction can be drawn among types of goods in a single market. *Ordinary goods* with a unique price in any given market may be contrasted with *personal goods* without unique prices, no matter how narrowly the market is confined. Personal goods are untraded goods in a single market. An example of such a good is leisure. A man who earns $100 per hour must, by definition, forgo $100 for the enjoyment of an additional hour of leisure. A man who earns $3.50 per hour must, by definition, forgo $3.50 for the enjoyment of an additional hour of leisure. This is true despite the fact that they each pay the same price for a watch, a bag of rice, or a pound of butter.

The value of life is like the price of leisure rather than like the price of butter. People can have different values of life because there is no mechanism, analogous to competition among grocers selling butter, to force them to be the same. To be sure, the prices of smoke detectors, safety belts, and medical services are the same for everyone in any given market. But in choosing which or how many of these items to purchase, people are displaying different values of life.

Diversity among people in their values of life is illustrated by means of the demand and supply curves in Figure 1. The unit of quantity is a .01 percent reduction in the mortality rate from some given base. The price is the cost or value of such a reduction, scaled up by a factor of 10,000 to make it commensurate with the value of life as I have defined the term. The supply curve summarizes the available mortality-reducing technology, ordered from the cheapest to the most expensive per unit of mortality reduction. Suppose that the cost of life is $100,000 when one buys a safety belt (as would be the

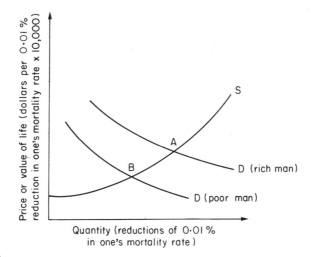

Figure 1

case if the safety belt reduced mortality by .03 percent at a cost of $30), $200,000 for a smoke detector, $300,000 for a visit to a doctor and so on, up to special and unusual medical tests which may cost millions of dollars for each life saved. This information may be summarized as a rising supply curve of mortality reduction. The curve itself would presumably be the same for everyone, though the points chosen on the curve may differ from one person to another.

Taste for mortality reduction can be represented by a demand curve which would probably be downward sloping. Demand curves may differ from one person to the next, and one would expect the demand curve of a rich man to be located to the right of the demand curve of a poor man, as indicated in Figure 1. The rich man typically buys more mortality reduction, just as he buys more of most every other good. What distinguishes the market for mortality reduction from the market for butter is that the rich man cannot buy more mortality reduction without at the same time paying a higher price for the marginal unit. In equilibrium, the value of life to the rich man (represented by the height of the point A) is greater than the value of life to the poor man (represented by the height of the point B).

Note, particularly, that these supply and demand curves refer to the individual rather than to the market as a whole. The supply curve of butter to an entire market may be upward sloping, but the supply curve to one person in that market is flat. The critical feature of the market for mortality reduction is that the supply curve is always upward sloping, for the market and for the individual as well.

Wealth is not the only source of variation among people in their values of life. People may differ in their taste for risk. One man may be particularly concerned to avoid unnecessary risk, another may be willing to accept risk at a modest price. The higher demand curve in Figure 1, which is indicated as belonging to the "rich man," could equally well be assigned to the "cautious man," and equilibrium values of life would differ accordingly. In fact, Viscusi, in the book cited in Table 1, argues that differences in taste for risk among workers can account for the discrepancy between his estimate of the value of life of about $6 million and Thaler and Rosen's estimate of about $600,000. People who differ in their taste for risk would sort themselves out in such a way that the more risk-averse get the safe jobs and the less risk-averse get the dangerous jobs. Consequently, the observed value of life would be lower among holders of dangerous jobs than among holders of relatively safe jobs. Viscusi attributes the discrepancy to the fact that Thaler and Rosen's study is based on a sample of more-than-normally-dangerous occupations, while Viscussi's sample is closer to the mean of the population as a whole.

It is difficult to say how the value of life would vary with age. An embryo contemplating his life to be would obviously place a higher value on a given reduction of mortality when he will be young than when he will be old, because a low mortality rate in one's old age is of no value to someone who dies in the meantime. On the other hand, the considerable wealth of many old people, together with their high current mortality rates, may give rise to a substantial value of life.

(c) *Externalities*. I cannot draw out the implications of the analysis of the value of life until one more consideration is introduced. A change in the probability of my death is of interest to others as well as to myself, and their interest may be relevant to the value of life for cost-benefit analysis.

Imagine a tontine in which a group of people, all of the same age, provide income and medical care for their retirement by saving money in a common pool. The amount of income is set to exhaust the principal and interest on the death of the last surviving member of the group. Suppose, when they reach 65 years of age, there are 1,000 members in the group, the total assets of the pool is $100,000,000, and each man's value of his own life is $500,000. The appropriate value of life for determining which kinds of medical treatment to provide and which to forgo is somewhat less than half a million dollars; it is in fact $400,000. Consider a preventable illness with a one in a thousand chance of killing each member of the group. If the group spends what it costs to cure the illness, each man's mortality rate falls by 1/1000. If not, each man's expected income increases by $100, which is his share of the equity in the pool of the expected victim of the disease. A man who would spend $500 to avoid a 1/1000 chance of death when there is no monetary compensation if he survives, would only spend $400 if he forgoes the $100 prize by protecting himself. Similarly, each member of the group would want the administration of the pool to employ a value of life of only $400,000, despite the fact that he himself would employ a value of $500,000 in his own behavior.

Implicitly, we are all like members of a tontine, because we provide for one another's old age and medical care through old age pensions and socialized medicine, and because a large part of the nation's assets are collectively owned. The value of life that each of us would want the public sector to employ is, therefore, less than his own personal value of life. It is ironic that public provision of services and the collectivization of assets, motivated presumably by a sense of fellowship among citizens, have the effect in practice of providing each citizen with an interest in the demise of his neighbors.

The relation between one's personal value of life, P^D, and the value one would want the manager of the tontine to employ, P^S, is illustrated in Figure 2. The height of the demand curve D^O is the value of life as it would be if future income each year were independent of one's probability of

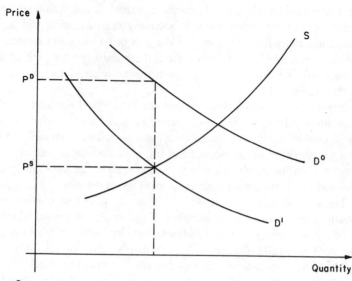

Figure 2

survival today, that is, if my income next year, contingent on my living to enjoy it, were independent of my probability of survival. The height of the demand curve, D^1, is the value of life corrected for the cost, to myself or to others, of an increase in the probability of my survival. The supply curve S is defined exactly as in Figure 1. The height of the supply curve is the cost of a small reduction in one's mortality rate. The difference between P^D and P^S is the externality. In our numerical example, P^D is $500, P^S is $400, and the externality is $100.

Even a personal mortality-reducing expenditure might take the externality into account. Suppose that, instead of joining a tontine, one purchases an annuity with an insurance company that is so observant that it can monitor one's mortality-reducing expenditure and adjust one's premium accordingly. The greater one's mortality-reducing expenditure, the longer one can expect to live and the more one must pay for any given annuity. The extra payment is like a shift downward of the demand curve from D^O to D^1, compelling the individual to absorb what would otherwise be an externality associated with a reduction in his mortality rate.[6]

There are several types of externalities in the reduction of mortality rates,

[6] See D. S. Shepard and R. J. Zechhauser, "Life-Cycle Consumption and Willingness to Pay for Increased Survival," in Jones-Lee, *Life and Safety*. Shepard and Zechhauser distinguish between the "Robinson Crusoe" case, where an individual is entirely self-sufficient, the "perfect market," where one can convert today's wealth into an annuity the amount of which increases with one's probability of death, and the "pensioner" case, where one's future income is independent of one's probability of survival.

some reducing the appropriate value of life for cost-benefit analysis and others increasing it. (1) The recipient of an old age pension imposes a cost on the rest of society when he acts to prolong his life, for the amount of the pension is independent of his expectation of life. This externality, which is in many respects like that associated with the tontine we have been discussing, creates a spread between the private and social valuations of the life of the old.[7] (2) The inheritor of one's property has an obvious interest in the length of one's life, which may or may not be matched by the interest of the giver of the bequest in the welfare of the recipient. (3) The saving of a life may result in the birth of extra children, who, one way or another, share the endowment of the nation. (4) On the other side of the coin is the grief of relatives and friends. This cost has got to be borne eventually, but its magnitude diminishes with the length of one's life. The death of an infant is looked upon as a tragedy; the death of an octogenarian is not.[8]

Economists have developed detailed mathematical models of the value of life for several purposes, among them (1) to see what relation, if any, there may be between one's value of life and his assets, the present value of his future income, the present value of his future consumption, and his expected mortality rates in every future year,[9] (2) to examine the response of a utility-maximizing individual to finite increases in his mortality rate, (3) to compute the externality associated with mortality reduction as a function of one's age, his expected future income (if he lives), and his expected future mortality rates, (4) to employ evidence of the value of life in the attempt to incorporate the observed historical reduction in mortality rates into the measure of a country's rate of economic growth, and (5) to estimate a value of life in circumstances where mortality reduction is only one of many determinants of a person's behavior.

---

[7] See B. C. Conley, "The Value of Human Life in the Demand for Safety," *American Economic Review*, vol. 66 (March 1976), pp. 45–55, and W. B. Arthur, "The Economics of Risks to Life," *American Economic Review*, vol. 71 (March 1981), pp. 54–64. Arthur compares the value to the survivors of the assets of the dead with a person's own value of life by incorporating both considerations into a growth model within which one can evaluate alternative steady states corresponding to different mortality rates. He derives a simple formula according to which the value of life appropriate for cost-benefit depends on four elements: one's value of living longer, one's valuation of the per capita reduction in consumption when the average length of life is increased, the effect of the loss of labor of the dead, and reduction in birth rates from the death of people in the childbearing age.

[8] See E. J. Mishan, "Evaluation of Life and Limb: A Theoretical Approach," *Journal of Political Economy*, vol. 79 (July 1971), pp. 687–705. So far as I know, the only attempt to measure one's valuation of another's life is a study of the willingness of relatives to donate kidneys to victims of renal disease. Lionel Needleman, "Valuing Other People's Lives," *The Manchester School*, vol. 44 (Dec. 1976), pp. 309–32.

[9] The relation between human capital and the value of life has been examined in detail by Linnerooth (1979), Arthur (1981), T. C. Bergstrom "When Is A Man's Life Worth More Than His Human Capital?" in Jones-Lee (1982).

Such models have been roundly criticized by E.J. Mishan as an attempt to draw facts out of thin air. They are "worth ploughing through for the intellectual diversion afforded one by observing misguided ingenuity, and also for the examples they provide of the proliferation of journal articles today a phenomenon that bears eloquent testimony to the current crisis in economic theory: much too much technique chasing far too few ideas." The alleged error in such models is that they cannot yield anything more accurate than the facts.

To test the figure for value of life produced by such a model, it is necessary to have some independent estimate of the value of life – which as indicated implies recourse to the individual's subjective valuation, in accordance with the basic maxim of normative economics. The test therefore requires a calculation of the individual's compensating variation for the gain or loss of life or, rather, for some predetermined gain or loss in chance of survival. No other test is possible. But, once we perform the required test – once, that is, we have calculated the individual's compensating variation by reference to revealed or expressed values – we have no need for the aforementioned sophisticated model. For by reference to the figure revealed by our direct test, we are compelled either to reject the model or not to reject the model. And, where we do not have to reject the model, we should save time and effort by simply deriving the value of life by the direct test.[10]

As the perpetrator of one such model, I cannot resist attempting a defense. In fact, the list of purposes two paragraphs above may itself be a sufficient defense. I admit straight away that models cannot be used as magic to invoke a person's value of life independently of evidence on what he does in life-threatening situations. They can be used as guides for assembling and interpreting the evidence. No observation of how people behave in life-threatening situations will tell us how to account for an externality such as that in our tontine example. This can only be accomplished with the aid of a fairly elaborate model of utility maximization in an intertemporal context, for the relation between private and social valuation of life becomes complex and difficult to quantify when one tries to take account of the age-structure of the population, age-specific mortality rates, and indirect effects of mortality on birth rates and labor supply. Models of the value of life are also indispens-

---

[10] E. J. Mishan "Consistency in the Valuation of Life – A Wild Goose Chase?" in this volume. The horrible examples are the papers by Conley and Arthur cited in footnote 7 and a paper of my own entitled "An Imputation to the Measure of Economic Growth for Changes in Life-Expectancy," in M. Moss, ed., *The Measurement of Economic and Social Performance*, N.B.E.R. Conference on Income and Wealth, vol. 38 (1973).

able when one employs historical evidence on reductions in mortality rates to impute for the increase in life expectancy in the measurement of the economic growth of nations. The models tell us how to use the estimated value of life to draw the appropriate equivalence between changes in income and changes in mortality rates, for both are components of the change in real income as a measure of the welfare of the representative consumer.

Cost-benefit Rules for the Public Sector

Governments cannot avoid the trading of lives for money, but they may establish the terms under which that trade takes place. The trade is unavoidable because governments take responsibility for activities – health, transport, environmental protection, civil order, and especially national defense – where lives can be saved at a price. The terms of the trade would depend to some extent on citizens' own values of life as demonstrated by their behavior in life-threatening situations, though it must be recognized that valuations differ according to age, income, and personal disposition.

One's assessment of how the government ought to behave in evaluating risks of death would depend to a great extent on whether one adopts a mundane or a celestial view of cost-benefit analysis. The celestial view is that someone out there is acting in the common interest, as represented by a social welfare function which enables him to trade off your benefit against mine in circumstances where they happen to conflict. On this view, the public sector may involve itself in any matter whatsoever as long as a balance of advantage can be identified. The mundane view is that citizens or their elected representatives empower the government to administer certain aspects of the economy and, implicitly or explicitly, instruct the government on the rules to follow. The distinction may be blurred in practice because the government may be instructed to take a more or less celestial view of certain matters – as would be the case, for example, if the government were instructed to follow simple utilitarian rules. Nonetheless, the mundane view takes cognizance of the fact that rules will have to be followed by men whose judgment is necessarily fallible and whose decisions may be influenced by considerations of self-interest, political expediency, and the special welfare of the ethnic groups or social classes to which they belong, as well as by the rules themselves. The social cost of human fallibility in decision making is nowhere more important than in matters of life and death.

There are several sorts of rules that the public sector decision maker might be asked to follow: he might, for instance, be instructed to do as he thinks best in the allocation of funds for road-building, medical care, and so on. This is to a large extent what we do now, for no single value of life is universally recognized in public sector decision making. Perhaps this procedure is rendered tolerable by our inattention, or by decentralization of decision making, so that lives in different regions or circumstances need not be explicitly compared. The danger in this procedure is that lives must be traded off, one against the other, whether we are aware of it or not. Without an explicit rule, lives in one place may come to be valued at more than lives in another, and the bond among the people that allows road-building and medical care to be financed collectively may dissolve when the disparity is finally recognized.

Alternatively, the public sector decision maker might be instructed to value lives, insofar as this is possible, according to the private valuations of the people at risk, with due allowance for the interests of the inheritors of the property of the deceased. In principle, he might be asked to construct values of life by income, age, occupation, region, ethnic groups, religion, color, and so on, though in practice he is unlikely to know enough about different groups to perform this task well. What can be said is that people with larger incomes usually place greater values on their lives. Thus, for instance, if one knows that people who travel by plane are on average wealthier than people who travel by bus, it would be appropriate to place a higher value per life saved for safety on planes than for safety on buses; a safety device costing $600,000 per life saved might on this principle be purchased for planes but not for buses. The same principle may be applied to the allocation of medical expenditure between cities.

This procedure may be defended on two grounds. First, it is what the private sector would do automatically. If bus companies and airlines are entirely in the private sector, then competition among rival firms would ensure that safety devices are purchased in each mode of transport up to the point where the cost per life saved equals the value of life of the users of that mode of transport. Second, this procedure is Pareto-optimal in the sense that, alone among the procedures we are considering, it leads to a situation in which not everyone could be made better off by a rearrangement of production and distribution of goods. Any other procedure could be improved upon by trades between rich and poor in which the rich pay the poor to allow the rich to have better access to lifesaving technology.

This procedure can be criticized from several points of view. First, since we do not have a system of "benefit taxation," in which the beneficiaries of each and every object of public expenditure are taxed according to their personal assessment of its worth, a public sector distribution of life-saving expenditure that recognized the greater value of life of the rich would necessarily widen the gap between the living standards of the rich and of the poor. Citizens would never vote for such a rule, and certainly not unanimously. Second, a public sector decision maker empowered to take account of differences in the value of life among citizens might employ his power of discretion capriciously, through ignorance or by putting interests of his own above the public interest. This is a possibility because individual variations in the value of life cannot be identified with certainty.

Third, and perhaps most important, the decision of citizens to undertake road-building or medical care in the public sector may be looked upon as a decision to remove these goods from the domain of property and to place them in the domain of equality instead. In political life, each person has one vote which, ideally, entitles him to an equal share of influence on legislation and policy. In economic life, each dollar has one vote in the sense that it commands an equal share of the goods and services produced. To place medical care in the public sector is to say, in effect, that income no longer counts in the allocation of medical care. It is to say that medical care is to be allocated according to the votes of people rather than to the votes of dollars. If so, differences in people's value of life which reflect differences in their wealth or purchasing power should remain unrecognized in the allocation of lifesaving expenditure in the public sector. Property is, after all, a social convention, and part of that convention is the specification of the limits of property rights. We cannot buy votes and we cannot buy slaves. Nor, unless we choose to make it so, do property-related differences in the value of life affect the rules of cost-benefit analysis.

Neither of the procedures we have so far considered – valuation of life according to the best judgment of the appointed decision maker and valuation according to personal valuations of the people concerned in any given project – is entirely adequate. A third candidate is the valuation according to the decisions of citizens as reflected by votes in the legislature. This procedure is obviously right in one sense, but virtually impossible in another. It is right in the trivial sense that there is no higher authority than the will of the citizens who pay for public sector projects with their taxes and for whom projects are designed. Cost-benefit analysis works perfectly when it undertakes or rejects projects where "a unanimous vote would have done so." The catch is that few projects would be accepted or rejected unanimously.

Nor can one appeal to simple majority rule. Virtually no project – no road, no hospital – would be undertaken if each project were voted on separately and if all votes were cast according to each voter's balance of costs and benefits of that project alone, for it is rare for any project to be beneficial to more than half the nation. Majority coalitions, however, may vote for sets of projects in which benefits exceed tax costs to the members of the coalition but not to the nation as a whole.

In sharp contrast to most projects which are financed through general revenue and are typically beneficial to well under half the electorate, the choice of a value of life for cost-benefit analysis is a single-peaked issue for which the will of the median voter might be expected to prevail. Voters may differ in their preferred values of life according to age, income, or disposition. The legislature can, nonetheless, be expected to choose a unique value because the median voter – the voter whose preferred value of life is half way along the scale from top to bottom in the sense that there are as many voters who would prefer a higher value as there are voters who would prefer a lower one – can form a coalition with either group to defeat any proposal but his own.[11]

The political basis of cost-benefit analysis is a real or imagined vote about rules to remain in force for a long time. Everyone knows that he will lose from some projects and gain from others, but he hopes that his gains will outweigh his losses in the long run. It is on this basis that people are content for the government to undertake projects when benefits exceed costs "to whomsoever they may accrue." Our problem remains to determine what rules self-interested and well-informed voters would accept for the valuation of life.

Taken literally, neither utilitarianism nor the minimax principle will do in this context, for they require more knowledge, integrity, and independence on the part of decision makers than administrators can reasonably be expected to supply. Imagine the predicament of an administrator of a county-wide medical service who is instructed to choose among alternative programs to maximize $\overset{N}{\underset{i=1}{\Sigma}}\ U_i$, where N is the population of the county and U_i is the utility of Mr. i. Whatever is meant by utilitarianism, it cannot be that!

On the other hand, there is some guidance to be had from the conceptual experiment in which one imagines oneself empowered to choose the rules for a society where one is destined to occupy a randomly-chosen station in life, with an equal chance of finding oneself in the shoes of anybody at all.[12] The best rules are the rules for that society which one would most prefer to enter in these circumstances. The experiment converts selfish calculations into prescriptions for the common good. With an equal chance of appearing as anybody in Canadian society, I would not want the administrator of medical services or transport policy to value lives from one project to another as he sees fit. Nor would I want him to adjust the value of life from one project to another according to his assessment of the subjects' own

[11] Duncan Black, "On the Rationale of Group Decision-Making," *Journal of Political Economy*, vol. 56 (February 1948), pp. 23–34.

[12] This framework for the establishment of rules for the public sector has been analyzed by John Harsanyi, "Cardinal Welfare, Individualistic Ethics and the Interpersonal Comparisons of Utility," *Journal of Political Economy*, vol. 63 (August 1955), pp. 309–321, and by John Rawls, *A Theory of Justice* (Cambridge: Harvard University Press, 1971). The fact that the former derives utilitarian rules while the latter derives *maximum rules* is irrelevant for our purposes.

valuations. Nor would I trust him with a utilitarian criterion. I would prefer to see him instructed to employ a single value of life for all projects in the public sector.

There is an ambiguity in this conceptual experiment which is particularly disturbing in the context of the choice of a value of life. To imagine myself as having an equal chance of occupying any post or situation in society may mean (a) that I have an equal chance of being born into anybody's life, or (b) that I appear on the scene to occupy the entire circumstances, age included, of someone who is now alive. For most purposes this distinction is irrelevant, but for the value of life it is crucial because an embryo would choose a vastly different schedule of the value of life by age than would an older person. An embryo behind the veil of ignorance would place a relatively higher value on reduction of mortality rates of the young than would someone with a chance of appearing at any age at all.

I am at a loss as to whether, and to what extent, the value of life for cost-benefit analysis should vary with age. Certainly the life of a person soon to die in any case should be worth less than the life of a child who can be expected to live out a normal span of years if he survives now. Perhaps the proper measure is not a value of life at all, but a value per expected year of life. Somehow that seems too strongly weighted against the old, though I cannot say what the right weighting might be. Fortunately, there are many projects involving the saving or losing of lives for which one cannot identify victims or beneficiaries as significantly younger or significantly older than the average of the population as a whole.

Is it Immoral to Exchange Lives for Money?

Though it seems reasonable enough to establish a value of life for cost-benefit analysis, there remains a feeling of unease about the enterprise that cannot be accounted for by mere squeamishness about the contemplation of death. One has a sense of tampering with matters that are better left alone, and of violating conventions that in some dimly-recognized way are necessary for the maintenance of society. Consider Ivan's challenge to Alyosha in *The Brothers Karamazov*.[13]

> "Tell me yourself, I challenge you – answer. Imagine that you are creating a fabric of human destiny with the object of making men happy in the end, giving them peace and rest at last, but that it was essential and inevitable to torture to death only one tiny creature – a baby beating its breast with its fist, for instance – and to found that

---

[13] Fyodor Dostoyevsky, *The Brothers Karamazov*, Modern Library Paperback (New York: Random House, 1950), pp. 291–292.

edifice on its unavenged tears, would you consent to be the architect on those conditions? Tell me, and tell the truth."

"No, I wouldn't consent," said Alyosha softly.

"And can you admit the idea that men for whom you are building it would agree to accept their happiness on the foundation of the unexpiated blood of a little victim? And accepting it would remain happy for ever?"

"No, I can't admit that, Brother."

We do feel that Alyosha is acting morally and justly in his refusal to accept the bargain. But why not accept it? Innocent children suffer regularly through deprivation, accident, and disease. Is it not worth the life of one child now to "make men happy in the end, giving them peace and rest at last?" More to the point, would not the kinds of considerations that lead us to propose a value of life for cost-benefit analysis require Alyosha to accept the bargain? Is Ivan's challenge any different from the ordinary comparison of lives lost or saved in road-building or medical care?

An embryo behind the veil of ignorance would willingly accept the bargain, for he has less chance of emerging as the victim than as one of the innumerable children to be saved from death or suffering. If the embryo's decision is the standard of justice, ought not Alyosha accept the bargain himself?

Two considerations might lead us to reject this inference. The first has to do with the nature of the bargain. It is a bargain that can only be struck with God or his secular equivalent. But God is not altogether trustworthy in such matters, as was revealed when he deceived Abraham about the sacrifice of Isaac. I suggest that the moral of the story of Alyosha and Ivan is not that the child that Alyosha refused to sacrifice is more precious than others God wantonly destroys. It is that *Alyosha* must never strike such a bargain, for God's part of the bargain will not be kept. If you believe that God has commanded you to sacrifice Isaac, to break the rules of normal human conduct so as to make the Messiah come or liberate mankind by revolution, don't do it. God has not so commanded or, if he has, he is less than candid about the reward. The point of the story is to inculcate proper habits of behavior as a defense against self-delusion.

There is at the same time a deep aversion to the placing of one's life in the hands of another. I will trust my fellow citizens to decide what cities to build, how much tax I should pay, or what my children should learn at school, but I draw the line at allowing them to decide when it is proper for me to die. I don't trust my fellow citizens with power over my life and I don't want such power over them. This is in part a lack of confidence in the ability of fallible men to administer such powers properly, and in part an unwillingness to see such powers in any human hands regardless of how honestly, carefully, and intelligently they are administered – for, like the Hobbit's ring, they are ultimately corruptive. Alyosha's response reflects our deep distaste for power over life and death.

Does this imply that we should desist from specifying a value of life for cost-benefit analysis? Quite the reverse. The specification of a value of life does not give powers over life and death to the administrators of public sector projects. It takes such powers away. Having placed the responsibility for road-building and medical care in the public sector, we have, knowingly or not, compelled ourselves to decide between your life or mine, and that decision must be twice delegated, from voters to parliament and from parliament to administrators of public sector programs. Our only remaining choice is how that decision is to be exercised. We can allow administrators to act as they see fit, in effect, requiring them to accept the bargain that Alyosha refused in the most favorable circumstances. Or we can bind decisions with rules that make those decisions less arbitrary, less subject to political influence, and less tragic. Specification of a uniform value of life constrains the choices of administrators of public sector programs and avoids many situations where one man must give or withhold the life of another.

For projects where there is no basis for supposing that the age distribution of lives lost or saved differs significantly from the age distribution of the population as a whole, a single value of life is all that is required. In view of the difficulties of deciding on an age distribution for the value of life in cost-benefit analysis, and to avoid the ugly implications of having the value turn negative for the very old, it might be best to avoid specifying an age distribution at all. From introspection, and from the table of observed values in the marketplace, one has a sense of what an appropriate value of life might be. The government can simply choose a number that seems reasonable, for it is better to specify a number a bit too large or a bit too small than to desist from specifying a number at all. A specified value of life maximizes the number of lives saved for any given amount of expenditure and minimizes the extent to which my life is at the mercy of others. Tragic choices cannot be eliminated altogether, but we should avoid such choices when we can. On the understanding that descretion will be exercised when the victim of a calamity is identified and in decisions involving the old and infirm, and that the chosen number will be increased each year in accordance with the rate of inflation, I recommend a figure of $750,000.

Economics, Queen's University, Kingston, Canada